ABBA
unplugged

ABBA unplugged

KARL FRENCH

PORTRAIT

Visit the Portrait website!

Portrait publishes a wide range of non-fiction, including biography, history, science, music, popular culture and sport.

Visit our website to:
• read descriptions of our popular titles
• buy our books over the internet
• take advantage of our special offers
• enter our monthly competition
• learn more about your favourite Portrait authors

VISIT OUR WEBSITE AT: www.portraitbooks.com

Copyright © 2004 by Karl French

First published in 2004 by Portrait, an imprint c
Piatkus Books Ltd
5 Windmill Street
London W1T 2JA
e-mail: info@piatkus.co.uk

Abba lyrics reproduced by permission of Bocu Music Ltd,
1 Wyndham Yard, London W1H 2QF.

Every effort has been made to identify and acknowledge
copyright-holders. Any errors or omissions will be rectified
in future editions provided that written notification is
made to the publisher.

The moral right of the author has been asserted

A catalogue record for this book is
available from the British Library

ISBN 0 7499 5034 X

Set by Action Publishing Technology Ltd, Gloucester
Printed and bound in Great Britain by
MPG Books, Bodmin, Cornwall

CONTENTS

ACKNOWLEDGEMENTS

Many thanks to the following for their help in completing this book: my agent, Pat Kavanagh; everyone at Piatkus, most of all my commissioning editor, the wonderful Penny Phillips, for her patience, sage advice and support throughout the project; copy-editor Richard Dawes for his diligent and intelligent work; Zak Reddan for invaluable and creative research, tracking down some arcane Abba-related material; Mary Fawcett; Marc Vaulbert de Chantilly for helping to clarify certain ideas despite his open and eloquently expressed distaste for Abba; John Tiberi for sparing the time to reminisce about his and Sid Vicious's peculiar encounter with Agnetha and Frida, about his days spent with Joe Strummer listening to Abba, among other, more esoteric artists, and much else besides; the staff at the British Newspaper Library in Colindale, Marylebone Library and Westminster Reference Library; my brothers Sean and Patrick for various pieces of assistance, not least access to their libraries; my parents for generous advice and my mother in particular for helping me out when my Swedish, inevitably and regularly, failed me; my Swedish family for advice and assistance, in particular my cousin Tobias Walldén and my aunt Marja Walldén and uncle John Walldén; my parents-in-law, John and Elizabeth Callaghan, for helping out when the going got tough; and Karin Petherick for pointing me in the right direction on a couple of issues and sharing her observations of life in Sweden in the mid-1970s. Finally, thanks for everything to Fiona, Martha and Toby, to whom this book is dedicated.

THANK YOU FOR THE MUSIC

It is now a little over 30 years since Abba burst on to the music scene with their barnstorming victory at the 1974 Eurovision Song Contest. The smart money would have been on their going the same way as previous winners and disappearing. There is, for instance, no musical playing to packed houses at theatres around the world built around the songs of Corry Brokken. No serious music writers make a case for the poptastic supremacy of Yizhar Cohen and Alphabeta. No opportunistic artists have made a living by impersonating Massiel.

So Abba, born out of a contest that thrives on the most ephemeral strand of pop music, pioneers of widely and justly reviled Europop, contenders for the title of worst-dressed band of the 1970s – a decade that spawned, lest we forget, Slade, the Bay City Rollers and the Rubettes – have transcended these perceived limitations. Having conquered much of the world in the seventies and disbanded at or very close to their collective creative peak, they have somehow grown even stronger over the past two decades, remaining commercially successful, and today

Björn Ulvaeus and Benny Andersson are perhaps more highly respected as composers than ever before.

Their back catalogue is vastly lucrative and has established them as serious musicians and songwriters, one of the precious few examples of a truly great pop band. So how did it all happen? How did they go from the musical backwater that was Sweden in the early 1970s and emerge – twice – as millionaire musical superstars?

INTRODUCTION

The house lights dim, and the stage lights come on to reveal a simple, central stage set. There is a palpable frisson, an audible collective shiver that ripples through the audience, something familiar from the moments before a band comes on at a concert for a particularly beloved pop star. For everyone knows, many because they have seen the show before, the delights in store; that by the end of the evening every single member of the audience in this respectable West End theatre will have abandoned their seat and will be dancing and singing along to the show's joyous encore. But this is all a couple of hours in the future.

To begin with, the curved wall situated in the centre of the stage represents the port on a Greek island where three young female friends are meeting, although in the course of the action it will be twisted, opened, closed and decorated to suggest the interior and exterior of a guest house, a beach and a nightclub. Sophie, the central character, is joined by her two best friends on the island where she grew up, on the eve of her wedding to a young man called Sky. She is blissfully happy at the prospect of her wedding, the only fly in the ointment being her continuing ignorance about the identity of her father. Her aching desire to find out exactly who her father is and to have him give her away at the wedding has been given a big boost by the recent discovery, as she explains to her excited pals, of her mother Donna's diary, written, as luck would have it, around nine months before Sophie's birth.

From this she learns that Donna was romantically involved with three men at the same time. So Sophie has contrived to get all three men to come to the wedding, each of them unaware of why exactly he has been invited. This is the, dare one say, Shakespearian premise of the brisk, indeed irresistible musical *Mamma Mia!* Over the course of two hours the action moves ahead as the characters, in their various groups of three, explore the themes of ageing, professional and romantic hopes and disappointments, and the yearning for adventure and self-knowledge.

The story itself is perfectly functional, if hardly inspired, but what it constitutes is a framework, a skeleton around which the show's appeal is built – the songs of Abba. In hindsight, and with the knowledge of the astonishing statistics attesting to the show's continuing success, it is hard to remember that when it was conceived, and even when it opened, it seemed a bit of a gamble. Abba, the band and their songs, had been the subjects of a dramatic shift in perception, journeying through levels of appreciation – pre-ironic, ironic, post-ironic – until, as became patently obvious, the group and their prodigious output were simply beloved.

The whole story of *Mamma Mia!* started with producer Judy Craymer's inspired idea that there was something in the catalogue of Abba songs that naturally lent itself to a stage show. Her association with Benny Andersson and Björn Ulvaeus went back a long way, as far as 1984, when she became managing director of Three Knights Ltd, the company formed by Andersson, Ulvaeus and Tim Rice to produce their own West End and, briefly, Broadway musical *Chess*.

Craymer found it a job to break down the resistance of the composers, but eventually they saw the logic in the plan, that there was an inherent narrative to many of their most celebrated songs, and that there was a secondary narrative in the way that their songwriting had become ever more mature and sophisticated – and gloomier – over the ten years that Abba made music together. Craymer turned to Catherine Johnson, an experienced writer for television and the stage, who, working in close collaboration with Ulvaeus, developed the central notion that the contrast in the mood of the songs from Abba's early and later periods naturally suggested two generations: a mother and daughter. All that remained was two and a half years of painstaking refinement and an international hit musical was born.

The notion of creating a musical around existing songs goes back at least as far as *Singin' in the Rain*, and has been used for shows and films as diverse as *Oh! What a Lovely War* and *All That Jazz*. *Mamma Mia!*, while continuing this tradition, is more closely related to other, more recent shows which give an audience hungry for nostalgia the opportunity to see, performed live, songs made famous by bands that, for reasons of death or dissolution, wouldn't be performing them themselves.

Willy Russell, who would go on to have notable successes in straight theatre with *Shirley Valentine* and *Educating Rita* and in musicals with the long-running *Blood Brothers*, filled the void left by the demise of the Beatles with the light-hearted *John, Paul, George, Ringo and Bert*, in which the last-named, fictional, character was ingeniously woven into what was otherwise a fairly straight retelling of the story of the Fab Four. *Elvis – The Musical* and the phenomenally successful *Buddy!*, a music-drenched dramatisation of the short and glorious life of Buddy Holly, would repeat or refine this idea of the stage musical biography. *Mamma Mia!* does something rather different, using the songs of a band to fashion a musical that has nothing whatever to do with the story of the band itself. This had been tried previously with varying degrees of success with the likes of *Labelled with Love*, based on the narrative-heavy songs of Squeeze written by Chris Difford and Glenn Tilbrook, and *Abbacadabra*, an early attempt to fashion an Abba-inspired musical.

In turn the success of *Mamma Mia!* led directly to the Madness musical *Our House* and the establishment of Ben Elton as a leading figure in musical theatre through his work on the Queen musical *We Will Rock You* and the subsequent Rod Stewart show *Tonight's the Night.* So it's not all good news.

But whatever its place in one or more musical traditions, *Mamma Mia!* stands alone for various reasons, not least the astonishing scale of its success. There are, at the time of writing, ten productions currently running in Europe, North America, Asia, Australia and New Zealand. This number is sure to increase – six further productions are in advanced stages of planning – and Abba's popularity in Central and South America has yet to be exploited. A good deal of the credit must go to the creative team behind the show, above all Craymer, Johnson, director Phyllida Lloyd, choreographer Anthony van Laast and production designer Mark Thompson. But the narrative structure is essentially a support system for the central appeal of the show, the music, which is brilliantly and imaginatively recreated. The palpable sense of excitement that precedes the opening and lasts throughout the show relies on the audience's playing the guessing game of trying to figure out where, and specifically to which wonderfully staged number, the action is heading next.

The show's global success – it has now been seen by well over ten million people around the world – underlines the sheer durability of Abba's music. They emerged from a contest that was almost designed to celebrate banal, throwaway pop music, and which year by year created one-hit wonders whose talents were scarcely worthy of even that one hit. After Abba's triumph and their apparent, but thankfully short-lived, inability to follow it up with further success, at least beyond Scandinavia, they were dismissed as glam-light – and you can't get much lighter than that – wannabe bubblegum popsters. But there was a profound commitment to success, a determination welded crucially to an undeniable talent for crafting exquisite and deceptively simple pop songs – and to save interminable semantic arguments we will eschew the easy use of the word 'genius'. What is indisputable is that Abba would become the dominant pop band of the second half of the 1970s, maturing and developing musically and lyrically through their years at the top, selling hundreds of millions of records around the world, creating, through painstaking writing and recording sessions, their own distinctive sound, however diverse their musical influences and inspirations.

Björn Ulvaeus and Benny Andersson, the group's songwriting duo, had eclectic tastes and would borrow from wherever they found inspiration. Both were from an earlier age of folk and pop music in what was, until their own emergence from it, the obscure musical backwater of Sweden, and had from their earliest days been immersed in not only folk and pop but also classical music. By the time of their first truly international success they had each enjoyed around a decade of pop stardom at home, and from relatively early on, with their own bands, had begun to compose their own music. With Abba, the songs, the sound and the lyrics may have became ever more sophisticated, as all four members grew up and grew apart, but even their early forays into the world of pure, disposable pop – and there is certainly no disgrace in great pop music – have endured.

Mamma Mia! has been described as the musical that Björn and Benny didn't realise that they had been writing at the time, and it confirms what many of us have known for a long time, that Abba were churning out a succession of dazzling songs, songs that were, though they so often appeared disarmingly simple, in fact carefully, meticulously crafted vignettes, ranging in mood, musically and lyrically, from exuberant celebration to world-weary resignation.

Abba sprang, as far as the outside world was concerned, fully formed from Sweden's small but thriving pop and folk music scenes, and, having moved in and out of fashion, have emerged as arguably one of the two or three greatest, most important pop bands of the twentieth century, and unarguably one of the half-dozen most successful in terms of record sales. How did this all happen?

CHAPTER ONE

'MAMMA MIA'

Just because you're small and blonde doesn't mean that you're completely stupid. Agnetha Fältskog

A IS FOR AGNETHA

Agnetha (pronounced Ahng-near-tuh, although she was in fact christened Agneta) Åse Fältskog, the girl with the golden voice, the golden hair and the most celebrated bum of the 1970s pop world, was born in the southern Swedish town of Jönköping on 5 April 1950. In her early days she would often refer to herself, especially in interviews with American journalists, as Anna, and would at other times be called, by design or otherwise, Agnetha. The 'h' stuck. She may well not have been in any obvious sense special nor ever have had much of a way with a joke, but not long after she had learned to walk and talk it was clear that her passion in life would be music.

She was born into a moderately creative family, her father something of an extrovert and a keen performer in local amateur dramatic sketch shows, her mother – in contrast naturally shy – a talented painter. It doesn't take a profound insight into the workings of the human character to see that the adult Agnetha, an obsessively private show-off, both shy and demanding, inherited these contrasting personality traits from her parents. The spark of Agnetha's lifelong love of music and performance was her discovery, at five years of age, of a piano belonging to an upstairs neighbour. She was instantly and for ever smitten and would spend as much time as she could familiarising herself with the keyboard. Two years later her parents gave her a piano of her own.

From the outset Agnetha was a composer, writing and performing her own songs for her family and, from the age of seven, in public. Her public debut took place at a Christmas party where, with her father's encouragement, she took to the stage to perform her rendition of 'Billy Boy', a hit in Sweden that year, which was somewhat marred by the fact that, according to Agnetha legend, her trousers fell down halfway through the song.

Agnetha continued to write and perform informally through her early teens and with a couple of friends formed a three-piece female close-harmony group called the Cambers, until, at the age of 15, she got her first professional gig after being taken on as the singer with a local dance band led by Bernt Enghardt. Leaving school shortly afterwards, she started work as a secretary and for a couple of years struggled to maintain the balance between the demands of her office job and life on the road. She finally gave up her day job a few months after achieving her first hit single.

While she sang covers on the road with the band – a mix of soul music and slower Swedish ballads – in her own time she composed a string of sweet, very personal songs, the best of them inspired by her active and generally, it seems, unhappy love life. From the outset her romantic adventures were marked by certain threads that would continue through her life, notably an attraction to relatively powerful men who, in the eyes of the outside world, would treat her condescendingly if not outright badly. This hardly makes her unique among women in general or female singer-songwriters in particular, and this mood of doomy romantic melancholy infuses these early compositions which also bear the mark of soft country influence. The key role model for the young Agnetha was Connie Francis. A native of New Jersey, Francis had a string of easy-listening hits from the late 1950s to the mid-1960s, her best records ('Stupid Cupid', 'Who's Sorry Now', 'Lipstick on Your Collar') being characterised, as Agnetha's work both alone and with Abba would be, by their slick production and the clarity of the singer's delivery. Agnetha was always precise in her enunciation even when she wavered musically.

The most important composition in Agnetha's early years as a writer-performer was 'Jag var så kär' ('I Was So in Love'), a sweet, personal if self-lacerating song, with a slightly French romantic lilt to it. It was written in the immediate aftermath of her breaking up with a boyfriend, one Björn Lilja, walking out on her. 'Jag var så kär' featured on a cassette sent to Karl-Gerhard Lundkvist, aka Little Gerhard, a briefly and only locally celebrated rock singer turned A&R man for the record company CBS-Cupol. Bernt Enghardt, who was related to Lundkvist by marriage, had by this stage left the band that still bore his name, but earlier had sent a tape to Lundkvist, only to have it rejected partly on account of a distaste for young Agnetha's supposedly flat singing – this would be a recurrent criticism of Agnetha's voice throughout her career.

When a second, and by all accounts haphazardly recorded, cassette was delivered to Lundkvist some months later, his reaction was altogether different. The good news for Agnetha was that, after listening to this tape, Gerhard was now keen, indeed determined, to record with Agnetha as soon as possible. The bad news was that he was equally eager for her to dump the backing band before hitting the recording studio. Agnetha may have seemed, and may very well have been, wide-eyed and innocent, but she was none the less focused, ambitious and not about to miss out on her big break. Here was a chance to realise the dreams that she had fostered since the time when, like countless millions of other girls and boys, she used to sing along to the hits of the day in front of her bedroom mirror, using her hairbrush as a mike.

Agnetha would continue to front the band for a couple more months and fulfil a contractual obligation to perform a tour of Sweden's *folkparket*. (These public parks dotted the country and hosted large festivals throughout the summer, events that would in time provide an outlet for the members of Abba both individually and collectively.) But, aside from this series of gigs, Agnetha had made a decisive break from the group that had nurtured her precocious talent. So Enghardt's band joined the ranks of music's nearly men – alongside the likes of the Beatles' own nearly man, Pete Best, early Rolling Stone Ian Stewart and, as we shall see, the various members of the Hootenanny Singers, the Hep Stars, Gunnar Sandevärn and his orchestra and the other three members of the Anni-Frid Four – people who would merit a modest footnote in pop history for having helped their colleagues, in some cases briefly and inadvertently, on the long and rocky road to stardom.

Agnetha's life-changing recording session took place on 16 October 1967 at the Philips recording studio in Stockholm and yielded four tracks: 'Följ me mej' ('Follow Me'), 'Jag var så kär', 'Utan dej mitt liv går vidare' ('Without You My Life Goes On') and 'Slutet gott, allting gott' ('All's Well That Ends Well'). Two men who would, in very different ways, play vital roles in the fate of Agnetha and Abba also featured in this session. Sven-Olof Walldoff, who would, while decked out as Napoleon, lead the band in Abba's Eurovision Song Contest triumph seven years later, had been consulted by Lundkvist about the possibility of calling Agnetha in for a session in the first place. In addition it was Walldoff who served as band leader when, after taking her first tentative steps into a recording studio, she was visibly nervous throughout the day.

'Följ me mej', a cover version of an obscure song, 'Hello Love', which had been recorded by the British singer Julie Grant (who had enjoyed minor hits in the mid-1960s with her versions of 'Count on Me' and 'Up on the Roof'), featured Swedish lyrics by one Stig 'Stikkan' Anderson. A specialist in translating foreign pop hits or simply rewriting the lyrics from scratch, Anderson was, more importantly, the man who would, within ten years, guide Abba from obscurity to international superstardom.

In November 1967 'Följ me mej', backed up by 'Jag var så kär', became Agnetha's debut single. The B-side turned out to be the more popular number and it was this song of heartbreak that dragged the record to number three in the Swedish hit parade on 28 January the following year, after Agnetha's debut appearance on Swedish television two weeks earlier. The single would make it all the way to the top of the charts, staying there for just one week. So, in quick succession and while still a teenager, Agnetha had achieved, and possibly already exceeded, her childhood dreams.

Famously reticent, at times reclusive, stubbornly unrevealing of her inner life in interviews and even in her touching if almost painfully cagey autobiography, *As I Am*, Agnetha would gush that she had never been so happy as when she first walked into the studio and heard a professional band rehearsing an arrangement of a song that she had almost casually knocked out at her piano. Again she would recall the giddiness she experienced when she heard her single played on the radio for the first time, a joy quickly surpassed when she achieved her first number-one single.

A pop star was born, and her first success led to further singles, among them the moving, lovelorn 'Utan dej mitt liv går vidare', and the release of a self-titled debut album, all of which reached the top ten in Sweden. But her record company had their eyes on the international market, or at least the German one, and encouraged a meeting between Agnetha and Dieter Zimmerman, an already successful young composer who had been chosen to oversee the launch of Agnetha's career in Germany.

From the start the relationship was as much personal as it was professional, and the couple were soon engaged. Neither Agnetha's liaison with Zimmerman nor her dogged, early attempt to crack the German market was destined to end happily. She recorded a succession of singles specifically tailored for Germany, but failed to make a mark there. These singles – eight over a period of two years – bore such unpromising titles as 'Robinson Crusoe' and 'Señor Gonzales' and were later recalled by Agnetha herself as 'horrible songs'. Her relationship with Zimmerman soon petered out, but her career back home continued to thrive, and as ever with Agnetha, there was someone waiting in the wings to ease her broken heart, and once again a slightly older man with greater experience in the music business.

The fateful meeting between Agnetha and the man who, more than any other, would shape her destiny had in fact taken place shortly after she and Zimmerman had first become an item. In the midst of her final tour of *folkparket* with Bengt Enghardt's band, Agnetha was booked at the Målilla Sports Park in south-east Sweden, where she was sharing the bill with another top pop act, although one that envied her own achievement in having achieved a number-one hit in the Swedish charts. The Hootenanny Singers were by this time veterans of the Swedish pop and folk circuit and while their lead singer had seen and admired Agnetha on her various appearances on national television – Agnetha recalled that the admiration was mutual – this auspicious, although by all accounts far from cordial, evening marked the first meeting in the flesh between the nation's favourite pop starlet and the young singer-songwriter and nascent businessman Björn Ulvaeus.

I don't have a brother but Björn is my brother.
Benny Andersson
It takes quite a lot of hard work to get rid of the rubbish.
Björn, reflecting on the songwriting process

B IS FOR BJÖRN

Studies have shown that one of the formative experiences common to many self-made millionaires is that of having in childhood witnessed their parents facing bankruptcy or another serious reversal of fiscal fortunes leading to a period of relative poverty. This is certainly true of Björn Ulvaeus, who would grow up to become a shrewd, wily businessman as well as a gifted musician and composer.

Ulvaeus was born on 25 April 1945 on the island of Hisingen, on the edge of Gothenburg, and spent much of his childhood in the small town of Västervik, in the southern province of Småland. In the immediate aftermath of the Second World War, his father, Gunnar Ulvaeus – born Andersson, Ulvaeus senior and his brothers had changed their name to rid themselves of this odiously common surname and in the process saved early Abba compositions from bearing the unwieldy writing credits 'Composed by B Andersson, B Andersson and S Anderson (né Andersson)' – launched a promising career as a shipyard owner, but by the late 1940s the yard was facing ever more urgent financial pressures and in time he faced a risk of bankruptcy. Salvation, albeit of a humbling kind, came in the shape of an offer of work from his younger brother, Esbjörn, who had himself become the owner of a small but prosperous paper mill.

So the Ulvaeus family decamped to Västervik, where Gunnar

took up his management post in Esbjörn's company and the family settled into a comfortable bourgeois lifestyle in this small but thriving town. In his early years Björn's musical interests were largely restricted to strumming on a mandolin, although not very effectively or tunefully, by his father's account. As Björn entered his teens and music began to exert an ever greater pull on him, his major inspiration came in the shape of imported skiffle records, the easily replicable home-made strand of proto-rock music that was proving equally inspirational to a generation of wannabe pop stars across the North Sea. As a result of pestering his parents, Björn was given an acoustic guitar on his 13th birthday, and although he was, by his own admission, at first no more talented on the guitar than he had been on the mandolin, very soon he formed a skiffle band with a group of friends.

Meanwhile, at school, having generally been no more than an average student, the teenage Björn found that things were beginning to take off for him, particularly in Swedish and English lessons, and his teacher in the latter is said to have remarked that Ulvaeus was the most gifted student he had encountered in 40 years in the profession. He continued to practise and perform with his band, who made a dramatic change of gear when they left skiffle behind and shifted instead into the then modish trad jazz, a form of music that was becoming increasingly popular in Sweden, Björn's appreciation of rock 'n' roll at this stage being pretty much restricted to Elvis.

At the age of 16 Björn was fortunate to be absorbed into a successful local skiffle band, the Partners, when his friend Tony Rooth insisted that he himself would join, as he had been invited to do, only if he could bring his buddy along with him. So Björn became a bona fide musician, playing guitar and banjo for the Partners in his last couple of years at high school. Spending much of their free time practising together, and with Björn gradually becoming the outfit's leader, singing and arranging their numbers, mainly American folk standards, they emerged as a proficient if not quite inspired pop-folk unit. With their having established a decent reputation among local music fans, there was a touch of Spinal Tap to the young band's story when the Partners learned that they were not the only group in the area to be graced with that name, a discovery that prompted their rebirth as the West Bay Singers, West Bay being a literal translation of their home town Västervik.

Björn had had little active encouragement from his parents – they assumed that he would in time pursue his academic career at least as far as university before finding a suitable outlet for his obvious business acumen – so he was surprised when one day his mother suggested that he and his band were sufficiently impressive, to her ears at least, to make it worth their while to enter a talent competition. This they did, and won through, along with the young Anni-Frid Lyngstad, to the final six.

Every story of the birth of a star or a whole group of stars is punctuated with decisive, fateful moments and first meetings. At this stage in the story of Björn and Abba came such an encounter. In its quiet way this event was the equivalent of the fateful day, specifically lunchtime on 9 November 1961, when, inspired by a customer's having come into his music shop and asked for a record by a group of whom he had never heard, Brian Epstein took his first, tentative steps into the dank Cavern Club in Liverpool and found himself transfixed by the sight and sound of the Beatles.

For the contest had come to the attention of Bengt Bernhag, the famous, talent-spotting head of Polar Music, who just happened to be looking for a clean-cut Swedish light pop-folk band, and he was supposedly attracted as much by their pleasing name as by the fact that they had made it this far in the competition. He contacted the band and asked them to send a demo tape, which they duly recorded and sent off. One of the tracks was 'Ave Maria No Moro', which made it on to the band's debut EP and, perhaps most significantly, contained within its lyrics a reference to 'Chiquitita' which Ulvaeus would store away in his memory and retrieve some 15 years later, when he was struggling with the opening of the chorus to a Hispanic-themed love song that he had planned to call 'In the Arms of Rosalita'.

Bernhag and Stig Anderson were sufficiently impressed to decide that the West Bay Singers should be the first band on their label. Stig headed off to Västervik to convince them that Polar should be their home. It wasn't that easy, but persuade them he did.

Bernhag's unerring knack for spotting talent had served him well once again. The band's first recording furnished them with their first hit single, 'Jag väntar vid min mila'. Speaking, nearly 40 years later, to Andrew Billen of *The Times* on 29 July 2003, Björn explained: 'A famous Swedish poet [Dan Andersson] wrote a poem and someone [Gunnar Turesson] put music to that. It means, I don't know, "I Am Waiting by My Mila". A *mila* is where you make charcoal in the middle of a forest. It is not something you do in England.'

The most important weapons in Stig Anderson's armoury were simply his blind faith in himself and his charges and his relentless ambition. He had some good instincts – and some lousy ones. His gut decision to go with the West Bay Singers – and, it must be said, Bernhag's determination was at least as crucial here – was one of his better moves. Having secured their services, Stig immediately decided that their perfectly acceptable name was too weak and insisted they change it at once. He was convinced that the current hootenanny movement, a trend of semi-informal folk-music gatherings that was happening in the US, was destined to last, and decided that rechristening his protégés the Hootenanny Singers would give them a boost and ensure a long and prosperous career. He was right about the length and success of the career, but hootenanny proved to be a flash in the pan, and for the following decade, through 30-odd singles, eight EPs and more than a dozen albums, Ulvaeus and his bandmates lumbered along under a name that they considered an embarrassment from the start.

A second condition imposed on the band on their signing up was that they should sing in Swedish, something to which the members, Ulvaeus, Rooth, Johann Karlberg and Hansi Schwarz, were all resistant. They rather thought of themselves, as the Hep Stars would with marginally less self-delusion, as a kind of Swedish Beatles, and wanted to sing in English. A compromise would be reached by the time of their first album, which was divided between Swedish- and English-language numbers (including a version of 'This Little Light of Mine'), with the Spanish 'Ave Maria No Moro' thrown in for good measure.

But the band's first recording, 'Jag väntar vid min mila' ('I'm Waiting by My Mila'), proved that, commercially speaking at least, Bernhag and Anderson's faith in them had been well placed, and that their insistence on courting an audience thirsty for soft pop-folk sung in Swedish was shrewd. The track that had helped the group to success on the talent show was equally successful when released as a single, providing the newly born Hootenanny Singers with a top-ten hit. Listening to the track today, you hear a rather touching, pretty version, graced with some of the light harmonies which would be the band's trademark, of an old light folk song, the performance coming over something like the Bachelors, but without the dangerous edge or the raw sexual energy.

What you don't hear in the early recordings is the obvious beginnings of a great pop career. This is clean-cut, very basic, marshmallow pop-folk. The group clearly didn't have a great deal of faith in their futures as musicians, all of them continuing their studies at the same time as pursuing their careers as Scandinavian pop stars.

Whatever the international limitations of the song's subject matter, and not least the untranslatability of the title, it was a pretty number and effectively launched the career of a band who would provide the backbone of Polar Music's success. The next couple of years were formative ones for the band and saw Björn take an ever more dominant role in their recordings. There was also a slight change in style and a general increase in professionalism, mainly as a result of the astonishing number of live concerts that the group performed.

Of more importance to the history of pop music was a decision that Björn made. In November 1963 the Rolling Stones enjoyed their second hit with 'I Wanna Be Your Man', a famously hastily penned song by Lennon and McCartney. Jagger and Richard had noted this and, finally acting on this seminal inspiration, collaborated on their first composition, 'The Last Time', which in 1965 provided the Stones with their first UK number one. The Beatles are the model for so much that followed, establishing the paradigm for the pop or rock band in terms of musical and career development. They themselves traced the evolution from a covers band, via tentative, derivative early compositions by the group's creative core, through the gradual, sometimes dramatic evolution of a musical style, the dabbling in movies, then, in a process that reversed the coalescence of the early years, a splintering leading to a bitter end involving recourse to law, and finally to the disappointments and occasional glories of the solo years. They were the models for much of what Abba did, not least in inspiring Björn, after he noticed the credits on one of their early albums, to have a go at songwriting himself.

The results were intriguing, moderately successful and modestly promising. 'Baby Those Are the Rules' is to some extent at least a risible piece of sexist nonsense:

Always be right on time, always give me kicks
It is not such a crime if I look at chicks.

Björn was responsible for the not-too-bad tune, which had about it a touch of 'You Better Move On', among other things. He couldn't be blamed for the lyrics, which came courtesy of Sandy Alexander, an American record producer and frankly obscure musical personage, the zenith of whose career in the business these lyrics seem to constitute. The appallingness of the words didn't prevent the song from being yet another hit for the band, early in 1967.

Just a little better was 'No Time', an anti-money number recorded some months before 'Baby Those Are the Rules' and dealing with breadheads rushing around 'to get to their employ-ment', the message being that 'this life was meant for living'. This was the first song that Björn had created all alone, and in June 1966 it became the band's sixth hit single. As Benny Andersson had done just a few months earlier, Björn had found a popular touch with his very first song. But a little over a week before 'No Time' hit the charts he bumped into the man who would become his writing partner for the following 38 years and counting.

We're quite different in many ways. He's more stable, I think.
He has an abundance of self-confidence in situations
where I have none. Maybe the two together make a
kind of whole. Björn Ulvaeus on Benny Andersson

B IS ALSO FOR BENNY

If Björn Ulvaeus was the galvanising spirit and, alongside Stig Anderson, business brains behind Abba's world-conquering success, then its quixotic, inspired creative force was Benny Andersson. As for the other members of Abba in childhood, music was a consuming passion for the young Benny, but in his case it was in the blood, his father and his grandfather both being accomplished, semi-professional accordionists who separately and together introduced the youngster to the instrument and nurtured his obvious musical talent from the outset. While the young Agnetha, Anni-Frid and Björn would all taste at least a degree of success in their pre-Abba pop lives, Benny would, almost by chance and through the sheer exuberance of his talent, find himself, while still a teenager, a member of what quickly became and remained for several years the most popular band in Sweden. Some described the group as Sweden's answer to the Beatles, although, as is often the case in such cultural translations, it is possible that they hadn't quite understood the question.

Benny, christened Göran Bror Benny Andersson, was born in Stockholm on 16 December 1946. Aside from being a modestly successful engineer, his father, Gösta, was a keen amateur musician who bought his son his first accordion for his sixth birthday. Even before then Benny had been immersed in music and had an abiding love for and knowledge of Sweden's rich folk-music culture. To this day the alternately jovial or sentimental tunes that constitute the mainstream of Swedish folk music are Benny's madeleines, songs that instantly transport him back to glorious childhood summers spent at the family's modest summer house on an island in the Stockholm archipelago. Thanks largely to his grandfather Efraim's patient efforts, Benny quickly became an accomplished accordionist and in time the three generations of Andersson men would perform together, alternating between traditional Swedish folk music and the *schlager*, the more modern style of sentimental folk song.

When he was ten Benny was given his first piano by his parents, and this instrument quickly became the centre of his life. He received some formal training but was essentially self-taught, sitting at the keyboard for hours at a time every day. While he always retained his love of all forms of Nordic folk music, he soon developed eclectic tastes and has recalled that one of his very earliest record purchases was Elvis Presley's single 'Jailhouse Rock'. Benny planned, or more likely it was planned for him, to follow in his father's footsteps and train as an engineer, so he left school at 15 and embarked on his engineering training. But these studies held little interest for him and the boredom he felt was relieved only by his musical adventures, in the early months at least. Well, it wasn't his only distraction – at the age of 14 while playing piano in a youth theatre group, he met 17-year-old Christina Grönvall, and despite the chasm between their ages the two embarked on a semi-secret romance.

Andersson was still just 15 and balancing his studies and his beloved music when he discovered that Christina was pregnant. Their son Peter was born on 20 August 1963. Galvanised into action, Benny took the apparently perverse decision to give up his engineering course and devote himself to music. Having been in various bands, he played his first serious gig when he was recruited into an outfit called Elverkets Spelmanslag (the Electricity Company's Folk Group – dreadful band names would be a prominent feature in Abba's prehistory). This jokey group were never going to be more than a stepping stone for the ambitious if unfocused young Benny, but they proved very effective in this role, bringing him to the attention of a band that really looked like they might be going places, albeit with a name perhaps even worse than Elverkets Spelmanslag.

The Hep Stars were already an established band with a small local following and a single release by the time they recruited Benny. Unlike Elverkets Spelmanslag, they could boast a professional and competent manager in the shape of Åke Gerhard, and when they found themselves in need of a temporary replacement keyboard player in the autumn of 1964 they didn't hesitate before turning to the teenager whose energetic and highly accomplished stage performances they had witnessed first-hand. Benny eagerly accepted the offer and became, almost from his first appearance on stage with the Hep Stars, their driving musical force. Just as Ulvaeus would when adopted by the band who eventually became the Hootenanny Singers, so Benny Andersson became a galvanising influence, and his move was soon made permanent.

In 1965 the Hep Stars released a succession of cheaply recorded cover versions as singles, among them Eddie Cochrane's 'Summertime Blues' and the more obscure and truly dreadful 'A Tribute to Buddy Holly'. Before long they hit gold with a reworking of Vince Taylor's 'Brand New Cadillac', which many years later was covered by the Clash, the influential political punk band led by the late, great Joe Strummer, who was, incidentally, an avowed Abba fan. With some sparse production and Svenne Hedlund's louche vocal performance, and boosted by the band's first TV appearance, this became the first of many national number ones for the Hep Stars. This first hit was soon followed by the revival of 'A Tribute to Buddy Holly', which somehow reached number five in the charts. The band's first, rough session then produced its second smash hit, with the reappearance of the Coasters-inflected 'Farmer John', which replaced 'Brand New Cadillac' at the top of the charts.

As the Beatles, the Rolling Stones and the Who had been in their early days, the Hep Stars were a super-energised covers band, in their case producing competent renditions live and, for their first studio album, gauchely called *We and Our Cadillac*, rough-and-ready covers of early rock-'n'-roll standards by Presley, Neil Sedaka, Little Richard and others. But, just as the British beat bands had done before them, the Hep Stars, and in particular Benny, quickly understood that if they were to have a sustainable career and develop a profile of their own they would have to start writing their own material.

As by some distance the group's most talented musician, Benny was the obvious, indeed the only, candidate to become their in-house composer, and his career began auspiciously with his first composition, 'No Response', which became a top-ten hit for the group. This song is pretty accomplished for a first effort at composition – a very simple, bluesy, skiffle sound, with an uncomplicated Beatles-y chorus. The Fab Four were patently Andersson's model and this is an OK Beatles pastiche, as demonstrated by the Beatles-quoting chorus: 'That's no response, no reply.' The track falls down badly with its lyrics, which scan perfectly but are otherwise incompetent, scarcely making sense, although clearly the lack of coherence was of no concern to the rest of the band, and anyway, at just over a minute and a half, it hardly outstays its welcome. Whatever the number's lack of sophistication, Benny had proved to himself that he could write a song of his own, and a hit to boot, for the song, released as the band's next single, reached number two in the Swedish charts.

His second effort, 'Sunny Girl', was, despite lyrics that Benny himself dismissed as 'lousy', an even bigger hit, reaching number one in 1966 and remaining there for six weeks. A sweet harpsichord introduction leads to the inept lines 'She's a sunny girl, a real girl', and later a chorus that boasts the magnificently, heroically bad 'She's domestic, she is property, she's slim like reed'. This time the inspiration seems not to be directly the Beatles, but more a Peter and Gordon vibe – the latter's big hit of the previous year, 'A World without Love', was a Lennon and McCartney composition. There are also, for those seeking the roots of the proto-Abba sound, strong echoes of the Searchers, especially 'I'll Never Find Another You', and, in the song's opening melody, just a hint of 'The Young Ones', Cliff Richard and the Shadows having been acknowledged as role models in the early days of the Hep Stars.

The identification of the many and varied inspirations in the composition of favourite artists' work is something between a diversion and obsession for fans and critics, but it is not merely an idle game. Particularly with a writing partnership like Andersson and Ulvaeus, whose own musical passions were so catholic – early American rock 'n' roll, American and European pop, classical, the folk music of Scandinavia, Germany, Italy and France, stage and screen musicals – it is telling to pinpoint how these influences are evident, sometimes too evident, in their early compositions, and gauge the process whereby they discover their own personalities and talents, gradually assimilate these influences and become distinctive songwriters in their own right, whose work in its turn may inspire and help to shape later generations of pop musicians.

Benny was now on a roll that has scarcely come to an end since. By the time of his next song, 'Wedding', co-written with the Hep Stars' lead singer, Svenne Hedlund, he was letting his already voluminous hair down, spreading his wings and producing a rather accomplished, classically influenced piece which, it must be noted, was a rather dismal reflection on the institution of marriage, coming as it did from a 19-year-old man who was at the time engaged and expecting his second child. Among its observations:

> *Listen to the preacher praying*
> *All the words he's saying*
> *Makes me feel very cold inside...*
>
> *... Now's the time when fun is over.*

But, then again, maybe something gets lost in translation in a song that includes the line 'Will you take this girl as wife?' As Steve Martin once observed: 'Some people have a way with words, and other people not have way.' Whatever the syntactical failings – and Benny made no secret of the fact that his English was all but non-existent and his early efforts were achieved with the aid of a dictionary, his ambitions never going beyond the exigencies of rhyme and efficient scansion – the words do seem to betray a certain cynicism about marriage. This makes it rather surprising that Benny chose to perform the song at the nuptials of Björn and Agnetha in the summer of 1971. It seems a little like a godparent standing up to recite Larkin's 'This Be the Verse' at a christening.

Perhaps it is no great surprise after all that neither of the Abba marriages stood the test of time. Back in late 1966, the writing was already on the wall for Benny's relationship, but, to look on the bright side, what was equally clear was that a songwriter of serious potential had begun his career. Andersson was helped by the fact that he began to write songs within the framework of an already, indeed instantly, successful pop band, but his record is nevertheless astonishing. Of his first three efforts at crafting pop songs, the very first reached number two in the charts and both of the follow-ups hit the top spot.

The run continued with 'Consolation', which, with its slightly trippy, late-sixties, Love-like feel, was a further development of Andersson's talents. The song benefits from the fact that the words are trickier to hear this time round and, when you can make them out, the fact that they don't necessarily make sense is much less of a problem – acid-tinged songs were supposed to be nonsensical – and there is a certain atmospheric menace in odd mentions of 'breakdowns' and 'burning bridges'.

Around the time that Benny wrote 'Consolation' – on Sunday 5 June 1966, to be precise – there took place a meeting every bit as significant in the annals of pop music as Paul McCartney and John Lennon's bumping into each other almost exactly ten years earlier, on 15 June 1956, at a fête in Woolton Parish Church in Liverpool, or, a few years earlier still, Keith Richard's bumping into Mick Jagger in the playground of Wentworth County Primary School in Dartford, Kent, or the moment when John Lydon, aka Johnny Rotten, met Simon Beverley, aka Sid Vicious (another Abba fan), in the corridors of London's Hackney Technical College in 1973.

The Hep Stars and the Hootenanny Singers were in the midst of summer-long tours of *folkparket* when both bands found themselves booked to play short sets at the end of a three-day festival at a site just outside the small town of Falköping, in southern Sweden. After briefly exchanging words as cars containing the two bands passed on a road near the venue where the Hootenanny Singers were about to play and the Hep Stars had already performed, these two stalwarts of the Swedish pop scene and the *folkparket* circuit seemed to hit it off right from the start, and the former invited the latter to a party they were planning for later that night in a hotel in Linköping, a town on the other side of Lake Vattern from Falköping. This party was in part planned as a send-off for the various members of the Hootenanny Singers, who were reluctantly about to head off and start their national service. After a confusion about the venue for the party – a confusion that reputedly saw the Hep Stars driving nearly a hundred miles in the wrong direction – the bands finally met up in the very early morning of Monday 6 June. The drinking continued at a nearby park, where the new fast friends Benny and Björn led the carousers in drunken renditions of shared favourites, notably Beatles songs.

As Benny said when interviewed in the *Independent* in 1996 about his first meeting with Björn: 'I think we got on well together – and we still do – because when we met we were both writing songs, we were the same age and we were sharing the same experiences in life.' Björn recalled in the same article: 'I can't remember much about that night except we talked, mostly about music, and he seemed a nice guy.'

Later that same day Björn and his bandmates turned up at their barracks for the beginning of their military service, but quickly found that a sympathetic commanding officer would allow the group plenty of time off to continue their musical pursuits. So it was that, less than three weeks later, Björn and Benny met up again, and this time, while also cementing their friendship with copious amounts of drink, the pair, the key song-writers in their respective bands, decided to have a go at writing something together. They also resolved that there was no time like the present and at once headed off to Björn's parents' flat, and from there to the family paper mill, an unglamorous if appropriately factory-like venue for the start of one of popular music's great compositional partnerships.

The result was 'Isn't It Easy to Say'. Neither composer has professed a lasting fondness for the song – Björn commented many years later: 'Let's just say it wasn't the best song we ever wrote' – which made it on to the next Hep Stars album, but it did mark one of the most significant developments in the careers, now suddenly intertwined, of two of the rising stars in Sweden's parochial pop scene. Listening to it today, you can't help feeling that they were unduly tough on their first co-composition. With the gift and curse of hindsight one may tend to overstate the true importance of events and the quality of creations, but 'Isn't It Easy to Say' is at the very least a promising, sweet, pretty song, a wistful romantic ditty instantly redolent of its pre-Summer of Love time, with a just slightly underworked verse leading to a rather lovely chorus. With a bit of tweaking, you could easily imagine this having provided a decent-sized hit for, say, the Monkees.

It wasn't just Benny and Björn who had become close – there had developed an instant rapport between the two groups, despite the folksiness of the Hootenanny Singers and the raucous pop of the Hep Stars. Aside from their shared fondness for early

American rock 'n' roll, the Beach Boys, the Beatles and Swedish folk music, the two sets of musicians were drawn together by their fondness for drinking. Various members, among them Björn and Benny, started to appear on one another's records, a symbiosis that progressed until, on the evening of 26 December 1966, Björn stood in as guitarist with the Hep Stars, a night that he still counts as one of the happiest, most purely enjoyable moments of his 40-year career. So Björn and Benny had now got drunk together, sung together, composed together and performed together in the studio and live on stage. Their personal and professional relationship would survive and thrive into the 21st century, and the cornerstone of the band that would organically emerge as Abba was in place.

> *She's achieved amazing things in Sweden, something she would never have been able to do had she stayed in Norway, where she would have been branded a freak.*
> Tor Brandacher, spokesman for Krigsbarnforbundet Lebensborn (an organisation established to protect the rights of the Lebensborn children), on Frida

A IS ALSO FOR ANNI-FRID

There is a temptation to regard the story of Anni-Frid Lyngstad – generally known from her early teens as Frida – as a real-life fairy tale, one in which the pretty and wilful orphan battles against the obstacles put in her path to find wealth and fame, and win for herself a real prince. But Frida's prince died young, as, tragically, did one of her children, and no conventional fairy tale so far written has told of a daughter born out of wedlock to a Nazi officer in an occupied country.

Frida's remarkable story began in the unprepossessing Norwegian coastal town of Ballangen, near Narvik, a small but tactically vital port, in the immediate aftermath of the Second

World War. German forces had invaded Norway on 9 April 1940 and exactly two months later, after an ultimately disastrous attempt by British forces to aid the Norwegians, the country fell; it would remain an occupied territory until VE Day, 8 May 1945. Ten days after Norway had finally succumbed to the invaders, Frida's mother, Synni Lyngstad, celebrated her 14th birthday.

Precious little is known about Synni's personality but it is said that the great passion in her short life, aside from her sole lover and one child, was music. Her father, Simon – who was reputedly sympathetic to if not actively involved in the Hjemmefronten (Home Front), the Norwegian resistance movement, which is said to have included as many as 50,000 members – grew ill and died in early 1941, leaving Synni in the hands of her apparently formidable mother, Agny.

Even with her father out of the way, there were plenty of friends and family members around to express their disapproval of Synni's first and only great romance, which began at the height of the occupation. Synni was just 17 when, in the autumn of 1943, Alfred Haase, a sergeant in the German army, was posted to Ballangen. This rather handsome 24-year-old was already married and had recently celebrated the birth of his first child, but neither of these facts prevented him from embarking on a romance with a girl seven years his junior, a relationship that would have been every bit as popular with Haase's superiors as it was unpopular with Synni's friends, family and neighbours.

One of the less examined aspects of the Second World War was the Lebensborn programme. Reacting in part to the dramatic loss of young lives across Germany and occupied territories, but more generally in a concerted effort to increase the number of Aryan children being brought up by approved families, Himmler put into action what was effectively an Aryan breeding programme on a massive scale. The Lebensborn programme had several constituent parts. In the late 1930s Lebensborn homes were established across Germany to which selected Aryan women impregnated by Aryan men could come to give birth in security, and then either bring up the children themselves or hand them over to carefully chosen families for adoption. From the start of the war there was a campaign to systematically kidnap children from occupied territories and rehouse them with Aryan families. Some authorities estimate that as many as 200,000 Polish children were kidnapped, perhaps as many as 50,000 Ukrainian children and a similar number from the Baltic states.

In Norway a wholly different strategy was implemented. Regardless of their marital status back home, Nazi soldiers stationed in Norway – and the German occupation forces numbered around 400,000 men – were actively encouraged to embark on romantic relationships with Norwegian women. Fifteen Lebensborn homes were established to care for the children – perhaps as many as 12,000 – born of these unions, as well as their mothers.

Back in Ballangen in the early summer of 1944, the nascent, illicit and therefore largely secret romance between Alfred Haase and Synni Lyngstad was edging towards consummation. The final romantic gesture on Alfred's part, one that served as a prelude, if not necessarily an irresistible enticement, to the couple's first love-making, was the rather unromantic-seeming gift of a sack of potatoes; but then it was wartime. Whether or not Alfred was, in his unconventional but ultimately effective seduction of the young Synni, acting consciously according to the dictates of Himmler's Lebensborn policy, one thing is clear: he didn't tell her that he was a married father until after they had made love for the first time. Nevertheless, the romance continued to blossom until, in the autumn of that year, it was suddenly and, it appeared, terminally broken off when Alfred was posted to the town of Bogenviken, some 30 miles north-east of Ballangen and therefore impossibly remote.

Had that been the end of it, the landscape of pop culture in the 1970s and beyond would have been unimaginably different, but fate dealt Alfred the opportunity for one final meeting with his young conquest. Sometime around 10 February 1945 – Haase himself was, when he recalled the events more than three decades later, somewhat hazy on the details – he was told that he and his regiment were being shipped out of Narvik and back to Germany. They were moved to Narvik, from where their ship was due to leave early the following morning. Alfred seized the opportunity and borrowed a comrade's bicycle, undertaking – and there is at least a suspicion of *post factum* romanticism here – the 60-mile round trip in the middle of the notoriously harsh northern Norwegian winter. Whatever the precise circumstances of this meeting, what is beyond doubt is that this was the last time the pair made love, and indeed, when he bade her farewell on the way back to his ship, this was the last that Alfred and Synni ever saw of each other.

What is equally certain is that Synni was left pregnant by Alfred. Again, from this point on, some of the details within the accepted version of events are at times either hazy or not wholly convincing or both. Alfred had apparently left his young girl-friend swearing that he would one day return, and it is claimed by some members of Synni's family that he had departed knowing that she was pregnant. It is clear that Synni wrote several letters to Alfred after he was back in Germany, declaring her undying love and either informing or reminding him that she was now carrying his child. Many years later Alfred would claim never to have received any of these, and further insist that he had himself written to Synni on several occasions. Whether or not they existed in the first place, his letters certainly never arrived in Norway, and having received no answer to her own various

25

letters, Synni, along with her mother and the rest of the Lyngstad family, ultimately concluded – why, it isn't wholly obvious – that the ship on which Alfred was being transported had been sunk on the way back to Germany.

Synni was, according to her family's account, overjoyed to be pregnant. But, whatever the extent of the now 18-year-old's naïvety, this bliss must have been tempered both by the loss of her unborn child's father and by the realisation that the fruit of this very dangerous liaison was unlikely to be warmly welcomed into the bosom of a community that, over the past four and a half years, had made patently clear its feelings about any form of collaboration. Synni was destined to discover just how violent was the Norwegian hatred of anything tainted by association with the despised German occupiers.

The Nazis' occupation of Norway finally came to an end in May 1945. Six months later, on 15 November, Synni gave birth to a daughter whom she named Anni-Frid Synni Lyngstad. Synni had, even before the birth, begun to sense the sting of rejection, often violent in nature, although in her case thankfully not physically so, that the children born of German fathers, known as *tyskebarna,* and their mothers were destined to encounter for many years to come. It is hard to describe the doomed Synni or her soon-to-be-motherless daughter as lucky, but they were less unfortunate than many of the *tyskebarna* and their families.

Norwegians are justly proud of the staunch and heroic resistance movement that sustained a relentless, albeit to a large extent ineffectual, guerrilla campaign against the occupying force. The treatment of the *tyskebarna,* who, as mentioned earlier, numbered perhaps as many as 12,000, has been, until the past few years, something of a dark secret in recent Norwegian history, a stain on the country's reputation for national propriety and its care for the weaker members of society.

The pattern of the oppressed, once freed from their shackles, mimicking the behaviour of their former oppressors, is a familiar one throughout history, and the bitterness felt towards the Germans by the Norwegians was given vent in the latter's treatment of the Lebensborn children and their mothers. By a cruel irony the Norwegians adopted the same view of the contentious study of eugenics as the Germans had in their treatment of Jews and the mentally and physically handicapped, towards their own despised enemy within. Under a government-sanctioned policy many of the children who had been born and kept in the Lebensborn homes were categorised as mentally retarded and dispatched to mental institutions. Only in recent years has this systematic abuse been acknowledged, following the documentation of cases of psychological maltreatment, as well as of physical torture and rape.

In Ballangen, Synni had been forced to cope with little more than ostracism from her community. It was her mother, the nearly 50-year-old Agny, who saw the potential dangers ahead and wanted better for little Anni-Frid. So, sometime in early to mid-1947, Agny took Anni-Frid across the border and into Sweden. They were soon joined by Synni, and by the late summer the three had moved to Malmköping, a small town outside Stockholm, where Agny made ends meet with a number of menial jobs.

Then, in September, just when Anni-Frid's turbulent short life seemed to be settling into something approximating domestic normality, Synni collapsed and was rushed to hospital with what turned out to be renal failure. After a couple of weeks on her sickbed, she succumbed to complete kidney failure and died on 28 September 1947 at the age of 21. Two months short of her own second birthday, Synni's beloved daughter was left an orphan – or so it seemed.

For much of her childhood Anni-Frid was a lonely child if not actually friendless, and her isolation was no less acute at home, for the bright but reserved child had little in common with her stern, though devoted and always solicitous, Norwegian grandmother, a woman who was prematurely aged by the efforts of caring for her granddaughter. In later years Frida would comment that her reluctance to display physical affection towards her two children was the result of her own loveless childhood. Anni-Frid would look for a degree of solace and comfort elsewhere. She was a prodigious reader, but found even greater joy in music, especially singing. Anni-Frid inherited her love of music from both her mother and, in a more concrete sense, Agny, who introduced her to the traditional folk songs of both her native and adopted countries.

In time Anni-Frid, having moved to the outskirts of Eskilstuna, a small town a short distance from Stockholm – years later her collaborator the jazz pianist Charlie Norman would remember how she was affectionately referred to on the circuit as 'that girl from Eskilstuna' – would sing at school and in local church choirs. Since before her teenage years Anni-Frid had determined with quiet resolution that her future lay in music, while elsewhere across Sweden the other future members of Abba had made similar decisions.

Although she would be, in purely commercial terms, the least proven of her bandmates when Abba was born, Anni-Frid was the most focused on her goal and also the most precocious when it came to securing what would be her big break in the music business. By the time she was 13 she had already been studying the piano for two years and regularly performing live, generally at talent shows. So, as a veteran of sorts, she felt sufficiently emboldened to approach a local band leader by the name of Evald Ek and offer to fill the vacancy of lead singer with his quintet. It was hardly the big time, but she was delighted to get the gig, and so Anni-Frid, only just a teenager, went on the road with a grown-up dance band, with her grandmother's blessing, as the singer of show tunes – Doris Day numbers were a special favourite of hers – as well as the folk songs with which she had grown up. By this stage she had also acquired the nickname Frida, by which she would be known personally, although not always professionally, from then on.

While Frida lacked the vocal delicacy that was Agnetha's speciality, in many respects she scored over the woman who would be her colleague and rival and, for a while at least, friend. Agnetha's very delicacy, so effective at portraying romantic pain and vulnerability, often spilt over into a rather less desirable brand of fragility, and the younger vocalist would be dogged by accusations of singing flat. Frida's voice was not merely more robust and reliable an instrument, it was also very much more versatile. Agnetha would, as Frida did, start out as a singer with a show band, but Frida, whose training, both formal and informal, had been more diverse, was called upon from her earliest days on stage to make frequent and dramatic shifts in musical form.

During the same period – and she sang with Ek's band for 18 months – Frida received advanced vocal training from Folke Andersson, an established opera singer. When Ek's band ran out of steam in the early summer of 1961, Frida accepted offers to front a number of dance bands on an *ad hoc* basis, before taking a job that, while merely consolidating her semi-formal vocal training, had a profound effect on her personal life. Taking the position with the Bengt Sandlund Orchester required Frida to broaden her vocal repertoire still further and branch out into jazz, which became her preferred musical genre for the remainder of the decade. More significantly still, the job introduced her to the band's physically unprepossessing trombonist, Ragnar Fredriksson, whose occupation away from music was in the distinctly unglamorous arena of his family carpet business.

A relationship between the two very quickly blossomed and in mid-1962 Frida, still only 16, found herself pregnant. On 23 January 1963 she gave birth to Hans Ragnar Fredriksson. Although she dearly loved her child, pregnancy and motherhood were something of an inconvenience for the fiercely ambitious Frida. She had to retire, at least temporarily, from the music scene. Things looked more worrying still on the professional front when Sandlund wound up the band in the spring of that year. But Frida never gave up hope, continuing her vocal training with Andersson, and in September came her biggest break thus far when she entered the talent competition Plats på scen (A Place on the Stage), winning her way on to the radio-broadcast final, alongside five other acts, among them the Hootenanny Singers.

While Plats på scen was the making of Björn Ulvaeus and his bandmates, for Frida it turned out to be a frustrating, tantalising brush with fame. She returned to the domestic life, in time married life, which she found ever more claustrophobic. At least there was still her music career, such as it was. Next up was the Sandevärn Orchester, a grand name for a small band, one that featured Ragnar on trombone. All the while Frida's ambition was to do something more, something else, and after she'd fallen pregnant again the joy of the birth of her second child, Ann Lise-Lott, later known as Lise-Lott, was tempered by the increased threat to the possibility of her fulfilling her dreams. Whatever the restrictions that motherhood entailed, Frida was as determined as ever to make it as a singer.

After the Sandevärn Orchester morphed into the Anni-Frid Four, her career finally suddenly took a dramatic turn for the better. She entered another talent competition, Nya ansikten (New Faces), which was broadcast on Swedish television on Sunday 3 September 1967 in a special show to mark Sweden's change-over from driving on the left to the right. The show was watched by a million people and Frida won the contest with her rendition of the popular song 'En ledig dag' ('A Day Off').

She attracted the interest of several record companies and was snapped up by EMI, but although her professionalism and technical ability belied her lack of previous experience in a studio, her recordings failed to win over the public. Her career plodded on at this level for the next couple of years, until there occurred a dramatic change in her circumstances. In early 1969, having accepted the offer of becoming the singer alongside veteran cabaret pianist Charlie Norman on an upcoming tour, Frida finally resolved to do what she had been threatening to do for some time: she left her husband Ragnar to look after their children, so that she could dedicate herself full-time to making her big break. Not long after she moved to Stockholm, her life took a dramatic upturn when she had an entry in the Swedish heat for the 1969 Eurovision Song Contest. Her effort fared poorly but the occasion marked the first fleeting encounter between her and Benny Andersson, who had written another of the entries, one that narrowly missed out on selection for the final.

It was not the last time that the two would meet, nor was it the last time they would share the disappointment of failing to qualify for the contest that would five years later propel them to international fame.

CHAPTER TWO

'SOMETHING'S ON THE WAY'

Swedish national service was not an especially arduous experience for the Hootenanny Singers, who were allowed to continue with their musical careers pretty much unbothered by the army. Aside from their extensive touring, the group were effectively the house band for Stig Anderson and Bengt Bernhag's young record label, and as such were selected to take on the Swedish versions of international hits that had become something of a speciality for Anderson. So they enjoyed a hit of their own with 'En sång en gång for längesen' ('A Song of a Time a Long Time Ago' – it's not a particularly good title in Swedish, either), a very rough translation of the Tom Jones hit 'The Green Green Grass of Home'. The recording of what turned out to be the band's biggest hit up to that time, January 1967, reached number two in the Swedish charts. This was especially significant, largely because it represented a major schism in the band, setting the seal on what had been apparent for some time: that the Hootenanny Singers had become Björn's own band in all but name. The single effectively launched him as a solo act, for although the song appeared under the name of the Hootenanny Singers, Björn was the only member of the band to appear on the track, the backing being provided by a small orchestra.

The summer of 1968, around the time Björn and Agnetha first met, saw the release of 'Raring' ('Sweetheart'), Stig's adaptation of the Bobby Goldsboro hit 'Honey', which was rather well performed by Björn and provided him with his first solo hit single. The follow-up was 'Fröken Fredriksson' ('Miss Fredriksson'), a jokey but not especially funny take on 'Harper Valley P.T.A.', which, like its predecessor, crept into the Swedish top ten.

'Saknar du något min kära' ('Are You Longing for Something, My Darling') was one of the most effective of Stig's many hit translations, this one a transposition to late-sixties Sweden of Peter Sarstedt's classic 'Where Do You Go to My Lovely', one complete with particularly Swedish references to, among other things, Ingrid Thulin's eyes. It would become Björn's third and thus far finest, if least commercially successful, solo effort. By the time it hit the lower reaches of the top 20 at the height of the summer of 1969, Björn had started to date Agnetha as discreetly as he could manage, their affair having blossomed after they took part in the same TV show. They couldn't keep the secret for long and within weeks of their affair beginning Björn and Agnetha had become the golden couple of Swedish tabloid newspapers. Their relationship with the Swedish media would not always be so harmonious.

By the time of the meeting between Björn and Benny, the Hep Stars were up and running, and while they would remain Sweden's most popular band throughout the decade, it was 1966, the year in which Andersson had learned that on top of his natural musical talent and showmanship he had a certain raw flair for songwriting, that proved to be the band's peak. Towards the end of that year the decision was taken to follow the path that the Beatles had taken two years earlier and transfer the band's appeal to celluloid. This would prove to be, as is explained at greater length in Chapter 14, something of a disastrous move, although it did yield the novelty hit 'Malaika' in 1967.

At the same time the band were embarking on what was a crucial, extended and, as it proved, terminal debate about their musical direction. As the Hootenanny Singers had already, and Agnetha would in time, the Hep Stars were confronting the question of how to translate their success at home, and in neighbouring countries, into a more substantial international breakthrough. They were to discover, following a couple of initially promising forays into the wider European market, that their appeal was fundamentally parochial. After all, who would want what was essentially an indifferent imitation of the Beatles, albeit a lively one boasting a songwriter of some promise, when the real band was still not merely around but at its creative peak?

But the Hep Stars had made their mark by singing in English, and in late 1966 took the apparently retrograde step of releasing 'I natt jag drömde', a fairly accurate translation of the old peacenik folk number 'Last Night I Had the Strangest Dream', a song which had significantly featured on the 1964 album *Wednesday Morning 3AM*, by Simon & Garfunkel, one of the key but little acknowledged influences on the early compositions of Andersson-Ulvaeus.

This inward movement was symbolic of a wider crisis in the band, both financial and creative. Their attempt to broaden into wider music-business concerns had to some extent failed. They had founded the Hep House organisation – and in this if nothing else they were ahead of the Beatles with their Apple company – as an umbrella operation to handle their business as a band, as producers overseeing other acts and also to serve as their publishing company. The company and the band members very soon reached financial meltdown, but at least Benny was exploring the broader possibilities of the business. He was a songwriter with a proven track record and was feeling increasingly at ease in a recording studio, as was Björn with his band.

The Hep Stars would continue to the end of the decade but only with significant changes in personnel. The year 1967 saw what should have been an auspicious moment in their development, musically and in terms of their potential marketability internationally, with the arrival of Curt Boettcher and his partner Steve Clark to handle their musical affairs. The pair, Boettcher in particular, had been key players as musicians and producers in the thriving West Coast soft-pop scene throughout the mid-sixties. Sadly, Boettcher and Clark fell out before the collaboration between them and the Hep Stars began properly. But then, for all their energy, their occasionally inspired moments of musicality and the emergence of Benny Andersson as a songwriter, the band were hamstrung by fundamental limitations. If nothing else, Clark recognised this problem and solved it with the brutal announcement that he would produce the next album, a work of soft 'sunshine pop', only if the group was stripped down to the bare essentials of Svenne Hedlund on vocals and Benny on keyboards, with session musicians performing all other duties on the record.

(The term 'sunshine pop' was coined to describe the musical genre that was effectively invented by Boettcher in his work with GoldeBriars, Sagittarius and the Millennium Cult, very uncommercial groups whose luscious harmonies influenced the Mamas and the Papas and Brian Wilson, the Beach Boys' resident genius. Boettcher would go on to sing backing vocals for the Beach Boys in some of their later recordings.)

The radical downsizing of the group resulted in *It's Been a Long Time*, a mediocre album which managed the negative double whammy of being a relative commercial flop in Sweden and failing to break the band in the US or indeed anywhere else.

By now the Hep Stars had decisively lost whatever focus or musical direction they may once have had, and their next attempt to extend their shelf life was scarcely more popular with the other members of the band than the humiliating treatment courtesy of Steve Clark. Svenne Hedlund's wife, Lotta, was brought in to share the lead vocals. (After the dissolution of the Hep Stars, Svenne and Lotta would form a musical double act and, under the guidance of Stig, Benny and Björn, enjoy a number of national hits, until the outside pressures of Abba forced the three increasingly to neglect them and the other smaller acts signed to Polar Music.)

It must be said that this decision didn't have any noticeably beneficial effect on the fortunes of the group, although 'Let It Be Me' is a rather sweet cover version of the Bécaud-Curtis track most famously recorded by the Everly Brothers, and 'Speleman' ('Fiddler') has a certain atmosphere and became a top-ten hit. 'Speleman' was an important record in the prehistory of Abba; the second of the Andersson-Ulvaeus compositions to become a hit single, it came shortly after the first to do so, 'Ljuva Sextital' ('The Wonderful Sixties'), which was recorded by Brita Borg.

However, by 1969 the Hep Stars had simply run out of steam, having some time before run out of inspiration. At the same time the Hootenanny Singers were in a similar crisis, riven by contrasting aims and ambitions which recall the confusion within the ranks of the Hep Stars, a lack of focus as to whether they were a pop group or a folk combo, and even in what language they should sing. By the time the Hep Stars called it a day, the Hootenanny Singers, although they would continue to record albums for the next couple of years, had themselves effectively finished as an active group, having given up the live performances with which they had established their reputation.

While Frida had risen to the level of a cabaret singer in urban nightclubs, the Hep Stars had been reduced to playing in the very same venues. It was at one such club in Malmö that Benny and Frida met properly a few days after their encounter at the Melodifestivalen, the show to select the Swedish entry for the 1969 Eurovision Song Contest. This time the pair got chatting and a connection was made but anything more than this seemed impossible, with Benny involved in another relationship at the time. But very soon they found that they were in love. These two young musicians – he already a star but with his career on a plateau if not on the way down, she progressing with frustrating slowness, still in search of her big break – had each found a soul-mate in the other. Aside from music, and a love of a good night out, they shared a similarly fractured domestic life, both having had two children as teenagers and both having left their partners in charge of the children, and work that made contact limited, although Benny was closer to a reconciliation with his young children than was Frida.

So 1969 was a key year for the various members of Abba. It was of profound importance on the personal level, witnessing the early stages of the two romantic relationships that would be at the heart of the band, but it also saw some serious low points as far as the musical careers of both Benny and Björn were concerned. But although their bands had effectively ceased to be, each man took solace in the growing working partnership with the other.

At the dawn of the 1970s, the decade in which Abba's manifest destiny would be realised in glorious Technicolor spandex, the various separate elements from which this force of pop glory would be formed were starting to coalesce. Björn Ulvaeus had been taken on as the protégé of the pop-management and production partnership of Stig Anderson and Bengt Bernhag, and from the outset had proved willing and able to learn from these more experienced figures, absorbing their knowledge of hit-making, songcraft, lyric composition, studio nous and, not least, business acumen. More significant still were the three over-lapping relationships from which Abba would grow.

Ulvaeus and Andersson had met, and formed an instant firm friendship based on complementary personalities and shared musical passions. This friendship had, almost from the beginning, leaked into their professional lives. They enjoyed, at times loved, performing together, but even more than this they experienced the same professional satisfaction – this more than anything that could be characterised in more joyous terms – from the careful crafting of a song. They were as critical – and, it must be said, sometimes justly so – of their earliest collaborations as they had been of their first solo songwriting efforts. But what they also noticed was that from the start, their compositions, wrought both separately and then together, had been at the very least competent, and, if not from the outset, then very soon, commercial.

They both struggled with lyrics in English and understood from the beginning that to sing in Swedish was fine for folk music but absurdly parochial in pop or rock, where English, specifically American English, was the *lingua franca*. Lyric-writing was hard enough for Andersson in his native tongue, and he confessed that his attempts at English composition were unpromising, whereas Ulvaeus had something of a gift for language, although it would take more than a decade of slogging away, his words aided and abetted by Stig Anderson in the early years of Abba, before he achieved anything approaching lyrical sophistication. But what was important as the 1970s were beginning was that Björn and Benny were a partnership, and were increasingly coming to believe that their friend, mentor and manager Stig was perhaps not too wildly optimistic when he insisted, as he often did, that they would one day write an international hit.

Of no less significance were the two romances that had blossomed in the previous year. From the very early days, when their budding relationship was the subject of speculative and, it soon turned out, accurate gossip in the national press, Björn and Agnetha were the golden couple of Swedish soft pop, and there was, of course, no other kind at this time. Although both were still young – Björn in his mid-twenties and Agnetha in her twentieth year – they were both seasoned professionals, hit-makers, blooded in life, in the studio and on the road. While Björn had been around slightly longer and was widely known, it was Agnetha who had enjoyed the first number-one hit, and she who was slightly more famous. With Benny and Frida it was he who was the real rock-'n'-roll star, as the second most prominent member of what had been for five years Sweden's most popular band, while she, although a gifted and versatile performer, was struggling to transform her talent into hits.

In retrospect the fusion of these two – or rather three – famous, talented twosomes into a pop foursome, and this band's progression into a hit-making outfit seem inevitable. But the formation of the band, while making sense to all four members from early on, was very far from inevitable. All of them were very ambitious and yet their ambitions seemed to be leading them in different directions. Already by 1970 the very fact that all four had been around so long meant that, even if they were not quite jaded by the prospect of performing live, then certainly life on the road had lost a great deal of its appeal, particularly the grinding routine of the summer *folkparket* circuit.

They had no way of knowing that what was waiting just round the corner was a recording that would further shape their destiny. The first-ever Abba album. Sort of.

CHAPTER THREE

'I HAVE A DREAM'

*I told myself that ultimately there could be a place for Stig
Anderson in the world of music.*   Stig Anderson

*The best thing that has happened to me was coming into contact
with Stig.*   Benny Andersson, speaking in 1976

As we will see, Bengt Bernhag would be vitally important to the
development of Abba, and his loss shortly before the band was
launched was keenly felt, particularly by his protégé Björn. But
for all his claims to the mantle, and those of studio maestro
Michael B. Tretow, there is really only one true candidate for the
title of fifth member of Abba, and that is Stig Anderson, Abba's
Peter Grant, Paul McGuinness, Kit Lambert, Brian Epstein,
even a touch of George Martin, all rolled into one.

Stig Erik Leopold Anderson (he was christened Andersson and
didn't drop an 's' until the early 1960s, and then without officially changing his name) was born in Mariestad, on the eastern
shores of Lake Vänern, in the southern-central province of
Västergötland on 25 January 1931. The twin motivating forces
in his early life were his illegitimacy – like Frida, Stig grew up
without a father, although he did eventually have a father figure
when his mother married the local tailor – and the humbleness
of his domestic circumstances. Stig was inspired by his mother's
tirelessness in taking whatever jobs she could in order to get by.

By day Ester Andersson worked in her home town of Hova, a few miles from Mariestad, as a hairdresser, but, as Agny Lyngstad would in the post-war years, she also took in washing, and once a week worked in a local sweet shop.

School held no interest for the young Stig. Even before he left – at just 13 – he had taken on the job of lighting the school's stove every day, a task for which he was paid a few kronor a week. When he did leave school he became a delivery boy for a local grocer, and then moved on to a poorly-paid menial job at the town's sports club. By this stage he had already proved that he was a grafter, but also, albeit on a lowly scale, a nascent entre-preneur. Using his contacts at the shop where he had his first job, he took on the concessions stand at sports events and quickly began to turn a tidy profit.

He was determined to get rich, but he had a very specific focus for his ambitions, being set from early childhood on achieving success in the music world. When he was five his mother had scraped together the money to buy a wind-up gramophone and a handful of 78s, at least one of them badly scratched. This paltry collection was enough to fire the boy, and as he began to sing along to these records he resolved to become a singer. Then, as he entered his teens, he would take any opportunity to sing that presented itself, at school or in local clubs.

Ester, seeing Stig's joy and determination and recognising the money-spinning potential of his great passion in life, bought him a guitar not long after he left school. Stig took to the instrument with complete dedication if no innate talent and enhanced the lessons he took at a local music school with dedicated practice at home. Soon he was ready to perform at local events, and right from the start he was utterly absorbed by everything that surrounded these occasions, the staging and the promotion as well as his own contributions to them. He would perform the sentimental *schlager*, a stock element of the Swedish and, more generally, the north-west European folk-music scene, but would soon add to his repertoire love ballads he had composed himself.

Stig had the drive, the chutzpah, but what he crucially lacked was a degree of technical proficiency, of composition skills, not to mention polish. He was recommended to enrol in the music course at the well-regarded Ingesund High School, just south of the town of Arvika in the province of Värmland. This he did in the autumn of 1949, and it was around this time that he met two people who would have a profound impact on both his personal and his professional life. A fellow student at the school was Gudrun Rystedt, a feisty farmer's daughter who would soon become his girlfriend. While maintaining his formal studies, Stig kept up his interest in musical revues in Arvika, where he was living. There two polar opposites – Bengt Bernhag was known as a taciturn, thoughtful, intelligent man – formed a friendship out of which a musical empire would be born.

At the same time Stig formed a musical trio with a couple of local friends, and continued to compose songs. One of these, 'Grädde på moset' (literally, 'Cream on the Pudding', but the sense is roughly equivalent to 'icing on the cake'), was taken up and recorded by a popular singer named Harry Brandelius. Sadly, the recording itself wasn't popular, and for the first but not the last time Stig would be frustrated at another's disappointing rendition of one of his songs. The next year another established performer, this time the comic Rolf Bengtson, recorded a version of another Anderson composition, this time his very first song, 'Tivedshambo' ('Hambo from Tived', a *hambo* being a folk dance), but with no more success.

In 1951 Anderson, who was training as a teacher, began his compulsory national service, but secured a short leave from this in the summer of 1952 to travel to Stockholm to record a single alongside his pal Bernhag, for the Philips label. Aside from giving Stig some brief early experience of the workings of a recording studio, the session's only substantial success was that Bernhag was offered a producer's job at the company.

After completing his military service, Stig, accompanied by Gudrun, headed to Stockholm, where he found work as a teacher while pursuing his musical dreams with undiminished determination. His songs, notably 'Det blir inget bröllop på Lördag' ('There Will Be No Wedding on Saturday'), continued to be covered by other artists, but true success evaded him until Nacka Skoglund's version of 'Vi hänger me' ('We're Still Here'), recorded in 1958, proved to be a fair-sized hit, allowing Stig and Gudrun, by this stage married with two children, to move into a more comfortable home.

The following year Anderson transformed his professional fortunes still more dramatically with his song 'Är du kär i mig ännu, Klas-Göran' ('Are You Still in Love with Me, Klas-Göran'). He had written this number for Lill-Babs, who was set to become one of Sweden's most enduringly popular singers. Lill-Babs was attached to Karusell records, where Bernhag was now working, and Anderson's old friend did indeed see to it that the song was given to the company's rising star. Written as a straightforward love song, it was transformed by Lill-Babs, under the express instructions of Bernhag as producer, into a broad comic number and as such provided Anderson with the first number one of his career.

As significant as the hit in itself was the impetus that the song gave to Stig's wider career in the business. Over the past few years his mixed experiences had confirmed for him the vital importance of maintaining control, both artistic and financial, over your own product. With this in mind he formed a publishing company to handle the rights of his compositions. This new company he modestly christened Sweden Music. In tandem with this new enterprise, he went into business with a Belgian entrepreneur, Robert Bosmans, setting up Bens Music, the company that would handle the rights for songs in the Netherlands and Scandinavia.

One element of this new deal was the acquisition of rights in foreign hits for the Scandinavian market. This gave Anderson an often lucrative sideline in penning Swedish lyrics to these hits, thus enhancing his profits from the publishing rights of these songs when they were recorded. It was only in 1960, after he had definitively established himself as a music publisher, that he finally felt able to leave teaching. Over the past decade he had managed to fit his work as songwriter and occasional performer around his classroom duties.

Aside from a contentious, although profitable, year spent as manager of the Spotnicks, Anderson concentrated on his growing publishing empire, continuing to enjoy success with his translated versions of American hits. But he saw that publishing wasn't enough, that if he really wanted to make his mark in the music world, the future lay in records. So it was that in 1963 he joined forces with Bernhag, who had over the previous decade established a reputation for himself as a consummate spotter of talent and hit songs, to form a record company. In the summer of 1963 Polar Music was born out of the Anderson-Bernhag partnership. Now all they needed was some talent to sign to the label.

It was at this time that Bernhag drew Anderson's attention to a report in the national newspaper *Expressen* about the talent show in which the West Bay Singers had shone, winning their way through to the final. Björn became, alongside his band-mates, the first artist to sign for Polar, thus entitling himself to a paltry 2.45 per cent royalty. This set in motion one of the relationships that would be vital to the formation and early years of Abba, and also marked the beginning of the complex financial negotiations and machinations that would be a prominent feature of the Abba story.

CHAPTER FOUR

'TAKE A CHANCE ON ME'

We were really christened Abba by DJs and people working for us. Björn Ulvaeus

By mid-1970 three of the future Abba members had already collaborated, Benny producing Frida's rendition of the Andersson-Ulvaeus composition 'Peter Pan', but the result was far from auspicious and the record flopped. Agnetha was ploughing on with her own solo pop career, Björn having firmly rejected her tentative suggestions that the two lovebirds, by now engaged, should collaborate on a composition, if not a recording. But June saw the start of the sessions for the album which would see all four future Abba members work together for the first time.

The album, *Lycka* (*Happiness*), was conceived largely as a showcase for the songwriting talents of the Andersson-Ulvaeus partnership. Their work together was, although far from fully formed, showing signs of improvement; the title track is a proficient tear-jerker that builds to a modestly rousing chorus, one that boasts a gentle burst of 'Penny Lane'-ish horns. The problem with the track, as with the album as a whole, is simply Björn's vocal performance: he has a decent, clear but almost characterless voice. Frida recorded a rather superior version of

'Lycka' which appeared on her self-titled album, produced by Benny, in 1971. *Frida* also contained a rather fine version of Simon & Garfunkel's 'Sound of Silence', but the album once more failed to give her any of the success that Benny, Björn and Agnetha had all enjoyed.

On the subject of Simon & Garfunkel, *Lycka* contained, among its other musical borrowings and homages, 'Lilla du, lilla vän' ('Little You, Little Friend'), a delicate, in fact rather too flimsy, Simon & Garfunkel pastiche. The duo are just one of the many late-sixties American groups whose work informed the feather-light 'Liselott'.

But the most pervasive influence on Andersson and Ulvaeus remained the Beatles, their fondness particularly evident on the appealing 'Någonting är på väg' ('Something's on the Way'). This recording is marked by some of the exuberance that would characterise the best of Abba's early material. Later on the band would be at or close to their worst when they somewhat self-consciously rocked out, but somehow or other it works here. The simple riff – very early Beatles, specifically 'I Feel Fine' – and the notion of something being in the air, and something being on the way, are surely Björn committing to paper some of his confidence in his creative partnership with Benny, which, after nearly four years, was still developing. The debt that Andersson and Ulvaeus owe to Lennon and McCartney cannot be overstated, but while it is often seen simply in terms of a more general example of pop-star behaviour, the Beatles having set a precedent as to how the best pop groups should develop, here the influence is more concrete. This song is a rather fine Beatles pastiche throughout, with a particular debt to 'She's Leaving Home' in a repeated chord sequence. Even so, for all its barely disguised borrowings, it is still a gloriously distinctive Andersson-Ulvaeus composition, their finest moment since their modestly auspicious beginning with 'Isn't It Easy to Say'.

Benny and Björn were, at the time of *Lycka*, perhaps just beginning to read the signs that are so clear in retrospect. If they were to achieve something remarkable, then it would be with their compositions, always focusing on the quality of the melody, and with the magic of Agnetha and Frida singing separately and, even better, together – something that they had noticed during informal musical sessions when the four of them holidayed together in Cyprus the previous year.

The record's final track, 'Livet går sin gång' ('Life Goes On'), is yet another pick-and-mix, spot-the-musical-reference effort, a less tuneful cross between the Beach Boys' 'Girls on the Beach' and the Mamas and the Papas' 'Dedicated to the One I Love', with just a touch of 'California Dreamin'' thrown into the mix. The sunshine pop of the West Coast in general, and of those two bands in particular, was a potent source of inspiration for Andersson and Ulvaeus in their early years.

The album, although not a success artistically or commercially, is significant in various ways. The project had begun for a number of reasons, not least to see if this superduo (a two-piece version of a supergroup) could replicate the success that they had achieved with their respective bands. For all its flaws it was a reasonably effective showcase for their writing talents, and they had clearly developed in this respect. There is a certain maturity to the album as a whole, although it has too many dull and otherwise weak moments. Its key importance is apparent when it is seen in retrospect as a staging post in the birth of Abba. In this respect the album's stand-out success was 'Hej gamle man' ('Hey Old Man'), a rousing ditty about youngsters seeking inspiration and the righteous path from a Salvation Army man. Abba-watchers will have spotted the recurrence of the Salvation Army in song lyrics in the vital early years of the band.

This is the true beginning of Abba. A reissue of the album featured another track on which all four of them perform. 'Tänk om jorden vore ung' ('Imagine if the World Were Young') is a limp thing, the sort that the Mike Samms Singers would have rejected for not being rock-'n'-roll enough, but it repeated the success of 'Hej gamle man', becoming a fair-sized hit single the following year.

After years of Andersson and Ulvaeus co-writing credits and their, though largely Benny's, involvement in Frida's solo work, 'Hej gamle man' is a historic moment in the prehistory of Abba in that it represents the first time that all four were on the same recording together. Of course, they haven't got the point yet, and Agnetha and Frida supply only backing vocals on the catchy chorus, with some fine harmonies from the second chorus, and some pretty, sub-Beach Boys 'la-la-la'-ing on the fade-out.

The band was slowly but surely beginning to coalesce, the pieces of the jigsaw falling into place. Of almost as much significance as the first appearance on the same record of Björn, Benny, Agnetha and Frida was the presence of sound engineer Michael B. Tretow, who, in his painstaking collaborations with Andersson and Ulvaeus on all subsequent records from the foursome, would help bring into being the Abba sound that would be fundamental to their success.

So *Lycka*, while far from a great album, scarcely even a good one, was eclectic by design, but patchy, with only the odd moment of inspiration and efficient but unremarkable production. But it was a key stepping stone in the development of Abba. The album didn't create much of a stir in itself, but 'Hej gamle man' became, on its release at the end of November 1970, in a sense the first Abba single, and a top-five hit in Sweden. The group were, in this early manifestation, close to recognising what would be their world-conquering pop formula, but had failed to understand fully the magic of which they were capable. Essentially, *Lycka* resembles an early Beatles album in which Ringo is the lead singer on every track.

The autumn of 1970 was in various ways a watershed period for the emerging foursome. Having finally come together as a studio act, albeit only in a limited way and on selected tracks, thus producing the wrong kind of album, they performed officially together on stage for the first time on 1 November. But they chose the wrong kind of live show. They made a move that reflected the then current crisis in Swedish pop music, a crisis of which the confused end of the Hep Stars and the entropy of the Hootenanny Singers, who were then still limping on as a folkie covers band, were symptoms. Björn, Benny, Agnetha and Frida, three best-selling pop stars and an established if not yet successful recording artist, chose to launch themselves collectively as some kind of novelty act. There are no recordings of their live act – a fact about which Björn, who considered this period a low point in his music career thus far, has expressed considerable relief – but it was, by all accounts, the performers' included, utterly dreadful.

The foursome, who, in all their various formations individually and together, would struggle to find a decent name, decided to perform under the title Festfolk (a pun meaning both Party People and Engaged People). This name gives a clue as to the nature of their act, with its unaccountable emphasis on broad humour. There is a tradition – not, admittedly, a noble one – of broad, slapstick humour in Sweden, and Festfolk seems to have been an attempt to fit into this entertainment lineage. There may be no extant recordings of the group, but there are photographs which show Björn and Benny in amusing costumes, complete with funny propeller hats, and there are stories of amusing songs, old records given new comedy lyrics, and bored audiences.

After the near-disaster of Festfolk it was back on track with the four's various projects, with Björn relenting and co-producing Agnetha's next album, *Som jag är* (*As I Am*) – which would nearly 30 years later inspire the title of Agnetha's insipid memoir – at around the same time that Benny was producing *Frida*. While Agnetha enjoyed some success with *Som jag är* and its follow-up in late 1971, Frida, despite continuing to prove herself a strong, versatile, expressive singer, was finding commercial success as elusive as ever. While Benny, Björn and Agnetha went on a tour of *folkparket* together, Frida toured as the singer with another act, suffering from a crisis of confidence and a depression of the kind that would recur throughout her adult life, even at the height of her success with Abba.

Things were going very much better for Agnetha, her soft, MOR pop finding a consistent if not massive audience. The summer of 1971 saw a collision of joy and misery. On 6 July Björn and Agnetha were married in what was supposed to be a private ceremony but turned into something of a public spectacle, with thousands of fans turning up in the small village of Verum to witness the union. The event was celebrated by Benny's performing the inapposite 'Wedding', followed by a performance at the reception by several former Hep Stars of 'Sunny Girl', with Björn taking to the floor with his new blushing bride, his domestic property, who was, judging by the pictures of the day, also 'slim like reed'.

The joy of the wedding was tempered the following day by the revelation that Bengt Bernhag, Stig's old friend and business partner and a mentor to Björn, had killed himself. Ever the pragmatist, Stig wasted no time in offering Björn the opportunity to become an in-house producer at Polar, an offer that Björn accepted on condition that Benny be employed as his partner.

That turbulent summer also finally saw the first hit single for Frida, who scored her breakthrough with 'Min egen stad' ('My Own Town'), a version of an Andersson track that had been recorded by the Hep Stars and appeared on the B-side of their 1967 hit single 'Malaika'. In the autumn of 1971 Frida, for all this belated success still unsure of her place in the music world, particularly when surrounded by high-achievers, secured a place in a long-running musical revue in a Stockholm theatre. The security of this work apparently did nothing for her confidence and, not for the first time, she seriously considered retiring from the music scene. Maintaining the symmetry of the growing partnerships, Agnetha won a stage role in the Swedish production of *Jesus Christ Superstar*, thus providing an early connection between Björn, Benny and the show's lyricist Tim Rice, a relationship that would come to fruition on the London stage 15 years later.

Agnetha's short run, just six performances of a scheduled nine, attracted at best lukewarm notices, but more important than her acting, to which she would return again briefly ten years later, was her recording of the song 'Vart ska min kärlek föra', a stirring Swedish version of 'I Don't Know How to Love Him'. This, probably her finest pre-Abba performance, showed what she could do with material suited to her particular talents, especially when handled by a sympathetic producer who knew her strengths and weaknesses, i.e. Björn. While Agnetha continued to bask in her various successes, Björn and Benny continued to ponder whether their future was as performers or as writing and production team, and Frida was still oppressed by her sense of failure, the four were about to have their careers entwined, all of them being on the verge of fulfilling, then exceeding, their wildest fantasies of success.

The recording sessions for what was to become *Ring Ring*, arguably the first Abba album, began in March 1972 and continued for nearly a year, this lengthy gestation period explained in part by the fact that all four members had outside activities at the same time – the Hootenanny Singers embarking on a lengthy tour at the end of April, at the same time as Agnetha went out on the road as a solo singer. At this time the band that would become known as Abba was still using the unwieldy collective name of Björn & Benny, Agnetha & Frida and would at times release records under the unlovely moniker Benny & Björn and Svenska Flicka (Swedish Girls). Moreover, Agnetha would have to endure the indignity of being officially known as Anna, the pronunciation of her real name apparently beyond the abilities of many non-Swedish speakers.

But it was in the studio that interesting things were really starting to happen, or at least the band was slowly coming together in its recognisable form, and Björn and Benny were growing in confidence and stature as composers. The title song, which opens the album, is patently a stab at Eurovision glory, and possesses an undeniable, insistent immediacy. It seems to have a touch of the faltering English that would, depending on your point of view, be a consistently endearing or irksome char- acteristic of Abba tracks throughout their career, although it was, of course, much more prevalent in the early days. There is some- thing gauche but charming about a ringing phone being 'the happiest sound of them all', but the clumsiness of the lyrics is hardly, or at least not entirely, the fault of Björn and fellow wordsmith Stig Anderson, seeing as Stig had sought help from Neil Sedaka. The veteran American soft rock-'n'-roller (one of the favourite artists of the young Agnetha) had had a string of hits in the late 1950s and early 1960s, among them 'Happy Birthday, Sweet Sixteen', 'Calendar Girl', 'Breaking Up Is Hard to Do' and 'Oh Carol', the latter covered by the Hep Stars in their early days. Sedaka had polished and/or rewritten Stig's translation of 'Ring Ring's original Swedish lyrics, and was apparently delighted with the results.

'Ring Ring' was a piece of pop composition which, in its production, was marked by many of the ingredients that, when further refined, would become staples of the Abba sound. Yet it is, as befits a song about someone desperately imprecating the object of her desire to call her, simply too insistent. The lyrical and musical repetition at the centre of the chorus, a feature that would become one of the central ingredients in Abba's early, intensely focused push for instant accessibility, is almost as annoying as it is catchy. Benny, Björn and Stig were certainly not going to be put off and would rely on emphatic repetition and alliteration during much of their career, although particularly in the early years.

Still, catchy the song certainly was – the rights to the single release having been sold by Stig around the world – and the confidence that Stig and the band had in it as a contender to become Sweden's entry in the 1973 Eurovision Song Contest seemed well founded. When the band came to perform it in the preliminary contest on 10 February, by which stage Agnetha was actually post-term with her first pregnancy, they already knew they had a sure-fire hit on their hands. But fate, in the form of the jury of experts, decreed that it wasn't to be their year. As Benny and Björn's composition for Lena Andersson, 'Sag det med en sang' ('Say It with a Song') had the previous year, 'Ring Ring', clearly the favourite with the audience, came third. This decision would lead to an immediate change in the selection rules which would ensure that by the following year a more democratic system was in place. As it happened, Nova and the Boys' 'You Are Summer', the Swedish song that won that night, went on to finish in fifth place in the Eurovision contest, two places behind Cliff Richard's tub-thumping but vacuous 'Power to All Our Friends'. Luxemburg's Anne-Marie David triumphed with 'Tu te reconnaîtras'.

'Another Town, Another Train', which incidentally shows Björn attempting to appear groovy by using the word 'groovy', is rather intriguing, if only because in its title, and to some degree musically, it is a forerunner of 'Another Suitcase in Another Hall', the touching, forlorn love song from *Evita*, composed by Andrew Lloyd Webber and Tim Rice, the latter the future writing partner of the Andersson-Ulvaeus team. Interestingly – for those interested in such things – the Rice-Lloyd Webber song seems to be a fusion, conscious or otherwise, of 'Another Town, Another Train' and Joni Mitchell's composition 'Both Sides Now', particularly in Judy Collins's version.

Next up is 'Disillusion', a rather tender little song of love and heartbreak, sounding, by some serendipitous case of reciprocal musical borrowing, rather like 'I Don't Know How to Love Him' from *Jesus Christ Superstar*, the Swedish version of which Agnetha had recently performed on stage and then recorded. The most notable aspect of the song, aside from Agnetha's poignant, tremulous performance, is the fact that it marks the first, and indeed last, time that one of Agnetha's own compositions made it on to an Abba album. Björn contributed the English lyrics to the song, which Agnetha had written and recorded in Swedish as 'Mina ögon' ('My Eyes').

'People Need Love' and 'Nina, Pretty Ballerina' are both marked by the emphatic – overemphatic – percussive beat that would, when allied with just a touch more musical subtlety, underpin some of the band's finest early hits. The first is a kind of trite, mini-lifestyle guide made exceptional, although not necessarily in a good way, by the surprise arrival of some yodelling from Agnetha and Frida in the final third of the song. 'Nina, Pretty Ballerina' was the first in a series of tracks ('Dancing Queen', 'Thank You for the Music' and '3 Scenes from a Mini Musical' being the most obvious other examples) in which Björn apparently writes about his wife in a heavily coded form. It is a song about a dull, ordinary girl who becomes special only when she dances 'just like Cinderella'.

The painfully slow, borderline unpleasant 'I Saw It in the Mirror' confirmed what was already very obvious: that Björn and Benny were big fans of the Beatles (check out the plaintive 'When this boy cries', which ends the chorus). The otherwise unremarkable 'Me and Bobby and Bobby's Brother' also contains an unmistakable echo of 'The Fool on the Hill'.

Perhaps the most promising track on the album was the cumbersomely titled 'Love Isn't Easy (But It Sure Is Hard Enough)', the subtitle suggesting, surely misleadingly, that Björn was indulging in a kind of risqué, *Carry On*-style *double entendre*. The borrowings are eclectic, and the 'Listen to that...' build-up to the chorus has a sequence that Björn and Benny would plunder a couple of years later – self-plagiarism being no crime – for the 'One more look ...' part of 'Mamma Mia'. Björn has spoken of how he and Benny would perform a kind of cut-and-paste operation on their own works in progress, fusing together the best bits from various compositions, a device that is illustrated in the extended 'Abba – Undeleted' track on the 1994 box set *Thank You for the Music*.

If the Andersson-Ulvaeus partnership has one significant weakness in its early output, aside from the occasional lyrical solecism, and the excessive percussiveness, and the preachiness... OK, among the failings in their early days – and in truth these also worked to their advantage to a degree – were their catholic musical tastes, their frenzied magpie borrowings and the almost frantic shifts in musical style in successive tracks.

On a shallow level there is something naïve about putting 'Me and Bobby and Bobby's Brother' (a trite little ballad – kind of 'Me and Bobby McGee' but without the moving lyrics and written for a German brass band) and 'He Is Your Brother' next to each other on a record. The second is, in terms of lyrics, rather too like 'He Ain't Heavy, He's My Brother' in its heartfelt, sophomoric plea for mutual respect for all humanity regardless of race, creed, colour, fashion sense or hairstyle. The triteness of the lyrics didn't prevent the song's being adopted as the official singalong in the Unicef gala in which Abba appeared alongside, among others, the Bee Gees, Olivia Newton-John and Earth, Wind & Fire.

Clearly the brother theme was no mistake because they chose to follow this double with 'She's My Kind of Girl' and 'I Am Just a Girl'. Basically, there's just too much Mittel-European oompah going on throughout the album, and much too much of Björn's vocals, although 'She's My Kind of Girl', with its slightly trippy, late-sixties pastiche, isn't at all bad and the use of the word 'fellow' in a pop song is oddly endearing. 'I Am Just a Girl', on the other hand, is truly insipid. Björn turns up again with the final song, 'Rock 'n' Roll Band', and he, Benny and everyone else should have been paying attention to the result. They may have had access to electric instruments and been able to turn their amps up when the mood took them, but they should have borne in mind the rule that some people should never let their hair down and rock out.

Abba were a *pop* band, albeit one infused with the spirit of various 1960s rock acts – and pop and folk, of course – from both sides of the Atlantic. They clearly wanted to be the Beatles, Simon & Garfunkel, the Beach Boys and quite possibly the Mamas and the Papas. Perhaps it was the desire to emulate the last of these that inspired the LP's back-cover photograph, in which the band are captured in a happy and hirsute pose, a pregnant Agnetha pulling off the impressive trick of looking uncannily like Michelle Phillips and Mama Cass at the same time. By this stage, before Abba had accomplished their breakout from the restrictions of a fame built on their popularity at home, they already had some international standing. And while the album and title single fared far better at home than abroad, they did notch up some fairly respectable sales, notably in Belgium, the home of perhaps the most loyal Abba fans in the world.

A little over a month before the release of *Ring Ring*, Agnetha gave birth to her first child, a daughter, whom she and Björn named Linda Elin, and within a month she was back in the studio recording, among other tracks, 'Disillusion'. The group supported the release of the album in late March with a promotional tour of Germany, Austria, the Netherlands and Belgium. Except they didn't: Agnetha stayed at home looking after her baby, her place being taken by a friend of Anni-Frid's called Inger Brundin, and the band's name was changed for the occasion to something like Biba.

The remainder of 1973 was taken up with Björn and Agnetha's adjusting to their new roles as parents, with a round of promotional activity to support the album and the single, the unsuccessful UK release of the single 'Ring Ring' coming in October, months after its appearance in every other territory. Aside from this, a commercially if not critically successful summer tour of Sweden's *folkparket* circuit and the recording of what would prove to be the Hootenanny Singers' penultimate album, *Dan Andersson på vårt sätt* (*Dan Andersson in Our Style*, Andersson having provided the poem that formed the basis of 'Jag väntar vid min mila', the band's first recording and first hit single nearly ten years earlier), the group's concentration turned to the need to make up for the disappointment of missing out on the chance to showcase the band at that year's Eurovision contest.

They were patently not the finished article at the time they came to record *Ring Ring* but there was a spark there, at least the suggestion, although this is obvious hindsight in operation here – it would have taken someone gifted with mystical powers to see a planet-conquering band in embryo – that something was just beginning to happen. They released the album under the name Björn, Benny, Agnetha and Anni-Frid, clearly more of a mouthful than Peter, Paul & Mary, although not nearly as tricky as Dave Dee, Dozy, Beaky, Mick & Tich. This had to go, and the obvious answer was to go to the opposite extreme and have as short a name as possible, but one that still encapsulated what was a foursome, and for Scandinavian audiences at least, a bona fide supergroup.

An acronym of their four first names was the obvious answer, and while Baab was seriously considered for a short while, many people had informally been referring to them as Abba for a while, thus taking away from Stig Anderson the credit for coming up with the name, something he habitually claimed to have done. Even then it wasn't altogether straightforward because the name had already been taken, Abba being the name of a Swedish producer of canned fish. Stig sought permission from the company to use their name and was told, rather delightfully, that they had no problem with sharing their moniker so long as the musical Abba did nothing to bring shame on the canned herring concern.

So the band were truly born at last, thus making *Waterloo*, depending on your attitude to *Lycka* and *Ring Ring*, the first, second or third real Abba album. Recording sessions had begun in September 1973 and continued for the next five months at Metronome Studios in Stockholm. By this stage Benny and Björn had established the patterns for working that would persist through their glory years. Stig had bought a small summer house on the island of Viggsö, in the Stockholm archipelago, in the late 1960s. Björn and Agnetha had bought a small place there in 1972 and shortly afterwards Benny and Frida joined them. There the two songwriters would retreat, keeping regular hours and knocking out their songs in a small cottage away from their main residences on the island. The pair collaborated on the music, although the chief creative force musically was Benny, Björn sorting out the words, helped in this task by Stig during the early years. Stig was genuinely important to their songwriting at this time in particular. He had come up with the melody of the song that would turn into 'Waterloo' (and for a while toyed with calling the song 'Honey Pie', in yet another nod, conscious or otherwise, to the Beatles).

The result of this lengthy recording process was a fairly indifferent album, although one that begins, as it happened, in magnificent career-making form with the title song. It remains what it always was, and that is a boisterous, attention-seeking device, the musical equivalent of their flamboyant, garish stage outfits, buoyant, instantly catchy, wilfully unsubtle but absolutely, resolutely impossible to ignore. At this early stage in their career together the band would regularly record alternative versions of their songs in various languages – Swedish, German, Italian, French – and the CD version of the reissued *Waterloo* contains among its bonus tracks the Swedish version of the title song, the one they would perform for the Swedish heats to decide the entry for the 1974 Eurovision Song Contest.

Aside from being an oddity, and a must for Abba completists, this track serves as a reminder that at this stage Ulvaeus and Stig Anderson weren't much good at writing lyrics in their native tongue, either, but, more importantly than this, that Swedish simply isn't a natural language for rock 'n' roll. It is not merely the unfamiliarity that makes the 'Jo jo...' and 'Men men...' at the start of the verses, instead of 'My, my...' and 'Yeah, yeah ...', sound faintly preposterous. As Björn admitted years later: 'English is by far the best language for music for rock and pop. It doesn't sound so good in Swedish.'

The overriding impression is that Abba was still a band struggling to find its identity. There are a couple of other tracks that are familiar to the casual fan, 'Hasta Mañana' and 'Honey Honey'. The first was for some time the only consideration with 'Waterloo' for the song that the band would choose as their Eurovision contender, and featured lyrics from Stig that he is said to have dictated over the phone to the band from Spain, where he was on holiday. The song is, alongside the habitual polyglot recording sessions, early evidence of the group's determined drive for success and international accessibility, their songs over the years alluding thematically, or in their titles, to

French, Spanish and Italian culture. What is rarely mentioned is the fact that their breakthrough success at the Eurovision contest was achieved thanks to a song that used as an extended amatory metaphor one of the great military glories in the history of the host country. Then again, if that was, consciously or not, the intention, it backfired somewhat inasmuch as the British jury was one of the few to grant Abba 'nul point'.

'Hasta Mañana' is actually a sweet song, but was passed over as a Eurovision possible for the, as it turned out, inspired reason that it was such an obvious choice. The intro echoes 'Tie a Yellow Ribbon round the Old Oak Tree', which had been a number-one hit earlier that year, and Stig surely knowingly quotes the 'don't know where, don't know when' from Vera Lynn's Second World War tear-jerker 'We'll Meet Again'. The lyrics are pretty wretched, and pedants surely resent the awkwardness of 'hasta mañana until then', i.e. 'until tomorrow until then'. Subtle it may not be, but alongside 'Honey Honey', it points to the developing Abba style, or at least one strand of it, a kind of sexy, or supposedly sexy, soundtrack to some fantasy Eurotrash lifestyle.

'Honey Honey' is one of the oddest of all Abba songs, something perilously close to pornographic, with its apparent attempt to recreate the sound of authentic love-making grunts that had been so effective for Serge Gainsbourg and Jane Birkin on 'Je t'aime (moi non plus)' and would be again on Donna Summer's seminal 1976 disco smash 'Love to Love You Baby'. Sadly, the very male huffing on 'Honey Honey' just sounds deeply sinister. There are hints of potential elsewhere. 'Dance (While the Music Still Goes On)' is almost a good song, and 'What About Livingstone?' could just have been an early and minor Abba classic if only the title and words had been changed wholesale. Perhaps Björn and Benny felt they were on a roll and were planning a song cycle based on great Englishmen of the 19th century but gave up on the idea when they couldn't come up with a decent rhyme for the Marquess of Salisbury.

Abba were generally a good source of material for collectors of lousy lyrics, and 'What About Livingstone?' contains the cherishably lousy couplet:

Tell me wasn't it worth the while
Travelling up the Nile

as well as the gauche phrase 'putting them on the test'.

Evidence of the band's lack of vision, certainly of focus, appears in the fact that there is no stylistic cohesion – or consistent quality – in the record. The sheer variety of their musical influences would always be one of the great strengths of the Andersson-Ulvaeus writing partnership, but here it comes across as something close to dilettantism, with the pounding power pop of 'Waterloo' followed by some wet, pseudo-reggae sound in 'Sitting in the Palmtree', which, admittedly, has a pleasant enough hook, and this in turn leading into 'King Kong Song'. With the gift of hindsight you understand the direction in which the band ought to have been moving, and in which they very soon would be moving, but by the time they recorded 'Waterloo' Benny and Björn were almost excessively versatile as songwriters who could easily shift from the cod-soul torch song 'Gonna Sing You My Lovesong' to the pleasingly jangly late-sixties pop-rock of the final track, 'Suzy-Hang-Around', a song that, uniquely on an Abba recording, features Benny on lead vocals.

There are also, in 'King Kong Song' and 'What About Livingstone' – and even to a degree in 'Waterloo' and the comic erotica of 'Honey Honey' – hints that things could have moved from this point in a very different direction, in that it seems, even after the disastrous supposedly comic tour of 1970, that the band still fancied themselves as in part a comic turn. Versatility and diversity would always be among the band's greatest strengths, but Benny and Björn (and Stig) hadn't yet achieved the consistency of quality in their songwriting.

Waterloo was nevertheless a smash hit in Sweden, where the album was released at the start of March 1974. By the end of the month it had shifted an impressive 125,000 copies. More importantly, it was led by the track that would finally, if not yet decisively, launch Abba as an internationally best-selling pop band.

CHAPTER FIVE

_____

'WATERLOO'

I thought it would be a push in our career, making people
in Europe aware that we actually existed.
Björn Ulvaeus interviewed on Radio Five Live,
Tuesday 6 April 2004

Looking again at Abba's performance of 'Waterloo' (sung in
Swedish) in the Swedish *Song for Europe* show, the most striking
thing is that it's not that great, certainly not that polished, a
rendition. Still, much of what would ultimately lead to their
triumph is already well in place. The outfits are pretty much as
they would be, their image eye-catching – although not necessarily in a good way. Sven-Olof Walldoff is there, leading the
band in his Napoleonic gear, while Benny and Björn, like so
many Swedish men, are in the midst of a bad-hair decade. But
Benny, sporting a silver jacket that suggests a glam rethinking of
the Beatles' *Sgt. Pepper's* look, with a white ruffle plume spilling
out of his chest, can hide behind his piano, and Björn can
distract viewers from his barnet with his rictal, John Denver
smile, his gleaming silver epaulettes and matching platform boots
in which he looks decidedly uncomfortable, his possible movements restricted to a nervous toe-tapping.

Of course, no one looked at the boys unless they really had to,
and there was plenty happening centre stage. Agnetha and Frida

are both, each in her own way, in post-hippie-chick mode. Frida's outfit suggests one of those children's mix-and-match card games in which somehow or other Terry McDermott's loose perm has been placed atop a garish country singer's bejewelled blouson, beneath which is an almost Summer of Love-style orange split skirt. Agnetha's look is at least colour-co-ordinated, everything from spangled hat to platform shoes in a uniform light blue that is, consciously or otherwise, borrowed from the Swedish flag. Her natural, endearing nervousness in live performance is enhanced by the height of those boots which, while incidentally creating a subliminal link to her similarly shod husband, limit her dancing to a very un-rock-'n'-roll shifting of weight from one foot to the other.

The spectacle, and the driving, insistent energy of Andersson's emphatically percussive playing cover up some of the shortcomings in the performance, notably Agnetha's singing, which is, particularly in some of the cruelly held notes, just a touch flat, as it occasionally was in live performances. More striking still than this, almost literally so, is one odd, almost flamboyant gesture – maybe they weren't used to singing that close to each other – when Agnetha raises her arms and comes close to hitting Frida.

There has been, virtually since the group emerged as an international pop phenomenon, an ongoing debate, among Abba-watchers at least, as to the precise nature of the relationship between the two women at the heart of the group. As will be apparent at this chapter's end, some – largely, it must be pointed out, men of a certain age – assumed that there must be some form of sapphic interplay between the two of them. A far more widely held, and from some of the evidence, more plausible theory is that the two had for some time, if not from the outset, perhaps resented each other. For adherents to this theory, the fleeting moment described above looks a little like one diva invading another's space.

But, whatever the small shortcomings of their performance, the group were, as they had been in the previous year's preliminary contest, by some distance the strongest act with the most instantly catchy song, and they comfortably achieved what they had set out to do. 'Waterloo' had won them a prized position as Sweden's representatives at the 1974 Eurovision contest, thus wiping out the bitter disappointment of the previous year's failure and setting them on course to become one of the era-defining bands of the seventies.

'Waterloo' had not been the group's unanimous choice for the contest. It could so easily have been 'Hasta Mañana', but eventually and rightly it was decided that what Abba should be aspiring to was to bring something that was uniquely themselves to the competition rather than perform a song like 'Hasta Mañana', which, while undeniably catchy and pleasingly lilting, was precisely the same kind of mid-tempo schmaltzy stuff that was typical of Eurovision. They figured that they could just as easily have won with either song – and confidence was never a real problem, with Björn and Benny's self-belief, boosted by Stig's encouragement. Incidentally, for a group that often and openly borrowed from other artists (and, of course, were in turn borrowed from), it was with 'Waterloo' that for a while they seemed to be facing the most persistent accusation of plagiarism. The charge was that the song's rhythm and indeed melody were similar to those of the Foundations' 1968 hit 'Build Me Up Buttercup'. As it happened, the accusations never came to anything, and although there is an undoubted similarity between the two songs, it is patently coincidental.

Britain, early April 1974. After the three-day week of the previous year, and the end of Edward Heath's government, Harold Wilson was elected, although compelled to lead as the head of a minority government. (He would be re-elected later with a small majority in that year's second general election.) The country had suffered the consequences of another miners' strike. In America Richard Nixon's inglorious presidency was heading inexorably to its premature implosion, Patty Hearst had recently been kidnapped by the until then obscure Symbionese Liberation Army, and the crew of the US Space Station Skylab had not long before returned to earth.

In sport, Red Rum won the second of his three Grand Nationals, Newcastle United would be outplayed in the FA Cup Final by Liverpool, who narrowly missed out on 'doing the double', having been pipped in the League by Derby County. In tennis, Björn Borg, although still two years away from his first Wimbledon triumph, was set to win the first of his six French Open titles and, significantly, was about to launch himself as a resident of Monaco, thus avoiding Sweden's punitive tax rates.

In the world of music, Cher and Bono had just got divorced, and in the UK singles charts Terry Jacks was at number one, as he had been in the US, with 'Seasons in the Sun', his schmaltzy take on the French-language original by the great Belgian singer Jacques Brel. (The translation and/or transposition of established hit songs was, of course, a money-spinning speciality of Stig Anderson.) Other hits in those weeks came from the Glitter Band, enjoying their first hit away from the then teen favourite Gary Glitter (how times have changed) with 'Angel Face', Charlie Rich's 'The Most Beautiful Girl' and Paper Lace with the Civil War-themed 'Billy Don't Be a Hero'. Queen had their own first chart hit with 'Seven Seas of Rye', and 25 years before it became an anthem for group hysteria, Elton John's 'Candle in the Wind' was on its way out of the charts. In the US, Blue Swede, led by Björn Skifs, Abba's friend and compatriot and himself also a Eurovision entry of the future, was enjoying a smash hit with his version of 'Hooked on a Feeling', a track that would, some 20 years later, enjoy a revival on the soundtrack to Quentin Tarantino's *Reservoir Dogs*.

It was the era when glam rock had been popularised and metamorphosed into glitter pop, a time of three national TV channels in the UK, all of which closed down before midnight, and was the early days of what would be a golden age of football violence. Jon Pertwee was Dr Who, David Hamilton did the afternoon slot on Radio 1, Terry Wogan had not long before moved across from Radio 1 to Radio 2, and on the cover of the *Radio Times* for the week of 6–12 April was a portrait of Olivia Newton-John alongside Cliff Richard under the headline 'Congratulations?', a reference to Richard's 1968 Eurovision Song Contest entry 'Congratulations', which lost out to Massiel with 'La La La', a song whose melody may long ago have been forgotten but whose lyrics have lost none of their resonance or power to move the listener.

It may not have mattered that Newton-John was Australian not British – nationality proved no bar to the American soft rocker turned DJ Katrina (of the Waves) winning for Britain in 1997 or the toothy Canadian songstress Celine Dion for Switzerland in 1988 – but what did ultimately prove something of a bar to her success in the competition was the wretchedness of the song with which she was chosen to represent her temporarily adopted country. For some reason England expected, or at least hoped, as expressed in an only mildly jingoistic preview article in that Saturday's *Sun* in which the headline posed the question on the nation's lips: 'Have we got the Eurosong at last?'

As the fateful weekend of the actual competition approached there were genuine fears about security. Various threats had been made, and coming only two years after the appalling events at the Munich Olympics, these couldn't be ignored. Of particular concern was the very real possibility that the IRA would, as they had been threatening to, continue their campaign of terrorist attacks on the mainland, and there were specific threats which suggested that the Eurovision Song Contest would be a target of just such an attack. These fears ultimately proved unfounded, but on 5 October and 21 November of that year the IRA would carry out devastating bomb attacks on pubs in Guildford and Birmingham.

So Abba and their small entourage came to Brighton, in a mood of quiet determination and confidence, checking into the Grand Hotel, by happy chance occupying the Napoleon Suite, which would itself become a target of the IRA on 12 October 1984.

Ignoring, presumably ignorant of, the rather graver dangers that they were facing that night, Björn and Benny were focused on the details of their performance; in rehearsals they had repeatedly asked for their sound to be tweaked, and they were just about satisfied by the time they came to take the stage. The problem had actually been a rather simple one: the BBC's equipment wasn't turned up to a volume sufficient to satisfy Björn and Benny and the particular requirements of their song. They wanted it louder, and by the time they came to perform in the contest itself they had very clearly got their way.

Abba were not quite unknown in the UK: copies of 'Waterloo' had been sent to record stations and the single was already receiving a decent amount of airplay. The competition itself seemed to be a four-horse race, the smart money being split between Abba, Olivia Newton-John singing 'Long Live Love' for Great Britain, Dutch entrants Mouth & McNeal (real names Willem Duyn and Sjoukje van't Spijker; hence the stage names) singing 'I See a Star' and for Italy, with 'Sì', Gigliola Cinquetti, who had the advantage of experience, having won the Eurovision contest ten years earlier as a 16-year-old.

So to the fateful evening itself. Saturday 6 April 1974. One thing that must never be forgotten about the Eurovision Song Contest is that it has been rescued from the dustbin of history in which it belongs only by its camp, ironic appeal. At heart it is a dismal celebration of songwriting mediocrity, an occasion at which are gathered, in some garishly and tastelessly decked-out auditorium, the cream – i.e. some gloopy, sickly and rather unhealthy mass – of what passes for talent carefully selected from the MOR hinterlands of a number of European countries. This number seems to increase annually, making the event ever more bloated, expensive and long, and, for some reason never made apparent, it includes Israel.

The Eurovision Song Contest was presumably not actually intended to be a camp festival of international blandness when it was launched in Lugano, Switzerland, in 1956, having originally been known as the Eurovision Grand Prix. In this inaugural contest, Switzerland, represented by Lys Assia, beat stiff competition from six other entrants. From 1958 the tradition, rather than strict rule, was begun whereby the winning nation is called upon to host the following year's contest.

In the first year of the competition the winners were chosen by a patently absurd system in which each nation would be represented by a jury of two who together decided to allocate between one and ten points to each competitor. This was changed, almost annually – a long and wholly uninteresting essay could be written about the many and arcane changes in the selection and voting in Eurovision. But from 1971 the system was tweaked to become slightly less ridiculous. Now each country would have ten jurors, each of whom had one point to allocate to any given song, aside, of course, from the representative of their own country. This system stayed in place until Abba's triumph, being replaced the following year by one in which juries returned votes of 1–8, then 10 for the runner-up and 12 for their favourite.

So, this was the competition that Abba were desperate to win, admittedly for quite sound commercial reasons, but one that in the nearly two decades of its existence had turned up perhaps one song of any genuine merit, 'Volare', under the title 'Nel blu dipinto di blu', performed by Domenico Modugno. And lest it be forgotten – although you'd have to know this in the first place in order to forget it – this song finished only third in the 1958 contest. The contest was not *entirely* without artistic credibility – of a sort – with Salvador Dalí having contributed to the publicity work for the 1969 contest, held in Spain.

After their triumph in 1973, Luxemburg had declined the dubious, costly honour of hosting the 1974 contest, so Britain had nobly stepped into the breach. When you look back on the event from a distance of 30 years – and I was one of the many viewers at the time – it is striking how desperately the whole affair needed an injection of irony. Our hostess was the polyglot people's aristocrat Katie Boyle, whose image, dress sense – on this particular evening she was wearing an outfit whose hue may well have been apricot – hairdo and indeed style of delivery must surely have provided some form of inspiration, however unwittingly, for the soon-to-be leader of the Conservative Party, Margaret Thatcher. Similarly the commentator in this pre-irony era was David Vine, a man who appeared to know little about and lacked enthusiasm for the music.

So it was Katie Boyle who served as our guide through the many lengthy and complex rules underpinning the Eurovision voting system, and David Vine who acted as a singularly gauche guide through the kitsch travelogue that constituted the filler between the 17 entries, in an event that was set to reach an audience of between 500 and 600 million in 32 countries. Vine was doing his best, trotting out the inane comments on the musical quality of the individual entries, but clearly much more at home when it came to making fatuous comments along the lines of characterising Spain as 'the land of the package holiday' and Norway as simply a 'tremendous country'.

There was no disguising the thrill when lovely Olivia came on to the stage, and Vine ejaculated, 'This is ours' ... and we were, of course, welcome to it. 'Long Live Love' was, according to Vine, a 'bouncy happy song' but also, sadly, dire, a fact that the singer herself noted in a rather embarrassing and, quite frankly, unBritish outburst the following day. The *Sun* on Monday 8 April reported on her disappointment in a story headlined: 'Olivia hits out: The song was wrong for Europe'. The piece talked of how she was close to tears at the reception after the contest, and had loudly branded the popular choice of 'Long Live Love' 'totally wrong'.

Meanwhile she was still, theoretically at least, in with a shout. Very much more realistic were the hopes pinned to the entries from Italy, who had the final song in the competition, and the Netherlands. The former was, at least according to Vine, who was an unashamed fan of this, 'the most beautiful song' in the contest, let down by the performer's nerves on the big night. It was and is a modestly sweet, sentimental little ballad, but the real challenge to Abba seemed instead to be emanating from the Netherlands' unlovely little-and-large duo Mouth & McNeal.

For those who can't or won't remember the events of that fateful night, McNeal was an anonymous chanteuse, at least set beside her porcine singing partner, who laboured under the illusion that his heft, his bearded face and his forced joviality – imagine a less endearing version of Dave Lee Travis if such a thing is possible – lent him a winsome air. Mouth had, according to Eurovision legend, lived up to his sobriquet on the eve of the contest, loudly and, to the female half of Abba, somewhat aggressively, proclaiming his absolute confidence that he was heading for musical glory the following night. He was in fact heading for short-lived fame, his unquestionably catchy song destined to reach the British top ten in the aftermath of the contest, but, blessedly, those to whom he had bragged would have the last laugh. If there was one moment when the

Netherlands duo blew their big chance it surely came with the couplet in which you would swear that Mouth sings:

You open up my ass for all the beauty
The beauty we're inhaling every day.

Whatever it was that turned the voters decisively, if not over-whelmingly, in favour of the Swedish entry, for the majority of those watching that night the emergence on to the stage of Agnetha and Frida was the first they knew of the band that was destined to dominate European pop music for the second half of the 1970s. English viewers may still have been reeling from Vine's observation concerning the nation from which they hailed – 'it's full of Vikings, of course' – and may have appreciated the genuine surprise in his clunky comment on the arrival of conductor Sven-Olof Walldoff in full military regalia – 'Oh, and it's Napoleon' – but there was something unmistakably different in this performance and this song.

The outfits were essentially unchanged from the Swedish contest, with Björn looking very glitter-pop as he strummed happily away on his star-shaped guitar, Benny pounding away on his keyboard and, in Vine's peculiarly inapt description, those 'two beautiful blonde girls' belting out the insistent, triumphant words. What is unmissable, and very deliberate, about the song and its arrangement is that it is so direct, so unflamboyant, so instantly engaging and wholly lacking in musical or lyrical subtlety, with Benny sledgehammering out the tune and Agnetha and Frida simply doubling up the vocals, eschewing any harmony.

Despite the fact that it lacked any vocal intricacy, the song was not without its hazards. Although the general performance is as infectious and joyous today as it seemed back in 1974 and is a considerable improvement on the rather restricted, restrained rendition in the Swedish contest, once again there are some problems with those painfully held notes leading up to the chorus. At one stage these proved too much of a test for Agnetha, who visibly winces as she fluffs her note; her autobiography could perhaps have been called *From Bum Note to Bum of Note*.

Whatever the minuscule deficiencies of the performance, there was something inescapably thrilling about Abba, and this is not simply the wisdom of hindsight in action. This was a band who had focused on this particular competition for several years as the best way to showcase first their songs and then themselves as a band. They had understood that there was no other realistic means for a Swedish band to gain recognition on the international stage, and both Björn and Benny would repeatedly refer in interviews to the realisation – one that clearly drove the foursome to become ever more focused in their determination to make it – that any tapes arriving from Sweden at British or American record companies would be immediately and unceremoniously binned. Having set their sights on the Eurovision contest, they had chosen the right song – 'Hasta Mañana', as was mentioned earlier, having been rejected as too conventionally a Eurovision-type song – and performed it with as much gusto and brio as a band in six-inch stacks could manage.

Now all that remained was the lengthy process of voting, which entailed an indescribably tedious explanation from Boyle, first in English and then in French, the second of which Vine felt no compunction in drowning out with his own trite wittering. Oh, and lest we forget for an instant that we are in the midst of the most unashamedly trashy decade of the 20th century, the entertainment – and as you will have noticed throughout this chapter, in an effort to conserve our ever-diminishing global resources, ink has been saved by the omission of ironic quotation marks – was provided by the poptastic Wombles. Womble-in-chief Mike Batt was himself destined to progress to further

Eurovision endeavours, with his collaboration with Lynsey De Paul on 'Rock Bottom' in the 1977 contest, as well as to have one of his compositions, 'Sometimes When I'm Dreaming', covered by Agnetha on *My Colouring Book*, her comeback album of 2004.

As Vine handed us back to someone he seemed briefly to think was Kenny Ball, the votes were at last, and at length, announced. Backstage the Abba crew were biting their fingernails with nerves, but things began well with a hefty five points from their generous neighbours Finland. Hindsight suggests that the powers of destiny were at work, but things got a bit hairy in the middle of the voting, the most nervous moments coming with the announcement of the British jury's vote of no points. This, ironically, was the jury that represented the people whose devotion to Abba, when it decisively kicked in a year later, would, with the possible exception of the Belgians', be the most enduring if not always the most passionate.

With Sweden granted no points, Italy were within just one point of them. But after that it was relatively plain sailing, and Abba had won, with a rather modest-sounding 24 points, beating Italy on 18, the Netherlands on 15 and Luxemburg, Monaco and Great Britain all on 14. Aside from being the first Swedish winners of the contest – they would be followed by the Herreys in 1984, the very lovely Carola in 1991 and Charlotte Nilsson in 1999 – they were the first *group* ever to win it.

Abba and Stig had met their destiny, but for a while it seemed as if some rather more worldly forces of order would prevent them from enjoying their first shared moment of international glory. Perhaps mindful of the security exigencies of the event, one overzealous official had bodily prevented Björn and Benny from taking the stage, thus leaving a clearly happy, but equally clearly bewildered Stig alone with the cherished prize for nearly a minute. Once the band did make it on to the stage they were able to perform their triumphal song, this time triumphantly. So began the first flush of fame that they had all previously experienced only on a local, parochial, relatively small scale.

They may have sold tens or even hundreds of thousands of records, and had a hatful of number-one hits at home and in their neighbouring countries, and a few thousand curious fans may have shown up to witness Björn and Agnetha's wedding, but they hadn't quite experienced the sort of media storm that engulfed them as soon as the credits had rolled on the broadcast of the competition. Photographers and journalists effectively stormed the stage and the band were bombarded with questions. They went directly to a champagne-drenched after-show party which led, with a brief interruption for a few short hours of sleep, to a champagne-drenched breakfast and then a photo-op on Brighton beach. Around this time, in a moment of respite from the attentions of the international media, the group, together with Stig, planned their tactics for the aftermath of their breakthrough success. Various television appearances on shows across Europe were arranged, and the round of press conferences, interviews and photo shoots continued.

On Monday 8 April the band consolidated the impact they had made in Brighton when they went to London to record their appearance on that week's *Top of the Pops*. Sales were accordingly boosted and the record shot up the charts, eventually reaching number one on 4 May and staying there for a further week. It was truly an international smash hit, and would remain their most widely successful single release for some years. Just number 14 in Italy, number three in France, Austria number two, the Netherlands number two, number one in Finland and Spain, nine weeks at number one in Switzerland, eight weeks at number one in Norway, five weeks at number one in Belgium, four weeks at number one in Germany, two weeks in Ireland. Outside Europe, and therefore away from the Eurovision factor, the single still performed extremely well. In the US it reached the giddy heights of number six in the *Billboard* chart, in Australia number four, New Zealand number three, number two in Zimbabwe and number one in South Africa, where the group's very obvious whiteness can't have done them any harm.

So the master plan had worked so far and, just as Stig had for many years promised the boys, who hadn't always believed him, that they would one day write an internationally successful song, so they had done in some style. So far, so good – but what was the next stage of the plan? At this time there was no real reason to believe, certainly for those unfamiliar with their status in their home country, that this garishly apparelled band, with the eye candy at centre stage, backed up by two gauche-looking, rather too clean-cut young dorks, peddling an irresistible but surely throwaway bubblegum novelty song, would do otherwise than follow the traditional path of the acts who find instant, continent-wide fame via Eurovision and then disappear gradually or suddenly after their brief moment in the spotlight. The song might be catchy, but you couldn't escape that more than faintly ridiculous image, and after all they were from the musical back-water of Sweden. They seemed set to be one-hit wonders, a novelty act, something of a joke.

For my own part I recall a family visit for a Sunday lunch party at the house of the eccentric political commentator Paul Johnson, when, almost the moment we walked in the door, the visibly refreshed host took a record from a pile, slammed it on to his turntable and announced: 'I must play you this terrific new song by these two wonderful Swedish lesbians...'

CHAPTER SIX
───────────

'THE NAME OF THE GAME'

The instant international success of 'Waterloo' was a hard act to follow, and when successive releases failed to emulate the sales of their breakthrough single, there was a certain relish in the way that the band was dismissed as a typical Eurovision one-hit wonder. But pop greatness was assuredly just around the corner.

There may have been a certain immediate sense of anticlimax as Abba and their entourage returned to Sweden, especially as their plane landed late at night and with no media frenzy to greet the band. But there was no time for indulging in post-climactic blues. The Eurovision victory had achieved precisely what the band and Stig had hoped it would, and what 'Waterloo' as a song was designed to do. The international success for which they had struggled for years in vain was theirs at a stroke. Now the important thing was to exploit this opportunity.

First of all, an understandable if fateful decision was made soon after their return, when Stig informed the 30 Swedish venues at which the group had been contracted to perform in the coming summer's *folkparket* tour that they had reluctantly decided to cancel all these engagements. This instantly set off, or at least added fuel to, a domestic backlash against the group, who had been as individuals and more recently together the darlings of the Swedish popular media. Stig cited exhaustion and their hectic schedules, which still included various solo projects: for Agnetha and Frida recording their albums, produced and partly written by their respective romantic partners; and for Benny and Björn these and other projects as Polar Music's in-house production and songwriting team.

Of immediate concern was the need to fulfil a number of international commitments and to reinforce the impact that their Eurovision glory had made. So, in the weeks following the victory, there were trips to record television appearances in Germany, the Netherlands, Belgium – where naturally enough their itinerary took in a visit to Waterloo – and Paris. In the French capital they also recorded a French-language version of 'Waterloo', produced and with lyrics rewritten by Claude-Michel Schönberg and Alain Boublil, the team who, a little over a decade later, would be responsible for *Les Misérables*, one of the most spectacularly successful musicals of all time, and would follow it up with *Miss Saigon* and *Martin Guerre*.

So, the big question in all this was, now that they had established themselves as an internationally recognised band, how to build on this, how to consolidate? The album was, of course, not that great, and it was certainly not enough to persuade international record buyers that they were anything other than some kind of amusing novelty act. The album signally failed to prove that they were an albums band, although it boasted respectable sales in what was already the group's Northern European heartland.

The vital thing was to come up with another hit song and try to prove that they could sustain the standards of their best numbers throughout two sides of an LP. The results of their endeavours would be the album *Abba* (rather than *Abba – The*

Album, which was still a couple of years in the future). *Abba* would, without quite constituting the finished article, the culmination of Abba as a pop band of genius, be another hugely significant step in their development as an authentic hit group, as songwriters, performers and an accomplished studio band. Most importantly, after a couple of false restarts, it included two songs that would, as single releases, banish at a stroke, or rather two strokes, the notion that had been gaining legitimacy over the past year and more: that Abba were a one-trick, one-hit act.

The recording sessions for *Abba* began in August 1974 and continued until the following March. Once again the style of the record was deliberately, consciously desultory. The variation from single to single, from album track to album track, was indeed a conscious ploy of the Andersson-Ulvaeus partnership, as Benny explained in the profile of him and his long-term professional partner in the *Guardian* in June 2002: 'Each song had to be different, because in the '60s, that's what the Beatles had done. The challenge was to not do another "Mamma Mia" or "Waterloo"'. So the joyous power pop of 'Mamma Mia!' leads directly into the stomping, subtlety-free 'Hey, Hey Helen', which boasts a weighty if not quite heavy guitar in the intro that sees Björn and co. once more struggling to fulfil their vain ambitions and prove the band capable of a full-on rock attitude.

From there, once again the band essays a reggae-lite vibe on 'Tropical Loveland', which has a rather pretty, lilting chorus, one that, as Abba devotees must have noted, contains an early instance of a particular verbal solecism of which Björn and Stig would be guilty several times – and indeed it is a common error among anglophone Swedes. The Swedish word '*roligt*' can, depending on context, be translated into English as either 'fun' or 'funny' (funny ha-ha and not funny peculiar, that is). So, in the second half of the chorus 'Life can be funny, happy and sunny', what Björn and Stig surely mean to say is that life can be fun, although here, and more particularly when they use the same rhyme in 'Money, Money, Money', this becomes something of a happy accident, lending weight and ambiguity to what is a very, even childishly, simple lyric.

Then they even have a fairly successful attempt at laying down a seriously funky groove in 'Man in the Middle'. But here and in the next track there are some lyrics that are almost criminally poor, and again there is something careless about the juxtaposition of tracks on Abba albums. Because just when you are recovering from the staggeringly awful ''Cause he's the man in the middle, Knows the way to diddle', you are confronted by something even worse in 'Bang-a-Boomerang', one of Abba's most irresistibly exuberant but also unashamedly ridiculous songs. The track, which had already been recorded, under Björn and Benny's supervision, by Benny's old colleagues from the Hep Stars the duo Svenne and Lotta (whose version of the song in Swedish, 'Bang-en-Boomerang', came third in the heats to find Sweden's Eurovision entry for the 1975 contest) is – and the process of exegesis isn't especially taxing here – a song-length simile/metaphorical ditty in which the boomerang is a symbol of the joyous reciprocity of love; lest we miss the point, 'a boomerang is love'. Incidentally, there is, so far as one can work out, no hidden meaning along the lines of an unspoken warning that if you bang a boomerang it will come back to haunt you.

Back to the lyrics themselves, and the fact that the song is so instantly catchy, so wilfully silly, means that you may feel inclined to forgive the contrived rhyming scheme of the chorus:

Like a bang, a boom-a-boomerang
Dum-be-dum-dum be-dum-be-dum-dum
Oh bang, a boom-a-boomerang
Love is a tune you hum-de-hum-hum.

Perhaps it really was a question of the paucity of Björn and Stig's combined vocabulary, because this leads directly into 'I Do, I Do, I Do, I Do, I Do', in which, appended to a decidedly MOR, Radio 2-friendly melody (and we're talking Radio 2 of the mid-1970s, not the radically revamped version of the early 21st century), are lyrics that are exceptionally repetitive even by the standards of Abba, a band who, especially in their early days, relied heavily on emphatic repetition. But, just as you're settling into this mood of breezy romanticism, the tempo changes dramatically once again and Björn does a reasonable Noddy Holder in the sleazy 'Rock Me', a track untouched by Stig, in which not for the first or last time Björn allows himself to shift into a more sexually explicit mode. Whether intentional or not, the image of Black Country lecherousness created by Björn's lewd vocal is oddly appropriate for a song that, in the tradition of the not impenetrable bluesy/hard rock sexual imagery of the sort brilliantly lampooned by Spinal Tap in the likes of 'Big Bottom', reveals its barely hidden meaning when you replace the word 'rock' with its Anglo-Saxon near-sound-alike verb.

To prove that Björn isn't the only member of the band with ambitions to rock it out, we have 'Intermezzo No. 1', a piece of extended piano noodling that featured prominently in Abba's live shows at the time. It was, Spinal Tap fans everywhere will be delighted to learn, initially inspired by Benny's passion for Bach and originally bore the title 'Bach-låten' ('Bach Tune'). It is a piece of engaging, although very nearly comic, cod-classical fluff, a work that falls in terms of musical indulgence somewhere between 'Lick My Love Pump' and 'Jazz Odyssey'. At the same time it is reminiscent of Paul McCartney's theme song to *Live and Let Die*, and also perhaps served as partial inspiration for tracks as diverse as Queen's 'Bohemian Rhapsody' and the title track on ABC's underrated but over-produced second album, *The Beauty Stab*.

The mood changes yet again with another stand-out track in the shape of 'I've Been Waiting for You', a torch song/rock hybrid itself featuring some dramatic shifts in mood as well as some soaring harmonies from Agnetha and Frida. What sounds every bit the perfect album-closer in fact yields to the more literally valedictory and subtlety-free but infectious 'So Long'. This, a song of the 'Waterloo' school of pounding keyboards, and one that – while bearing some grunting backing vocals in the chorus that suggest that Björn, Benny and engineer Michael B. Tretow still hadn't twigged that 'King Kong Song' had been a horrible mistake – carries a distant and rather unlikely melodic echo of 'Hangin' Round' from Lou Reed's album *Transformer*.

So *Abba* is, in some senses, very reminiscent of *Waterloo*, with Björn, Benny and Stig (whose influence on the lyrics, never profound to begin with, was becoming ever weaker) essaying a number of diverse musical forms. But it is a significant advance in many ways, not least because, although the album is still unarguably uneven in terms of the quality of the tracks, the band had become very much more confident as performers, Björn and Benny's songwriting was beginning to take off and, together with Tretow, the pair were gaining mastery of the recording studio.

While the album was being recorded and mixed, the band continued their painful attempts to follow up their first international success. 'Ring Ring' had scraped into the UK top 40 and their next release, 'I Do, I Do, I Do, I Do, I Do', fared even worse, peaking at 38, and this despite an elaborate, indeed ridiculous, PR campaign based around the theme of weddings and involving models turning up at radio stations in meringue dresses and morning suits, and DJs being subtly wooed by gifts of champagne. Success was just around the corner in the UK, which was always avowedly the key territory for the Anglophile band, but 'I Do...' did significantly better in the US, reaching number 15, and would prove a breakthrough success elsewhere,

Saturday 6 April 1974: Abba's date with Eurovision destiny – the triumphant band members joined on stage by Abba's *éminence grise* Stig Anderson and conductor Sven-Olof Walldoff.

Here's a story of a group called Abba: *above left* Agnetha in squaw get-up, *above right* Björn in full rock-out mode, *below left* Benny and his beloved accordion, *below right* Frida modelling an item from a range of Abba-themed jewellery.

bba and their followers: *above* Abba in their pomp and in their much celebrated, rarely
nitated day pyjamas and, *below,* Erasure paying homage, simultaneously sincere and camp,
) their great idols.

Above Abba in seasonal if not necessarily festive mood and, *below,* their arch-imitators Bjorn Again promoting their 1992 Christmas single 'Santa Claus Is Coming to Town'.

hitting the top ten in Austria, Belgium, West Germany, the Netherlands, Norway and South Africa, and topping the Swiss charts. But the success of the single was most notable in Australia, marking the beginning of a spectacular cultural phenomenon (see Chapter 13).

Abba was released across Europe on 21 April 1975, and was a hit in all of the band's reliable territories – across Scandinavia, West Germany (where it was released under the title *Mamma Mia*), Switzerland, Belgium, the Netherlands – but just missed out on the top ten in the UK, the last Abba album proper to do so, indeed the last not to reach number one in the UK charts. Here the band were still, of course, fighting against the reputation, where they had a reputation at all, of being one-hit wonders. But that was all about to change. Through spring and summer the group criss-crossed Europe fulfilling various promotional duties and also began to take their first decisive steps into the Eastern European market, shifting hundreds of thousands of copies of their records in Poland and East Germany.

By the autumn 'S.O.S.' had been released and become a considerable hit across mainland Europe, as well as in Australia, but Epic, Abba's UK record label, was painfully aware of the band's current standing in this crucial market and delayed the release until the middle of September. This reluctance was, it very soon became clear, ill founded.

The track opens with those few tentative, unmistakably sad piano chords leading to the introduction of the guitars and then Agnetha doing what she always did best: evoking an instant sense of great sadness. She pleads:

> *Where are those happy days?*
> *They seem so far behind.*

There is something almost unforgivably crude but at the same time touching and naïve in the use of 'so nice, so good', clearly a function of a lack of linguistic ease, even vocabulary. The verse flirts with despair and then the spiralling, baroque synthesiser leads in the chorus, which explodes into a mood of glorious affirmation, as many of the great examples of populist art do – think *It's a Wonderful Life*, or almost every Hitchcock film – where the tension as everything is irretrievably awful yields to the relief of some *deus ex machina* saying everything is perfectly OK after all. But there is something of the Beatles' 'Help' about the song. The Beatles were at their fab peak at this time and everyone hummed along to what was expressly a cry of despair from John Lennon, but one couched in a catchy tune. So 'S.O.S.', for all the manifest exuberance of its chorus, offered a hint of what was to come, of the complexity of which Abba were capable, indeed a kind of gloom, particularly in the realm of romantic relationships.

The ambiguity of the song was enhanced by the video, and the importance of Lasse Hallström to Abba's success shouldn't be understated: the way in which his images pointed already, at this early stage in their careers, to the schisms within the band's relationships, out of which many of their greatest achievements would be born. From early on he understood – how could he have missed it? – the very Swedish sense of melancholy that underpinned the group's music. But, then again, it is also simply – and it is the kind of simplicity that is achieved through the application of talent and hard work – a great pop song.

From their earliest days, at times through their various solo projects, and as a band, the members of Abba had faced accusations of excessive musical borrowing, at times of outright copyright infringement, notably with the brief furore surrounding the supposed similarities between 'Waterloo' and the Foundations' 'Build Me Up Buttercup'. Most, if not all, of these accusations had been either patently absurd or at least blown up beyond their merits, but they did point to the fact that Abba, more particularly the Andersson-Ulvaeus composition team, like virtually all artists in every field, are to an extent the products of everything to which they have been exposed.

The creative process is a blend of inspiration and, depending on the quality of your creation and the ingenuity of your copyright lawyer, imaginative recycling, homage or theft. Until now Björn and Benny's compositions had been marked by their eclectic musical borrowings. But they had been gaining in confidence all the time, and 'S.O.S.' marks the first obvious instance of an Abba track that in its turn inspired their peers. In this case, ironically, the payers of homage were the brothers Gibb, the Bee Gees being one of the 1970s MOR, disco-inflected bands with whom Abba would so often be bracketed. Their song 'Islands in the Stream', which provided Kenny Rogers and Dolly Parton with a monstrous hit on both sides of the Atlantic in the autumn and winter of 1983, by which stage Abba were defunct, contains at the end of its chorus an uncanny and very neat tribute to 'S.O.S.', transforming into a nine-note section the 12-note sequence at the end of the latter's chorus:

When you're gone
How can I even try to go on?

Bjorn described 'S.O.S.' as 'Our first really exceptional song' but, sadly, he and his bandmates wouldn't know until they had ceased to exist as a band that it represented another vital stage in the development of Abba. The stature of the song and the complex importance of the group, their relevance as multi-layered as the studio sound for which they became famous, is emphasised by the appearance of 'S.O.S.' in the film *Tillsammans* (*Together*, 2000), Lukas Moodysson's masterpiece, a wonderfully bittersweet, tender, sad, funny and brutally honest evocation of Sweden in the mid-seventies. The story of life in a commune, rooted in Moodysson's own childhood experiences, begins and ends with 'S.O.S.' being played on the soundtrack, in both cases the lyrics standing in part as a literal commentary on the on-screen action. At the start of the film the song, with its lament for a love lost, is a direct echo of the split-up of two central characters. Its reprise occurs over the sudden cautious optimism of the climactic scene when, for all the impossibility of communal living and the characters' dogged adherence to a rigid political orthodoxy, a collective game of football in the snow brings all of them together, suggesting a nostalgia for a time of idealism and hopefulness.

Moodysson's choice of Abba was no accident; indeed, interviewed by Stephanie Banbury in the *Sydney Morning Herald* on 22 June 2002, in the run-up to the film's Australian release, the director believed that the band could have had a beneficial effect on the communards in the film and the real ones among whom he had lived as a child: "'If they had opened up and started listening to Abba then they would have had a bigger potential for changing the world." Abba was the key? "Abba and the people who listened to Abba, yes.'"

As has been said, and as Björn, and to a lesser extent Benny, often repeated in interviews, the UK was always the essential market in which Abba had to prove themselves. From the early days of their compositions, when Stig had insisted that the boys would one day produce an international hit, their eyes had been set on making it in the UK, and there was never any pretence that the experiences of the previous 18 months had been other than painful. Björn subsequently and repeatedly spoke of the hurt he felt when he contrasted the treatment the group experienced in the immediate aftermath of the Eurovision victory and over the following year, when their dwindling stock was reflected in the diminishing quality of the cars that the record company used to ferry the group around.

'S.O.S.' was embraced with almost the same enthusiasm as 'Waterloo' had been the previous year, and now the band were established. The single peaked at number six in the UK charts, but its success was in its way as important as that of 'Waterloo' and, after the awkward post-'Waterloo' hiatus, was the first in an unbroken line of 19 consecutive top-ten hits in what would become their adopted home; in first Frida's and then Björn's case, literally so.

Meanwhile the Abba bandwagon rolled on, the band members jetting from England to Italy, to the US and across Scandinavia, with their recorded appearances on TV shows and their, as it turned out, prescient if not quite revolutionary use of video clips standing in for the rigours of touring, to which all four members were reluctant to submit themselves. This innovative technique certainly seemed to be paying off in what were already established territories, each with its own Abba fan base. But could it work in America?

The success or otherwise of Abba in America has always been a slightly confused and confusing issue. Abba were always an Anglophile band, and at least by the time 'S.O.S.' and 'Mamma Mia' made it clear that the band were there to stay, the mutual affection between Abba and a significant proportion of the UK was very resilient. But for every pop and rock act, and despite Robbie Williams's hollow protests of indifference to the whole issue, cracking America is of vital importance in terms of both stature and hard cash. The received wisdom even at the height of international Abbamania was that in the US the band had signally failed to replicate their massive success, and to a degree this is true, although there are many acts hailed as having broken the American market who would be delighted with the sales that Abba achieved and continue to achieve there: 14 singles hitting the top 40, four of them reaching the top ten, five albums in the top 20, all climaxing in the monstrous success of *Abba Gold* –

three million sales and still counting – and the box office and Tony-winning triumph of *Mamma Mia!*

But what remains clear is that they didn't at their peak become the cultural phenomenon on the other side of the Atlantic that they were elsewhere, and this selective appeal was surely a result of their stubborn insistence on their own form of promotion. It has long been accepted that in order to make it in the US you need to undertake the back-breaking slog of relentless touring, criss-crossing the country and backing up each live show with as many appearances as possible on the nation's myriad local radio stations.

That Abba were determined to ignore this traditional path presumably cost them sales, but the profile that they had gained from the success of 'Waterloo' – and this despite the fact that Eurovision means precisely nothing in the US – allowed them access to some networked chat shows, and these appearances in turn boosted sales of 'S.O.S.', which peaked at a respectable if unspectacular number 15 in the *Billboard* charts. This was a quite different time in the history of singles sales, a market that has experienced some serious troughs over the past decade and more. Despite failing to break into the top ten in the US, 'S.O.S.' managed the impressive feat of shifting over a million copies in that territory alone.

The band had been no slouches in the recording studio, and the start of November saw the release of *Frida ensam (Frida Alone)*, which, while resolutely MOR, is nevertheless one of the strongest of the many solo projects undertaken by the members of Abba. Then again, to call it a solo album is misleading in that it is to an extent an Abba album, the only missing ingredient being Agnetha. As well as playing piano and keyboards, Benny produces and once again reveals his fondness, one that he always shared with Ulvaeus, for the sound of the Beatles and the Beach Boys, the track 'Som en sparv' ('Like a Sparrow') sounding, in terms of its production and backing vocals, uncannily like a cross between the Beatles' 'Sun King' and the Beach Boys' 'Girls on the Beach'.

The Beach Boys make a less oblique contribution to the record via 'Skulle de' va' skönt' (a Swedish-language version of 'Wouldn't It Be Nice' from *Pet Sounds*, featuring, unusually for these transpositions, a relatively precise translation of the original). The album is essentially an eclectic collection of such cover versions and translations, ranging from the closing number, 'Var är min clown' (a sweet, affecting version of Sondheim's 'Send in the Clowns', a track that Bono was fond of dipping into during live shows in the years before he rediscovered the joys of 'Dancing Queen'), to 'Liv på Mars' (an odd reimagining of David Bowie's 'Life on Mars', which, while highlighting the technical virtuosity of Frida's voice, provides a reminder that English is a far more natural language than Swedish for rock and pop).

Among the other selections is 'Guld och gröna ängar', a Swedification of 10cc's hit 'Wall Street Shuffle', co-written by Eric Stewart, who ten years later would produce Agnetha's second post-Abba solo album, *Eyes of a Woman*.

The sense of *Frida ensam* being an Abba album in all but name and Agnetha is enhanced by the contributions of Michael B. Tretow, as co-engineer and mixer, and Ulvaeus on acoustic guitar. Indeed the recording features virtually the entire group of Abba regulars, with Rutger Gunnarsson on bass, Roger Palm on drums and Janne Schaffer and Lasse Wellander on electric guitars. More significant for Abba fans is the opening track, a Swedish-language version of 'Fernando' which, while recognisably the same song, suffers just a touch from thinner, less warm production and a slightly less inspired vocal performance than features on Abba's more familiar English version.

The album, with its peculiar, decadent, faintly Richard

Hamilton-like image of Frida decked out in a flouncy, lacy outfit, sitting beside a table holding an opulent meal for one, her hand disconcertingly placed between her splayed legs, suggesting that she is quite happy to be alone, was released only in Scandinavia. If anything, the record is excessively varied, a fault to which Abba were prone particularly in their early days. Moreover, some of the production flourishes seem to have been added just for the sake of making the sound distinctive, not least the Swingle Singers-style backing vocals on the track 'Jag är mig själv nu', which is anyway a somewhat redundant reworking of Gary Puckett & the Union Gap's risqué 1968 hit single 'Young Girl'.

Three weeks later, on 1 December, launching an informal and purely domestic battle of Abba's lead singers, Agnetha's latest solo album was released, and as with Frida, it was one that would prove to be her last effort until the dissolution of Abba in 1982. *Elva kvinnor i ett hus* (*Eleven Women in One House*) is a concept album, the concept being that each song represents the story of one character, the character in each case assumed by Agnetha in her vocal. All but one of the songs were co-written by Agnetha and her sometime writing partner Bosse Carlgren, she being responsible for the melody, he for the lyrics. The record, produced by Agnetha herself and engineered by the ever-reliable Michael B. Tretow, underwent, like *Frida ensam*, a protracted gestation period because of the overwhelming success of Abba – in the case of both solo projects 18 months elapsed between the start of recording and the eventual release. In Agnetha's case the result of all this time and effort was rather more uneven, and certainly less well received both critically and in terms of sales, than Frida's solo breakthrough.

Among the album's stand-out tracks is 'Tack för en underbar vanlig dag' ('Thanks for a Wonderful Ordinary Day'), on first listening a syrupy, happy-clappy paean to everything, which emerges with successive hearings as an irony-heavy song pointing to the impossibility of such optimism, hardly 'Perfect Day' maybe, but pleasingly cynical nevertheless.

Tellingly, by some distance the strongest track on the record is Agnetha's solo take on 'S.O.S.', boasting, though boasting isn't quite the word, Swedish lyrics from Stig Anderson. The latter constituted Agnetha's last Swedish solo hit for seven years. But the near-simultaneous releases of *Frida ensam* and *Elva kvinnor i ett hus* confirmed Frida as arguably the more talented and unarguably the more versatile of Abba's vocalists. With *Frida ensam* she finally scored a true solo hit, the album staying at number one in the charts for six weeks and shifting more than 100,000 copies in Sweden alone, around twice as many as Agnetha sold of hers.

Sandwiched between these two album releases in what was a hectic period for the band was a release that led to yet another important milestone in Abba's development. On 14 November Epic released 'Mamma Mia' in the UK. Had it not been for the astonishing success of this when it was eventually released in Australia, which was in its turn thanks largely to the Lasse Hallström video clips (see Chapter 13), 'Mamma Mia' would likely not have been released as a single in the first place. As it was, this reluctant release finally made it into the UK charts in the middle of December. Then, after hanging around in the upper reaches for the next month and a half, for much of which time Queen's 'Bohemian Rhapsody', the track which alongside 'S.O.S.' and 'Mamma Mia' helped usher in the age of the pop video, hogged the charts, it finally replaced 'Glass of Champagne', by two-hit wonders Sailor, at number one right at the end of January 1976, hitting the top spot nearly two years after the chart-topping 'Waterloo'.

Nineteen seventy-five had been an astonishing year for Abba, and 1976 would be even better.

CHAPTER SEVEN

'ARRIVAL'

*When we make an album, we try to record ten or twelve
really good songs.*   Benny Andersson

Abba, and in particular Björn and Benny, have throughout their
careers been frustrated with one thing or other, most often the
artificial constraints imposed upon them and their careers by
others, generally journalists. First there was their inability to
break into the international market, and then, when they had
done so, their contemptuous dismissal as one-hit wonders – and
this was a particular if understandable phenomenon in Britain –
and then their characterisation as solely a singles band. The
above quotation comes from a UK press conference held by
Benny and Björn to celebrate the chart success of 'Mamma Mia',
and afforded the pair the opportunity to excoriate the gathered
hacks for their neglect since the highs of Brighton in April 1974.

The gripes about being dismissed as a singles band were only
partly justified. Although they were improving, thrillingly for
some at least, album by album and single by single, the albums
were still bitty. But things *were* getting better, in terms of quality
and consistency of the recordings and also in terms of how the
band was received. And if Benny's words were as much an exhor-

tation to himself and his bandmates to change the way the band was perceived, as to journalists to address their own attitude to the group, it was a successful tactic. Piggybacking on the success of 'Mamma Mia', sales of *Abba* picked up markedly and it finally peaked at number 13 in the UK charts. This would be the last Abba album proper not to reach the number-one spot: over the following 16 years the five studio albums and four official compilations spent cumulatively more than a year at the top of the album charts.

The frenzy of activity in which the band had become involved over the past 18 months and more had already resulted in lengthy delays to Frida and Agnetha's solo projects and had done the same for what would be the group's fourth studio album (the third to be released under the name Abba). The sessions had begun as far back as August 1975, but the album, *Arrival*, wouldn't be released until the autumn of 1976. To fill the gap, and to capitalise on the success of 'Mamma Mia', following on from 'S.O.S.', the cheeky but, as it turned out, enormously lucrative decision was taken to release a greatest-hits album, despite the fact that of their five UK releases up to then only three had made it to the top 30, although, admittedly, two had been number ones.

So, on 26 March 1976, *Greatest Hits* was released in the UK, with 'Waterloo', 'Ring Ring', 'I Do, I Do, I Do, I Do, I Do', 'S.O.S.' and 'Mamma Mia' padded out with the likes of 'So Long', 'Hasta Mañana' and 'Bang-a-Boomerang'. Significantly for Abba-watchers, the album sleeve included Bengt Malmqvist's dramatic, even theatrical, shot of the band on a park bench. Benny and Frida are caught on the left of the picture in a passionate embrace, while immediately to their left Agnetha, at her most beautiful and just slightly out of focus, stares directly at the camera, her feet pointed inwards to enhance the image of her as a vulnerable little girl. Beside her sits Björn, miserably engrossed in a magazine, in jeans so flared they are virtually loon pants, and stacked heels that must add a good three inches to his modest height, his body language, with his legs crossed directing him away from Agnetha, portraying a kind of hostile indifference.

The image is carefully contrived and posed, but it is meaningful in various ways, not all of them factors of which the group were necessarily conscious. What it reveals at its basic level is the growing sophistication of Abba. As a carefully composed single-shot drama it points to their awareness of the power of image, how that image, chiefly in the videos for which they were already becoming famous, can be manipulated to reflect and enhance the increasing complexity and intelligence of their songwriting. For the group were turning out singles that, while always adhering to the crowd-pleasing exigencies of melodic pop, were becoming ever more involved, ever darker. In retrospect, this photograph, taken while Björn and Agnetha were outwardly as solid a couple as ever – indeed were a couple of years away from having their second child, Christian, a younger brother for Linda – seems to play with the theme, as Björn was himself increasingly with his lyrics, of romantic desolation, and conjures up the atmosphere of emotional chilliness as a relationship falls apart.

After Frida's domestic success with her solo version of 'Fernando', which had proved to be the most popular track on the album, although never actually released as a single, the group had gone into the studio to record their own version of the track, the first Abba single release to constitute a self-contained drama, and the single entered the UK charts the day after the release of *Greatest Hits*. The song, with its Andean-piped intro reminiscent of Simon & Garfunkel's 'El Condor Pasa', and its Spanish Civil War vibe, has echoes, conscious or otherwise, of *A Farewell to Arms*, famously filmed starring Gary Cooper and Ingrid Bergman, alongside Greta Garbo, Sweden's greatest movie star.

If not quite, or necessarily, constituting simple accretions of great moments, the underlying magic within the most treasured music, films and books can reside in certain fleeting, almost hidden moments.

Abba have their own fair number of these tiny, perfect musical epiphanies. The list, of course an unashamedly subjective one, would have to include the addition of a brief 'and' before the line 'the love you gave me' in the third chorus in 'S.O.S.', creating a melodic drum-roll effect; the acoustic guitar making its first appearance in the chorus of 'The Name of the Game'; and, perhaps subtlest, most beautiful, most effective and affecting of them all, Frida's voice cracking, almost yodelling, towards the end of the sustained final 'o' in the second mention of the name in the opening of 'Fernando', a tiny, heartbreaking moment that almost subliminally prepares you for the wistful romanticism of the song, even though its tender message is couched in a some-what woolly narrative – it could just as well be set against a backdrop of revolutionary Mexico as the Spanish Civil War. You can almost excuse the 'since many years I haven't seen a rifle in your hand' as something this Swedish freedom-fighter might whisper to her ageing lover and former comrade-in-arms. But, then again, maybe it's just bad writing. Despite the indifference of some of the lyrics, it is a wonderful, evocative, sentimental ballad, although one that, for the obvious reason of the song's subject matter, Catherine Johnson somehow failed to weave into the action in *Mamma Mia!*

After a steady climb up the UK singles charts 'Fernando' reached number one on 8 May, staying there for four weeks. Interestingly, the song that 'Fernando' replaced was the wretched Eurovision winner 'Save Your Kisses for Me', which had been at the top for six weeks and would end up the biggest-selling UK single of the year. It was performed by Brotherhood of Man, a bunch of Abba-imitators who would enjoy their second chart-topper in August of that year with 'Angelo', a low-grade pastiche of 'Fernando'.

'Fernando' finally and decisively banished any lingering doubt as to Abba's stature. It was a monstrous hit single internationally, hitting number one in virtually every country where their records were sold. It is almost easier, and in some ways telling, to list the places where 'Fernando' *didn't* make it to the top of the charts, among these America, where it stalled just outside the top ten, and the home territories of Sweden, Norway and Finland, in all of which it peaked at number two. Later versions of the first volume of Abba's *Greatest Hits* would reflect this phenomenal success and include 'Fernando'. The album went to the top of the UK album charts on 10 May and remained there for nine weeks, and then returned to the top for another two weeks on 16 October, becoming the biggest-selling LP of the year. In all, the record remained in the UK charts for 130 weeks, shifting more than three million copies and becoming the group's most successful album release until *Abba Gold* 16 years later.

So that's where Abba were in mid-1976, an outfit growing in confidence, gradually exerting a benign, spandex-clad stranglehold on the international pop market. If they needed any further proof that they had ceased being mere musicians and become instead genuine pop icons, this came with a bizarre unaccountable rumour that sprang up in the early days of that year's very hot summer. In the aftermath of Beatlemania, when the group had taken the decision to give up live performances and dedicate themselves instead to turning out meticulously produced pop masterpieces, the Beatles and in particular Paul McCartney became the objects of a succession of ever more crazy rumours as to what was really happening with the band, most of which were built around the notion that Paul was dead. Starved of the opportunity to see their idols in the flesh, the Beatles' more extreme fans were left with plenty of time to subject the evidence, principally the vivid sleeves of *Sgt. Pepper's* and *Abbey Road*, to a degree of drug-enhanced scrutiny the intensity of which their creators could not possibly have anticipated.

This surely unhealthy pastime reached its apex/nadir with a particularly inspired piece of interpretation of the famous cover of *Abbey Road*, in which final confirmation of McCartney's tragically early demise was found in his shoelessness – don't ask – and the final giveaway sign of the number plate on one of the cars in the picture's background, which included the digits '28 1F', i.e. 28 IF, suggesting, to the easily and imaginatively suggestible, that the 27-year-old pop star would never make it to 28. (Twenty-seven, incidentally, is the preferred age for all self-respecting and self-destructive pop and rock stars to make their early exits, among them Jimi Hendrix, Jim Morrison, Janis Joplin and Kurt Cobain).

So, perhaps to prove that Abba were matching the status of one of the bands whose success they sought to emulate, there started to spring up reports, perhaps somehow or other inspired by Agnetha's avowed distaste for air travel, that the group had been involved in a plane crash. The rumour spread across mainland Europe, picking up, like a large-scale game of Chinese whispers, ever more grisly details as it went, until it was widely believed that three members of the group had indeed died in this non-existent air disaster.

If they were indeed dead, then the automaton look-alikes who replaced them did a superb job, their first duty being to perform at the heart of a tacky extravaganza to celebrate the imminent nuptials of King Carl Gustav and his intended, Silvia. That Abba chose this glitzy gala event to showcase one of their newest compositions, 'Dancing Queen', for the very happy couple led some commentators to the understandable, if entirely erroneous, conclusion that the song had been written, even commissioned, for the soon-to-be-royal Silvia. She was physically not dissimilar to Frida – who would herself marry into royalty 20 years later, thus becoming a friend of the King and Queen – and was, like Frida, a polyglot commoner of German blood. Another congruence was that both women, as they entered their middle years, increasingly immersed themselves in charitable work, Silvia with disadvantaged children, Frida with environmental matters.

The work-related matters for the rest of the year revolved largely around organising a live show for the following year, to take place at London's Albert Hall, and work on a large-scale Swedish TV documentary on the band entitled *Abba-Dabba-Doo*. This programme, along with a series of five radio documentaries on the band scheduled for the Christmas and New Year period, and the official anointment suggested by their appearance in the royal wedding celebrations, pointed to the fact that the group had regained the affection at home after the immediate problems in the aftermath of 'Waterloo's success and the cancellation of the 1974 *folkparket* tour. There was also a flying visit to Poland to bolster their growing popularity there, and another of their whistle-stop tours of American and Canadian chat shows.

At last, in a staggered campaign, *Arrival* was released across Europe, first in Sweden, then in France, Belgium, Germany and, on 5 November, in the UK. Between the first and last countries, the band's actual home and their adoptive one, the album had shifted more than half a million units in advance copies alone. As writers, as performers, as a studio act, and the production team of Benny, Björn and Michael B. Tretow, the whole Abba machine displayed an ever-increasing confidence fuelled by their comfort in their various roles and their accomplishments. The confidence, even arrogance, suggested by the album's title was patently justified. This had been clear long before the release of *Arrival*, from the success of the single that had entertained the Swedish royal couple and which, when widely released in advance of the album, provided further proof of the group's talent and astonishing versatility.

The notion of Abba's collective progress and enhanced fiscal clout is illustrated by the two cover photos from the successive albums. On the front of *Abba* the band are pictured dressed in elegant, 1920s-style glad rags, sitting in the back of a plush limo, with fans peering in through the window, all four members happily toasting one another and their success in champagne. By the time of *Arrival* the band are wearing very modern, perhaps faintly religious-cultish, all-white overalls, and drop in from the heavens, transported by bubble helicopter.

The album opens with the rip-roaring 'When I Kissed the Teacher', a track that once again points to the influence that the production techniques of the Beach Boys and Phil Spector exerted on Abba. As evidenced by the record's lush, full sound and particularly the complex vocal layering, and the harmonies, the group have taken these models and created a sound that is by now instantly, unmistakably identifiable as their own. Björn's lyrics were improving to keep up with the prodigious advances that he and Benny were making in terms of basic melody and harmonic inventiveness. That said, Abba were still capable of pure, inane pop and almost wilfully ridiculous lyrics, as evident in the dumb but irresistible form of 'Dum Dum Diddle' – featuring in the chorus 'Dum-dum-diddle to be your fiddle' a rhyming scheme achieved by what is effectively foul play. For all the upswing in terms of consistency and overall quality – and successive albums improved until the golden age of the band that began with *Arrival* – many of Abba's foibles and weaknesses, and even a kind of structural template, are as evident on this album as they had been on previous efforts.

'Waterloo' and 'Bang-a-Boomerang' had proved that Björn couldn't resist an extended metaphor representing the joyous complexities of relationships and romantic love. On *Arrival* there are two examples of the type. The first is 'Dum Dum Diddle', in which Björn uses the notion of a woman wanting to be meta-morphosed (and this is one metamorphosis that Ovid for some reason failed to explore) into the fiddle belonging to a violinist with whom she is in love, so that 'we'd be together all the time'. Here Ulvaeus, interviewed in the *Guardian* in June 2002, must be allowed to come to his own defence: 'I'd been working all night trying to come up with a decent lyric. And I thought, "Well, I'd better take in something to prove that I've been working." I showed them this song, thinking they'd say, "Oh, no! We can't do that!"' Actually the tune is rather wonderful in a cheap, bubblegum way, something of which the Chinnichap writing team (Mike Chapman and Nicky Chinn, who churned out hits for the likes of Suzi Quatro and Racey, Chapman even-tually also writing for and producing Agnetha in her solo career) would have been proud.

The second piece of extended love imagery comes with 'Tiger', which was, as shown by their performance of the number in *Abba – The Movie*, a staple of the group's live shows. Then again, this could simply be a song about the threats lying around every corner in the ferocious modern metropolis, but casting Frida and Agnetha together as the titular, predatory felines gives the song a certain unmistakable *frisson*, not least in a mini-couplet that in the mid-seventies must have struck a mixture of terror and a strange inexplicable, or perhaps easily explicable, excitement into the hearts of countless boys of an impressionable age: 'And if I meet you, what if I eat you'.

An unwritten rule stipulated that each Abba album must contain one atmospheric, tropical-themed throwaway number ('Sitting in the Palmtree' on *Waterloo* and 'Tropical Loveland' on *Abba*). Accordingly, there is another, albeit ghostly, example on *Arrival*, at least for anyone with the 2001 CD reissue, whose two bonus tracks include 'Happy Hawaii', a working version of the obligatory Björn-sung track 'Why Did It Have to Be Me?' This last number is the weakest on the album, some kind of cross between a Germanic oompah song, a musical form for which Benny always had a fondness, presumably because it allowed him to hit his piano keys with unfettered ferocity, and a dirgey rock number, something like mid-career Status Quo on Mogadon. Since we've touched on Benny's pianistic enthusiasm, it should be said that there are strong links in terms of percussive beats between certain strands of Central European folk music and the Swedish equivalent of which he was so fond (see the discussion of his post-Abba albums in Chapter 17).

Elsewhere there is Agnetha singing the lively 'That's Me', another of the tracks from the fast-maturing Andersson-Ulvaeus partnership, its surface brightness belying something more complex, darker, even actively sinister going on lyrically. The song tells the story, very briefly and efficiently, of the nocturnal adventures of a woman called Carrie. The perhaps unconscious nod to the eponymous, telekinetically gifted heroine of Stephen King's best-selling horror novel, Brian De Palma's film adaptation of which had been released earlier that year, gives the number a sense of danger that undercuts the inherent pathos of the words.

The song's first-person narrator is addressing a potential mate, presumably in some bar, and is warning him not to mistreat her. It is possible that her innocent exterior conceals a sexually voracious temptress: 'I'm Carrie not the kind of girl you'd marry.' The lyrics have a certain intriguing ambiguity, so that it's not entirely clear whether she is more the pursuer or the pursued – in the song's words, the eagle or the dove. Either way, this track, in which she shares the lead vocal with Frida, was always one of Agnetha's personal favourites, and was one of only three Abba songs, along with 'The Winner Takes It All' and 'Slipping Through My Fingers', that were selected for inclusion on her

English-language greatest-hits collection – indeed the song lent its name to the collection.

Agnetha's enduring fondness for 'That's Me' is in itself rather intriguing, as is the fact that it merits inclusion in her favourite performances alongside two other Abba songs that are so expressly personal and both written by Ulvaeus with her in mind. 'The Winner Takes It All' is yet another extended metaphor inspired by the miserable dissolution of their marriage, and 'Slipping Through My Fingers' an expression of the regret that the workaholic Björn felt when he belatedly acknowledged that his concentration on Abba had meant that he missed a lot of the early life of both his daughter Linda and his son Christian. Aside from the obvious fact that 'That's Me' afforded Agnetha the opportunity to adopt a persona – and role-playing within the context of songs was something that her work on the ambitious *Elva kvinnor i ett hus* proved she enjoyed – it is tempting to see 'That's Me' as a work of autobiography, or autobiography by proxy at least.

The temptation to analyse song lyrics, no matter who the composer, for hints of autobiographical truths is irresistible, doubly so when the chief lyricist is married to one of the vocalists through whom he speaks. Björn is, throughout Abba's recordings, repeatedly drawn to lubricious, at times creepy, sexually charged encounters between men and women, the implied venue generally being some imaginary, sleazy chat-up joint. One can't help but wonder at the inspiration for this song, although there is something uncomfortable about Agnetha's playing this role at her husband's bidding, within a scenario that evokes certain rumours, almost certainly unfounded, of sexual infidelity. For example, Agnetha was said to have had an affair with her therapist, something she angrily denied, while other rumours suggested that in the aftermath of her marriage break-up her appetites while on the road – and there is, of course, something of the fan's fantasy to these reports – were the match for those of any of her notorious male counterparts in the seventies music scene.

The album is rounded off with the soaring, portentous instrumental title track, admittedly an instrumental in which Agnetha and Frida's voices are used as instruments, while Benny's synthesiser impersonates the drone of bagpipes. The bagpipes made alarmingly regular cameo appearances in the UK singles chart in the 1970s, the most obvious examples of this egregious tradition being 'Amazing Grace' by the snappily named Pipes & Drums & Military Band of the Royal Scots Dragoon Guards, Wings' 'Mull of Kintyre' and Rod Stewart's 'Sailing'. At various times Benny and Björn would, in interviews, align themselves with the punk movement, claiming an unlikely brotherhood, at least inasmuch as they were, with their direct pop attitude, diametrically opposed to the self-indulgence, grandiosity and pomposity of the prog-rock movement exemplified by Yes, early Genesis and ELP.

Their opposition to prog rock should not be confused with their opposition to progg rock, the second being a uniquely Swedish musical form, one particular to the political orthodoxy that reigned in the country in the early to mid-seventies and to which the synthetic, apolitical pop of Abba was inimical. Progg, short for *progressiv musik*, was marked by an engagement with political ideas, especially a left-leaning political idealism. Although politics, and more specifically progg, and Abba were hardly natural bedfellows – the bland anthemic 'People Need Love' and the romanticism of 'Fernando' representing the closest that they ever came to tackling socio-political subjects in their songs – Stig did make one ill-advised attempt to court one of the movement's key players. His attempt in 1975 to sign Mikael Wiehe ended, perhaps inevitably, in a legal dispute and lasting mutual mistrust.

In fact Abba's avowed antipathy to prog rock looks pretty hollow in the context of 'Arrival', which, like the Bach-inflected

'Intermezzo No. 1' on *Abba*, constitutes the kind of onanistic, crowd-pleasing – so long as the crowd in question is sufficiently goofed – synth-noodling of which Yes or ELP would have been proud, although Rick Wakeman or Keith Emerson would have stretched out the tracks to several times their lengths. As it was, Abba's new album very soon came to the attention of Mike Oldfield, prog's own boy genius, whose debut masterpiece of conceptual electro-muzak *Tubular Bells* vied with Pink Floyd's *Dark Side of the Moon* for the title of most stubborn, chart-hogging album of the early to mid-1970s. Oldfield instantly added *Arrival*'s title track to his own repertoire and, through his version, the number has survived as something of an underground classic, and has become, in several variations, a staple of the trance music scene.

All of the above points to the fact that Björn and Benny had fulfilled their ambitions, and once again confounded the group's critics, establishing Abba as specialists in albums as well as singles. At the heart of *Arrival* are three nuggets of pop genius which individually and cumulatively cemented Abba's status as the world's premier pop band and Andersson and Ulvaeus's reputation – and this recognition was almost entirely retrospective – as a songwriting team to match the greatest partnerships in pop history.

This mighty trio of tracks begins with 'Dancing Queen', the single whose global triumph heralded the album's release in virtually every territory, and the song that is almost objectively the most significant work in Abba's repertoire. Björn and Benny had sat down to compose this song using as their model George McRae's 'Rock Your Baby', the seminal disco single and a UK number one in the summer of 1974. The structure of 'Dancing Queen' is innovative, the brief piano flourish, which leads directly, jerkily into the short-lived, lilting, lush intro of wordless harmonies and rich backing, evoking a DJ's almost clumsy segue. This in turn moves into the chorus, a musical gimmick that suggests that we have, as if entering a club in full swing, stumbled into the midst of the track. It's MOR but not as we knew it; the song is a fusion of rich, flawless, Carpenters-style composition and production, but underlaid with a beat, enhanced by the simple story of the lyrics, that makes anyone, almost everyone, want to dance. This is attested to by an avalanche of anecdotal evidence – the reaction that the song gets at any of the countless weddings, and nightclubs retro and otherwise, ironic and otherwise, where 'Dancing Queen' has become a crossover staple; for it is, quite possibly uniquely, one of the very few selections that is guaranteed to fill the dance floor, appealing right across the board.

Björn and Benny, with a little help from Stig, may not have been the obvious masters of the dance scene, but in the lyrics they tackle the central idea of the desperate hedonism of dance culture. The same premise is central to *Saturday Night Fever* (1978), the cinematic apotheosis of the disco movement, in which the erotic possibilities of club life, the brief exhibitionistic/voyeuristic joy of dancing and being seen dancing together, constitute the sole avenue of pleasure in certain people's lives. This basic idea allows Björn to explore further the theme – one that he had previously played with in 'Nina, Pretty Ballerina' and to which he would return in 'Thank You for the Music', and tellingly always with Agnetha in mind as the vocalist – of a woman, shy or otherwise unprepossessing, who would come alive only in performance of some kind. For once, the lubricious sexual longing within the words, which elsewhere can come across as uncomfortably lecherous, is appropriate for what is, alongside 'Money, Money, Money', one of the album's two informal anthems to the aspirational, vulgar, *arriviste* lifestyle. The incongruous mention of 'a bit of rock' music can be generously overlooked in the context of what is an almost flawless gem that transcends the despised genre of disco.

Despite being backed up by one of Lasse Hallström's weakest videos, set in an irredeemably naff disco, 'Dancing Queen' proved to be Abba's biggest-ever hit single, reaching number one in Australia, Belgium, West Germany, Ireland, Mexico, the Netherlands, New Zealand, Norway, South Africa, Sweden, the UK – where it was the band's third consecutive single release to top the charts – the US, where it was their sole chart-topper, and Zimbabwe.

With the obvious *double entendre* of the title – double at least for listeners who can still imagine the words referring to a woman – the song would, alongside 'Gimme! Gimme! Gimme! (A Man After Midnight)', be at the heart of the group's gay appeal. To confirm this, as if it needed confirmation, the song became a staple of gay icon Kylie Minogue's live set, a version appearing on her 1999 live album *Intimate and Live*. Aside from having seeped into the collective consciousness, as confirmed by the song having provided Elvis Costello with an unlikely source of inspiration (see Chapter 8), it has become perhaps the most widely covered of all their tracks. Ever the Abba fan, Costello quotes 'Dancing Queen' in 'When I Was Cruel No. 2', from his 2002 album *When I Was Cruel*:

> *The ghostly first wife glides up on stage whispering to*
>   *raucous talkers*
> *Spilling family secrets out to flunkeys and castrato walkers*
> *See that girl,*
> *Watch that scene*
> *Digging the 'Dancing Queen'.*

A conventional cover of 'Dancing Queen' by the A* Teens made it on to the soundtrack of the 2000 Sandra Bullock vehicle *Miss Congeniality*, a film that has acquired a certain obscure, crypto-gay kudos after being named by Chandler from TV's *Friends* as one of his favourite films. A more interesting cover was recorded by Luka Bloom, the brother and sometime collaborator of Christy Moore of Moving Hearts fame, to round off his 2000 release *Keeper of the Flame*. Bloom's rendition of the track as a straight, slow, folkie ballad sits alongside his covers of tracks from more predictable candidates for the stripped-back-to-basics treatment, among them Bob Dylan, Joni Mitchell and U2.

When U2 themselves belatedly discovered a sense of humour and one of irony, both of them hidden inside an oversized lemon apparently, they confirmed their new light-hearted and knowing approach to life and art by incorporating a rendition of 'Dancing Queen' into their live set throughout their 1992 Zoo TV Tour, and it would remain a regular feature of their live repertoire for the next five years. But on 11 June 1992, in the course of their second and last night at Globen in Stockholm, the band were joined on stage by Björn and Benny for the song, prompting lead singer Bono to prostrate himself uttering several 'We are not worthy's in the then current, post-ironic show of *Wayne's World*-style mock obsequiousness and genuine respect.

'Dancing Queen' represents the zenith of Abba's career as a singles band in terms of sales, and is quite possibly the group's best-loved song, not least by Frida herself, whose favourite it always was from the very beginning. She recalled driving from the studio during the recording sessions for *Arrival*, and listening to the backing track for the number, and this alone was enough to reduce her to tears.

For their next single release in most territories, a song was chosen that strongly pointed first to Björn and Benny's growing talent for creating mini-narratives within their compositions, and by extension and more pertinently to their attraction to, and seemingly instinctive facility for, musical theatre. Aside from anything else, 'Money, Money, Money' was in some senses Abba's most subversive recording, its extended fantasy-paean to wealth going against the grain of the socialist, ultra-high-taxation orthodoxy of Sweden in the mid-1970s. There is also the sledgehammer irony of lyrics in which a group, already by this stage the most successful in Europe and beyond, indulged in the supposedly impossible dream of being rich. Benny and Björn have always insisted that the song was, to this extent at least, a joke.

The songwriters admitted from the outset that the number was inspired by 'Money, Money', itself a whimsical fantasy song from the Kander-Ebb musical *Cabaret*, the film of which was directed by Bob Fosse and provided Liza Minnelli with her career-defining role as Sally Bowles. It was clearly not just this song that they had in mind when they created this musical playlet, in which a woman dreams of escaping the drudgery of her life by striking it lucky in a game of chance or getting herself a wealthy man. Musically, the song evokes the decadence of 1930s Berlin, at least as captured in *Cabaret*, and there is something of that show's song 'Liebe Herr' in Frida's sustained note on the word 'ball' leading up to the first chorus. By this stage the band were wearing the studio-craft and meticulousness of each creation lightly, and the exquisite harmonies between Agnetha's soprano and Frida's mezzo have an almost effortless quality to them – the appearance of effortlessness in art generally being a sure sign of prodigious effort.

The song's retro roots are enhanced by Lasse Hallström's accompanying video, which is one of his and the group's finest collaborations while also having an unmistakable air of camp that makes it impossible to imagine they didn't come across as a partly kitsch act even at the time. To set the scene of the grey life endured by the song's narrator, Frida is first seen wandering in a state of obvious anxiety through the streets of central Stockholm, before she is magically transported to her fantasy stage, where, sporting an almost Sally Bowles-style hat and standing at the edge of a circle of light, she sings the song, at times with a Beckettian *Not I* close-up on her mouth, emphasising the precise diction that was always one of Abba's underacknowledged strengths, as well as some frankly un-American teeth.

Intercut with this are various shots of money – a pile of dollars and a rather paltry stash of Swedish kronor – and best of all the first appearance of the group's infamous Japanese kimonos-cum-day pyjamas. Aside from featuring the first instance of Abba's much-mocked 'a-ha' ejaculation, the song contains a good example of Björn's very Swedish use of the word 'funny', which conveys a sense that a rich man's world must be a strange place to be, while the use of this translation of the Swedish word '*roligt*' together with the notion that it is 'always sunny' surely suggests that life is always fun for the rich.

Whatever the linguistic nuances of the lyrics, the song, while not quite as monstrously successful as its predecessor or its follow-up single, was still a big worldwide hit and, significantly, the band's last Australian number one, reaching the top of the charts in Belgium, France (where 'Dancing Queen' had stalled at number three), West Germany, Mexico, the Netherlands and New Zealand, and reaching the top ten virtually everywhere else. It remains a cherished, minor Abba classic, and one of Benny's favourite Abba recordings.

While 'Dancing Queen' was at the time the most successful Abba single, and is the most enduring of them all, their follow-up to 'Money, Money, Money' was in its way no less important in the development of the group's identity, constituting yet another leap forward in terms of songwriting, performance and production.

The *Oxford English Dictionary* defines melancholy as, aside from the condition of having an excess of black bile (the literal meaning of the word, as classicists won't need reminding), a general irascibility or depression, a 'tender or pensive sadness'.

Without wishing to sound too much like Roland Huntford (see A Very Brief History of Sweden in Chapter 14), I can say that one of the things that Swedes do really well, aside from suicide and depression – and around this time Frida was finally coming out of a year-long period of profound self-doubt and depression – is divorce. Having given a hint of the glorious melancholy to come in the career-making double whammy of 'S.O.S.' and 'Mamma Mia', this strand within Abba's music reached the first of its twin peaks of joyous misery with 'Knowing Me, Knowing You' – the second being Abba's other divorce masterpiece, 'The Winner Takes It All'.

Abba were capable of creating works of relatively simple, hedonistic pop exuberance, as their breakthrough 'Waterloo' proved, but that was always more of a pragmatic attention-grabber than a true sign of the band's talents. The mention of Abba, for the many with any degree of affection for the band, tends at first to excite feelings of a kind of pure happiness, wrapped up in recollections of simple, infectious pop, campily enjoyable videos and garishly outlandish outfits, but all this is symptomatic of the flattening out of memories and the glow of nostalgia. For it's preferable to remember the 1970s as a time of kitsch, of laughable sartorial nightmares, of innocent, pre-Aids sexual freedom rather than of, depending on where in the world you were, the paranoia of Vietnam and the cynicism of Watergate, Cold War tension, repressive political orthodoxy, industrial action and international terrorist atrocities. But, through it all, and certainly at their best, Abba, for all their surface gloss, were continually and inexorably drawn to everyday human sadness, the pain of romantic disillusionment, and regret at time passing, better times recalled with an aching fondness.

The attraction of the gloomier realms of life had been at least suggested in earlier work, but with 'Knowing Me, Knowing You' (the sole contribution to this effort of Stig Anderson, credited as

co-writer in many of the group's early and mid-period compositions, was its title) it came to the fore of the song. It was here that
the twin influences of the Beach Boys and the group's shared
culture, particularly as filtered through the masterpieces of
Ingmar Bergman, collided. The Beach Boys were models and
idols principally because of their distinctive harmonies and
layered sound. These effects, like Phil Spector's famous 'Wall of
Sound' productions from around the same period in the early to
mid-1960s, Björn, Benny and in particular Michael B. Tretow
had emulated by replicating vocal and instrumental recordings
on separate tracks and then incorporating fractional time delays
and distortions on separate tracks to conjure up a fuller sound.
But the Beach Boys were influential to Abba in more than just
their expertise in the studio and their accomplishment of a
distinctive sound rich in complex harmonies. (Incidentally, one
of Stig Anderson's more lucrative licensing deals in his early days
as a music entrepreneur in the early 1960s was to secure the
rights to the Beach Boys' songs, rights he held on to, despite
strenuous efforts from other interested parties, throughout the
group's golden years.)

The Beach Boys' songs, written almost exclusively by Brian
Wilson, are often casually remembered as relentlessly upbeat,
optimistic ditties, but this impression is just as illusory in their
case as in Abba's. In fact the trajectory of the two bands is oddly
similar, if in a general rather than specific sense. There is no
suggestion that, during the creation of, say, *Voulez-Vous*,
Agnetha and Frida were so out of it that they performed their
vocal harmonies while lying down on the floor, or that Björn and
Benny were turning out their polished pop gems from a sandpit
built in the studio, after consuming dangerous quantities of
industrial-strength hallucinogens. But both bands were built on
intense, increasingly strained emotional connections between the
members, and both emerged as pure pop acts before moving on

to more complex, ever darker subject matter. The prevalent mood was always one of longing for times past, the band taking their fans along with them only part of the way on this musical journey, before almost wilfully losing their commercial edge and then fizzling out, in each case the group ending in a whimper and not a bang.

So, at this crucial stage in their career, Abba were beginning to establish a singular gift for songs bathed in a mood of exquisite sadness, a thread that would run through many of the high points of their prodigious output, from the obvious examples of 'The Winner Takes It All' and 'The Day Before You Came', to lesser-known gems such as 'The Way Old Friends Do', 'Our Last Summer' and 'Slipping Through My Fingers'. The mood of 'Knowing Me, Knowing You', emphasised by what is perhaps the finest, the most camp, the most Abbaesque of all their videos – it is hard to watch it, and especially the awkward choreography of the band members as they move from position to position, without being reminded of the cruel and acute, if not especially funny, *Not the Nine O'Clock News* parody *Super Duper* – must have been influenced, however subliminally, by the films of Ingmar Bergman, two of them in particular.

The Swedish director's grim masterpiece *Persona* (1967) had provided the key inspiration for what would become the iconic look of Abba videos. The idea, first used in the video for 'Mamma Mia' and returned to strikingly in the 'Knowing Me, Knowing You' clip, of capturing the faces of all four members, but most potently of Frida and Agnetha, in close-ups and appearing in different spatial relationships to each other, both facing the camera, perpendicular to it or to each other, is lifted from *Persona*. In this, perhaps Bergman's most complex film, the central characters, the tortured nurse played by the Swedish Bibi Andersson, the mute actress by the Norwegian Liv Ullmann, build, through the alternately bitter and nostalgic outbursts of

Andersson's character, to a communion of personalities, their faces connected via a series of close-ups before ultimately merging.

Aside from the borrowing of this visual trope, the song, with its melodic but mournful vignette of divorce, is thematically linked to Bergman through his 1973 film *Scenes from a Marriage*, a condensed version of the TV series *Six Scenes from a Marriage*, in which the descent of Marianne and Johan's (Liv Ullmann and Erland Josephson) marriage into bitter divorce is subjected to Bergman's scrutiny. The video captures Agnetha and Frida at their most beautiful and best-dressed, at least for those who can cope with Frida's decidedly non-PC fur coat. Frida's slightly tired look, clearly the result of her intense work schedule and the long period of depression from which she was beginning to emerge, fits with the mood of the song. Hallström, using the four Abba members to portray versions of themselves, deliberately plays with the idea that the song is somehow autobiographical.

Interspersed with shots of Agnetha and Frida striking wistful poses in the wintry landscape are rather potent shots of the two couples, at times intercut with one another with near-strobo-scopic jump cuts, and a succession of slo-mo embraces which lead to close-ups on the women, in each case revealing with varying degrees of subtlety the depressed undercurrents in these relationships. On one level the video here is as much a piece of fiction as the photo shoot of the previous year in which Agnetha and Björn are depicted as being no longer able to communicate. At this stage Björn and Agnetha were still several years away from their divorce, while Frida was singing with conviction about the pain of separation several years before she and Benny had finally got married.

Björn would for years reject attempts to interpret the lyrics as a simple reflection on his own marriage, in much the same way that other artists would react frostily to interpretations of their art as thinly disguised autobiography. In his authoritative history of the group, *Bright Lights Dark Shadows*, Carl Magnus Palm quotes Björn as commenting: 'Even if the roots are somewhere deep inside, from something that has happened to you, it's still 90 per cent fiction ... I was just working from images. I saw a man walking through an empty house for the last time as a symbol of divorce. I just described what I saw. I certainly hadn't been through that myself then.' This is a fairly gentle example of what is known as the Woody Allen Defence, Allen's films and life being the objects of an intense and ongoing game for fans and critics hoping to find direct links between the two – links between Allen's films and life, that is, not between his fans and critics.

Allen has always insisted that there is virtually no autobiographical nature to his work despite ample evidence to the contrary, but compare the above quotation with the words of a mellower 58-year-old Ulvaeus, speaking in a profile in *The Times* by Andrew Billen on 29 July 2003. Perhaps it was just a matter of being worn down by the relentlessness of the enquiries over the preceding 25 years, because, asked which of his Abba compositions was drawn from his own experiences, Ulvaeus happily volunteered: 'An example is "Knowing Me, Knowing You". I think we had just gone through, or were going through, the divorce, Agnetha and I, and I had this image of a man walking through an empty house with boxes, you know, and hearing to himself what had happened in those rooms and seeing what had happened in those rooms for the last time.'

The song is at the heart of the notion that Abba are terminally naff, as exemplified by the *Not the Nine O'Clock News* pastiche and the more damaging fact that the song had inspired the title of the fake, post-modern, kitsch chat show hosted by Alan Partridge, Steve Coogan's glorious caricature, an amalgam of several vacuous, self-important TV presenters. The hijacking of the title by Coogan points to a natural association – one bolstered by the episode of *Knowing Me, Knowing You* in which he and regular co-star Rebecca Front performed a memorable medley of Abba hits – between Abba and conservative England. The not unreasonable suggestion is that Abba, at the time that the punk movement was emerging from the suburbs, was happily providing the bland soundtrack to the empty lives of suburbanites and Middle Englanders. But the track, for all the unquestionable kitsch quotient of the video, transcends this image of naffness, or rather, succeeds in being simultaneously naff and glorious.

Nor would parents with children of a certain age have failed to notice the source of the loving pastiche 'Knowing Now How I Know You', performed by frizzy brunette Fizz and her fantasy friend the blonde pop-star toy Penelope Pink, complete with faces perpendicular to each other, in the Tweenies' Christmas special feature-length video *The Enchanted Toyshop*.

Sure enough, 'Knowing Me, Knowing You' proved to be yet another monster hit and million-plus seller, reaching number one in Germany, Ireland, Mexico, South Africa and the UK. Significantly, it just about scraped into the Australian top ten, its relative failure signalling the beginning of the end of Abbamania down under (see Chapter 13). Still, the single added to their reputation as a four-piece hit factory, a tour was in the offing, and although cracks were beginning to appear in the Ulvaeus-Fältskog union the couple would soon be announcing the imminent birth of their second child, while, after Frida's black period, her relationship with Benny was looking pretty solid. All in all, divorce had never sounded so good.

CHAPTER EIGHT

THE SHAME OF THE NAME

You realised that Abba represented everything you were going to hate. It seemed ... to deny your purpose as a new generation, to deny your point of view, and the thought that Mum and Dad might be whistling that tune in the bathroom of your suburban home made you want immediately to commit arson.
Malcolm McLaren, interviewed in
The Winner Takes It All – The Abba Story

... when the Sex Pistols' 20th anniversary reunion tour came to London, John Lydon decided that the band should enter to the strains of 'Dancing Queen' – the plan being to remind us how terrible music had become when the Sex Pistols came along. The idea backfired. On instant recognition of that piano flourish, the entire audience cheered and broke into spontaneous dancing.
Peter Paphides, the *Guardian*, Saturday 8 January 2002

The 4 December 1977 issue of *Melody Maker* carried a generally enthusiastic review of *Arrival*, beginning with the declaration: 'There is no doubt that Abba are the classiest pop outfit around Europe at the moment.' The reviewer pointed out a certain chilliness that emerges after six or seven listens, but overall the impression is a favourable one of what was, without question, the band's finest LP to that date, leaving aside both its stature compared to the later, even slicker productions and its standing as one of the high points in pop history.

But what is especially striking about this review, graced with a photograph of the foursome, posed and smiling, is that opposite it there is a full-page advert for the Sex Pistols' Anarchy Tour. The juxtaposition of Abba, the consummate creators of their own brand of lush pure pop, with the poster boys of anti-authority, pro-destruction anomie, seems at first jarring, the notion that they shared the same period of history and music incongruous, but these impressions are misleading and the gulf between the two was not as wide as it seemed at the time.

The era of punk was a short-lived one, and dating its birth and demise is an inexact, arbitrary task. But punk as we know it didn't begin until the early, grunting rumblings of the Sex Pistols in early 1976, although they'd formed the previous year, and was effectively dead by the time its clown prince, Sid Vicious, took his final, fatal overdose in February 1979. So, at the height of what seemed this seismic movement in the history of popular music, one that banished the moribund rock and pop scene at a stroke, what was the dominant musical force?

The answer is Abba. In 1976 the group spent a total of 12 weeks at the top of the singles charts, and in 1977 another nine. Their *Greatest Hits* album was the biggest-selling LP of 1976, just as *Arrival* was the following year's biggest seller, the two albums topping the charts for a combined 21 weeks. Their supremacy was under no threat from any direction and they would go on to enjoy chart-topping albums in each of the following four years.

But, for all their unrivalled commercial success, Abba did not enjoy universal adoration in their mid-to-late-1970s heyday. One is tempted, with hindsight, to recall that the breakthrough Eurovision triumph led seamlessly to the establishment of Abba as an instantaneous chart-topping band. In the same way one could imagine that, because of the band's current status with the continuing success of their *Gold* album, its admittedly less successful follow-up, the re-release of their entire back catalogue on CD and the monstrous global triumph of the musical *Mamma Mia!*, Abba always enjoyed today's widespread, although still far from universal, critical acceptance, which takes in all those who appreciate their music whether in a spirit of pre-irony, irony or post-irony.

Credibility was always a problem, and there was always a sense in interviews that for Benny, and perhaps even more for Björn, that level of acceptance, of credibility, was enormously important. They were hindered at the time by various problems inherent in the band, chiefly related to image, perception and style, both musical and sartorial, all of which were exacerbated by the fact that it was during the punk era that Abba reached their musical peak.

For part of this problem of how they were and, to a degree, continue to be perceived is that they are partly frozen in time, stuck in the public imagination in the risibly unfashionable mid-seventies. And the fact that to this day all four former band members, or rather the three that still speak to the press, have to address some or other question related to Eurovision in virtually every interview they undergo confirms this impression. Björn in particular insists that the bad clothes were intrinsic ingredients of the band only for the first couple of years – which is incidentally contradicted by the appalling blue (Arctic-themed and thus apparently representing the band's origins at the top of the world) outfits worn throughout the 1979 tour. But when one is contemplating Abba it remains all but impossible to this day to shake off thoughts of skin-hugging Lycra, of stacked glitter heels, of star-shaped guitars, of squeaky cleanliness, of, for want of a less naff word, naffness. Even before the arrival of punk and new wave, the notion of selling out constituted, for many punters and almost all music journalists, an important and vexed question. In this at least Abba were perversely fortunate in that no one could ever criticise them of selling out because they had never been remotely *in* in the first place.

To give a very brief, personal illustration – and this is not an anecdote so much as a simple personal epiphany – of the ridiculous schism between what was deemed acceptable and what unacceptable, I remember the horror I felt at being asked by one of my brothers – it must have been late November or early December in 1977 – to pick up a couple of records for him. I was already going – as a painfully self-conscious born-again, but strictly plainclothes, follower of punk, or at least new-wave orthodoxy – on a record-buying mission. I can't remember what I was going to buy, although judging by the time it could have been something along the lines of Elvis Costello's 'Watching the Detectives', 'Complete Control' by the Clash, perhaps 'The Modern World' by the Jam, i.e. something angry, in its own way tuneful and not least right on, something unquestionably, unmistakably credible.

The absurd thing that to this day sticks in my mind is the pain I felt when my brother specified exactly what records he wanted me to get him. His request was for Glenn Campbell's 'Wichita Lineman' – a song of which I was at that stage entirely ignorant but which had incidentally been covered by the Hootenanny Singers, although Campbell was to my mind at that time utterly unacceptable – and, more perilous still, the current number-one single, 'The Name of the Game'.

It is ridiculous to recall now that this suddenly seemed to me something approaching a hazardous mission, but it crystallised the tension that is created by all orthodoxies between what you know that you are supposed to like and want, and what you actually do like. Punk seemed and probably was a necessary and inevitable cultural phenomenon. The previous generation of rock stars had become bloated zillionaires, their live shows overblown and ultimately sterile events. What was needed was something young, something new, although those who had tracked the pub-rock scene or the New York proto-punk movement, or had a look at the Stranglers' drummer Jet Black's birth certificate, understood that it wasn't that new or particularly young. What punk and new wave brought was loudness, a dirty approach, an apparently hastily knocked-off, careless sound and, generally and crucially, an attitude that saw as despicable anything old, established, slick and corporate, all of which explains how Motörhead somehow managed to tag along on the first wave of punk.

The results of this movement were at their best thrilling; the first albums by the Sex Pistols, the Clash, the Jam, the Stranglers – although purists dismissed them as too old and too old-fashioned dirty rock-and-rollers to qualify as true punk – and the Damned were and remain exhilarating, if flawed masterpieces. But that orthodoxy, one to which I and many others ascribed, was ridiculous and invidious. The arrival, or at least the brief supremacy, of punk in the summer of 1977 was a kind of musical Year Zero. For a while, long-standing affection for the likes of the Beatles, Led Zeppelin, the Eagles, Pink Floyd and, God help us, glam or bubblegum pop, had to be suppressed. I was, like many others, a closet Abba fan, and it was as such that I went out on this dangerous mission.

Having gruffly acquired these forbidden fruits, I took them back home and listened to these records that seemed so contrary to the punk ethos. But with my fondness for Abba now – and I had retained a fondness for the group, however reluctant, since first seeing them in the 1974 Eurovision final – a strictly secret affair, I do recall a small jolt, some kind of guilty pleasure, no doubt, at the sheer lushness of the production, the clarity of the singing, the reminder or revelation that this supposedly candyfloss outfit had once again turned out a piece of shimmering, lustrous, direct but also subtle and sophisticated pop.

One is tempted to impose a pleasing narrative arc on one's own life and I would like to say that that moment, that little epiphany, saw me come to a very obvious conclusion: that, while not all styles of music or art are of equal value, and that by the same token there is generally very little to be gained from comparing artists and artefacts from different fields – has there been a more pointless debate in the history of cultural criticism than the Dylan versus Keats battle? – there can be merit and beauty in any work of art, and to avoid a protracted argument, let's see it as a given that pop music is a form of art. I suspect that, again like many others at that time, I in fact came to this realisation rather slowly.

I can, for instance, still remember experiencing something of a shock when I first heard Clive Gregson, the lead singer of the post-punk pop band Any Trouble, announce on a live recording on the B-side of their single 'Second Choice': 'This is a song by my favourite band', before launching into a rather gruff cover version of 'The Name of the Game', the lyrics tweaked to fit with the change in the singer's gender. Admittedly, neither Gregson (who was generally lumped together with the vocally similar angry young men of the post-pub-rock scene Elvis Costello, Joe Jackson and Graham Parker) nor his band was remotely danger-ous or cutting edge, but even so there seemed to be something almost daringly transgressive about this, tantamount to standing up and saying: 'My name's Clive Gregson and I'm an Abba fan.'

With their crystalline productions, the clarity and careful harmonies of Agnetha and Frida's vocals, and their, albeit decep-tively, sweet pop music, Abba seemed almost diametrically opposed to everything about the punk ethos. But this again was illusory.

Even the leaders of punk gradually – sometimes reluctantly, sometimes not – came out as Abba fans. In the booklet accom-panying the Sex Pistols' three-CD box set, Scott Murphy interviewed the surviving members of the band about the sources of their musical inspiration. Talking about 'Pretty Vacant', their third, arguably their finest and certainly their most poppy single, writer Glen Matlock recalled: 'To cut a long story short, I was short of a riff. Abba's "S.O.S." came on the jukebox and hey presto! I had it. But you've got to know where to look.' Drummer Paul Cook was still not convinced after all these years and said: 'Glen reckons the original riff was influenced by Abba's "S.O.S.". I can't see how he worked that out.'

Matlock wasn't the only Sex Pistol who retained a strong, almost taboo-busting fondness for the forbidden fruit of Abba's wistful, melodic pop genius. John Tiberi was, during their brief glory period, the Sex Pistols' road manager, and indeed, in the words of Sid Vicious, the 'fifth Pistol'. Tiberi, aka 'Boogie', recalls the Pistols' tour of early spring 1977. It was a time for regrouping, literally, with the recently drafted-in Sid Vicious needing some relatively inconspicuous gigs in order to blood himself – something he had done literally in his early days as a band hanger-on – as the band's new bassist, replacing Matlock, who had been their musical driving force.

With Matlock having been asked to leave the group, and now with their new member, and following on from the celebrated gig at London's Screen on the Green cinema, the band embarked on a short, bonding trip to Berlin. After this short break, and consciously or otherwise taking advantage of the calm before the almighty storm that would await the band on their return to the UK with the release of 'God Save the Queen' as the alternative anthem to mark the Silver Jubilee, Tiberi and the group set off for three weeks of concerts in club venues in Denmark, Norway and Sweden. The atmosphere throughout the tour was harmonious and there was a sense of renewed optimism and creativity among the band members, who relished the enthusiasm of the fans, although there was nevertheless a decisive split between the two halves of the band, lead guitarist Steve Jones and drummer Paul Cook on one side, Vicious and Rotten on the other. Towards the end of this mini-tour there occurred a very quiet, fleeting and oddly poignant meeting between two bands, between two musical cultures.

Tiberi, John Lydon and Vicious were heading into a small airport terminal in Oslo after the short flight from Trondheim. While Lydon was hanging coolly in the background, Tiberi and Vicious spotted two strangely familiar-looking women, whom Vicious quickly identified as Agnetha and Frida. While Lydon remained aloof, Vicious, who, for all his attraction to manifold forms of self-abuse, always had something of the cheeky, exuberant schoolboy about him, marched up to the astonished pair and effusively, though not necessarily articulately, declared his undying admiration for them and their band. Taken aback by this patently sincere, if unlikely, expression of fandom, Agnetha and Frida made brief remarks about how they were themselves looking forward to a shopping spree in London and then made off. Thus ended this very brief union between what were perhaps the two major musical forces, in the UK at least, of the second half of the seventies.

You could have scripted it better, something wittier, or indeed witty, could have been said, there could have been the suggestion of some spark between Sid and Agnetha, but that's the way it happened, and this encounter lasted barely a minute. But, aside from the apparent oddness of these people's briefly sharing the same air, what seems at least a little surprising is the fact that at this time Vicious should so openly have expressed his love of Abba. But the more you look, the more you see that few people even within the very heart of this supposedly iconoclastic movement were immune to the charms of Abba's meticulously crafted pop gems.

Tiberi also remembers many occasions sitting around at Joe Strummer's place during the period when he had worked as the road manager for his pre-Clash band the 101ers: 'We used to share musical tastes quite strongly, actually, me and Joe. We used to sit around, playing records, smoking dope and that's about the only thing that we did together. I mean he didn't do much together with anybody, like go the pictures, or down the pub, or to the art gallery or whatever. But we did do smoking dope and playing records, and the more esoteric the better. Abba? Oh, yeah, absolutely.' A shared favourite was, incidentally, 'Dancing Queen'.

To confirm this still incongruous notion that the leader of the most politically engaged band of the punk era, the band who refused to sell out by playing *Top of the Pops*, was an unabashed Abba fan, there is the extract below from Vic Garbarini's joint interview with Strummer and fellow guitar hero who emerged in an earlier generation, King Crimson's Robert Fripp, which appeared in the June 1981 issue of *Musician*. The interviewer talks of having mistaken the backing musicians (actually the members of the Clash) on a recent Ellen Foley recording for Abba:

> Strummer: That's a compliment.
> Fripp: Abba are very, very good.
> Garbarini: I agree, but I'm surprised to hear both you say that. What you like about them?
> Strummer: They hardly ever lay a turkey on you. They've kind of hit a rut these days, but they were in there just blammin' 'em on to the charts for ages, which is admirable ... also the girls are nice-looking!

Another devoted Abba fan of the time was Elvis Costello. One of the figureheads of the new-wave era, Costello was a master of angry, urgent pop songs or narrative ballads, as comfortable writing about politics as about romance. His biggest hit, 'Oliver's Army', was, unlikely as it sounds, inspired by 'Dancing Queen', as he has freely and often admitted, inspiration for the tune coming when he was suddenly struck by the potential of his regular pianist Steve Nieve's messing around with the Abba hit's melody on the piano. Costello would once again refer to the song, much more recently, in 'When I Was Cruel No. 2' and, waxing lyrical on the subject of the track in the course of answering a fan's enquiry on the askelvis website on Saturday, 8 June 2001, he insisted that it contained 'the second greatest "yeah" in all pop music after the Mamas and the Papas' "I Saw Her Again"'.

Elvis Costello's fondness for Abba was no passing phase. He offered several of his compositions for Frida's 1982 Phil Collins-produced solo album *Something's Going On*, and was keen for Agnetha to record a version of his 'Shatterproof', an appropriately poppy, melodic song about the fragility of romantic love, with, as often in his work, violent undercurrents, for her 1983 album *Wrap Your Arms Around Me*. It wasn't selected for the album and instead became a minor hit for Billy Bremner, of Rockpile fame.

Costello's 2002 collaboration with the great Swedish mezzo-soprano Anne Sofie von Otter, *For the Stars*, included, among other cover versions, a rendition of 'An Angel Passing through My Room', from Abba's *The Visitors*, and also featured, alongside other guest musicians, a contribution from Benny Andersson on accordion. Costello has included *Abba Gold* in his eclectic selection of the 500 records that 'You Need'. So Abba sit comfortably alongside everyone from Chet Baker to the Bee Gees, Bartók to Grandmaster Flash, Mozart to Robert Wyatt. He had initially intended to annotate every entry but gave up after the very first one, in favour of a more general overview of his diverse musical leanings. This one entry is for *Abba Gold*, of which he says succinctly: 'Fast songs for entertaining your Australian friends, or playing with the dressing-up box. Slow songs: a pop-music version of Bergman's *Scenes from a Marriage*.'

So, of course, the idea of punk and new wave being musically isolated, springing fully formed in 1976/7 created and inflected by nothing more than the spirit of ennui, allied with a general, burgeoning anti-establishment, anti-rock dinosaur passion affixed to the imported New York proto-punk scene stretching back through the New York Dolls to Iggy Pop and Lou Reed and beyond, was always short-sighted. Looked back upon, and listened to, from today's perspective, nearly 30 years on, the whole punk scene seems much more innocent, less cohesive, often more melodic, and far less isolated than it seemed at the time, absorbing ideas from what were apparently the most unlikely sources.

While for some Abba may have represented a faintly embarrassing secret passion, for others there was never any shame in being a fan of these purveyors of great pop music. As Michael Bradley, bassist and regular songwriter for the mighty Undertones (whose magnificent self-titled debut LP *Melody Maker* assessed as 'a competitor for Abba's *Greatest Hits*') writes in the sleeve notes for the band's *True Confessions*, a collection of the group's A-sides and B-sides: 'Pure pop was Abba.'

CHAPTER NINE

ABBA – THE ALBUM

*I admit there was a strong sense of competition within both
of us. I don't want to hide the fact that Frida and I had opposite
backgrounds, temperaments and personalities. We could get
furious and tired with each other, so we had our
moments.* Agnetha Fältskog in *As I Am*

As 1977 began, Abba were arguably at the high point of their
collective career, and Björn and Benny were knocking out hit
songs with little apparent effort. But this was a highly deceptive
phenomenon, for their compositions were accomplished in the
course of what was a nine-to-five job for the pair either in Abba's
offices or in a cottage on the island of Viggsö, where both couples
had holiday homes. These songs were coming off the back of a
succession of hit singles and their most inspired, most consistent
album so far, with which, aided by their idiosyncratic promotional philosophy, they had apparently cracked the notoriously
difficult American market – although again this impression was
misleading.

It was in January that year that Lasse Hallström shot the
video for 'Knowing Me, Knowing You', and at the same time
the Abba organisation, headed by the ever-pragmatic, ever-ruth-
less Stig Anderson, was putting the final touches to the band's
imminent tour. It is a measure of the dedication to the Abba
cause of all four members, and especially Björn, that when he

127

and Agnetha decided to try for a second child – Linda was nearly four – he felt obliged to inform Stig of even this preliminary decision.

The image of the band was so squeaky clean, and for those who hadn't taken the time to seek out the not-so-hidden clues to a deeper angst contained within the lyrics of even their biggest hits, the Abba story seemed too good to be true. The yin-and-yang pairing of the group's two lead singers, which had led early, idle commentators to intuit some lesbian undertones to the group's structure – these two goddesses surely couldn't be attached to those two physically unprepossessing backing musicians – now inspired journalists, specifically those writing for the *Sun*, desperate for a story, any story, to imply some mutual enmity fizzing just below the surface between the two singers.

The gist of the story was that these twin divas were continually at each other's throat when away from the public eye, their personalities incompatible. Agnetha was portrayed as prissy, uptight and infuriated by Frida's slapdash timekeeping and fixation on hideous outfits, and Frida, the smarter, more musically sophisticated, indeed generally more sophisticated of the pair, as frustrated by Agnetha's inability to grasp the musical instructions so patiently given by their romantic partners. The hostility between the two singers is a given in *Abba – The Name of the Game*, the breezy story of the band co-written by Tony Calder, Colin Irwin and Andrew Oldham, the last-named of Rolling Stones fame and infamy. There was perhaps some truth in this mildly muck-raking story, if only in that it pointed to some general, contrasting character traits in the two women.

There really was a marked contrast between the personas and personal histories of Agnetha and Frida. Agnetha had emerged from a perfectly normal, almost perfectly happy childhood, a shy extrovert whose role model Connie Francis was a bland heroine only slightly more rock and roll than Sandra Dee. Success had come easy and early to Agnetha, as had, after an early romantic hiccup or two, her dream man.

Frida, on the other hand, the bastard offspring of a small-town Norwegian girl and a Nazi, and effectively an orphan from the age of two, had been brought up in humble conditions by a grandmother who, while determined to raise her well, was far from being a cuddly, nurturing earth grandmother. While Agnetha was Sweden's golden girl of pop and in time half of a golden couple, Frida's early career was something of a slog, which saw her paying her professional dues as a singer with various dance bands in the course of which she fell into the arms of Ragnar. Maybe the photographs don't do him justice, but the man was hardly a catch and, as with so much in Frida's early adulthood, indeed her early life, there is something desperate about this union. It was patently ill judged, or at least doomed not to last, her ambitions leading her to take the radical decision to leave much of the parenting of her two young children to Ragnar while she headed for Stockholm to pursue her dreams.

This is another moment that crystallises the stark contrast between Frida and Agnetha. Agnetha couldn't bear to be parted from her children, something that became very obvious to her when she and Björn returned to their family home after the Eurovision adventures and found that Linda scarcely recognised them after their extended separation. From that moment she had resolved to put her family life first, a decision that, along with her much-publicised distaste for flying, threatened to harm her career.

In the early days of the two couples, when their collaborations were on a more informal basis, they had socialised happily together, but this had been a short-lived phase and over the years they went out less and less often as a foursome, particularly after the birth of Linda. This was not just a matter of the two women's not being bosom buddies, but as much to do with the increasingly intense professional collaboration between all four. While always the best of friends, and there is scarcely a hint of a major split between the two over the past 35 years, Björn and Benny needed regular breaks from each other, with their compositional duties being carried out within the rigid structure of regular working hours. Perhaps toeing the band's official line, the two women themselves almost invariably protested that they got on perfectly well, although they never tried to pretend that they were actually the best of friends, yet the simple fact is that they had contrasting personalities.

Frida was known, certainly as far back as her days with Charlie Norman, as a woman who enjoyed a lively social life. She was gregarious and talkative, although Norman remarked on the fact that she never opened up about the circumstances of her child-hood when they were hanging out together. There is nothing unnatural in this, especially in light of the strange truth of her early years.

Agnetha, by contrast – although there are rumours about a wild streak that came out in the aftermath of her divorce – for all her directness, her talent (unlike Frida, she was an accomplished composer and producer) and her fierce temper, something she did share with Frida, was essentially a private person; in the post-Abba years, increasingly and notoriously so.

Then there was the not so small matter of Agnetha's general standing in the group and in particular the extraordinary and surely not entirely healthy focus on her bum. This was the most famous backside in show business until the arrival on the scene in the late 1980s of fellow gay icon and Abba-covering Oz popstress Kylie, the pair of them being eclipsed, as was much else besides, by J-Lo's celebrated behind. The attitude of many, though by no means all, Abba-watchers was summed up in the *Not the Nine O'Clock News* parody in which Pamela Stephenson (Agnetha) and Griff Rhys Jones (Frida) cruelly sang:

One of us is ugly
One of us is cute
One of us you'd like to see in our birthday suit.

Agnetha was the latest in a long line of Swedish starlets – Greta Garbo, Ingrid Bergman, Anita Ekberg, Britt Ekland – to become internationally famous. These women were objects of fascination, studied as much for their colourful private lives as for their work, the prurient interest in their professional and private lives fuelled in part by a version of the answer that Hitchcock routinely gave to interviewers who asked why he was always attracted to working with blonde actresses. In his *The Dark Side of Genius – The Life of Alfred Hitchcock*, Donald Spoto quotes Hitchcock as averring: 'The perfect "woman of mystery" is one who is blonde, subtle and Nordic.' Hitchcock always insisted that what made blonde women appealing to men, certainly as film stars, was a surface purity concealing darker desires that would become apparent if ever one found oneself, in Hitchcock's creepy image, in the back of a taxi with one of them. Agnetha was created from this template of Scandinavian beauty, emerging as the very ideal of Nordic, Aryan womanhood.

Beside this eye-catching package squeezed into some Lycra outfit or other was Frida, who was absurdly and unaccountably dismissed as unattractive, in some quarters at least, solely by dint of not being blonde, this despite her supposedly being the result of a Nazi eugenic breeding programme designed to produce perfect Aryans. That there were occasional tensions within the group was not disputed, but the fiercest of these, by their own accounts, were even then happening within the two romantic relationships, Björn and Agnetha's marriage being characterised from the outset by regular domestic spats.

But, for all the occasional disagreement, the working and personal relationship between Agnetha and Frida seems to have been generally totally functional and cordial, a fact that led the group to take legal action against the paper to scotch this rumour which they felt was damaging their carefully constructed pure white image. With this issue dealt with temporarily at least, the band could turn their attention to their imminent tour of Europe and Australia, and after that the recording sessions for what would be their fifth album, blissfully unaware that a far more sensational tabloid story was waiting for them, specifically for Frida, just around the corner (see Chapter 15).

Abba had always had problems of one kind or another with the whole business of touring. They had begun as a musical foursome with the disastrous live shows of 1970, experiences that would have proved terminal to less determined artists. On the domestic front they had endured the repeated slog of *folkparket* tours, and their only previous attempt at even a limited international tour, the 1974 jaunt across Denmark, Germany and Austria, had been at best a serious disappointment, at worst a disaster, one alleviated only by the relative triumph of the Swedish dates which rounded it off. That previous experiment had failed largely because, established as they were in their home territory, by late 1974 their international stature was essentially limited to the public awareness of them provided by their recent Eurovision success. Since then, however, Abba had become close to claiming the spot as the biggest band in the world – the US excluded – and certainly the biggest pull across Europe and in Australia. The change in their circumstances was reflected in the scale of the tour and the appetite of their fans around the world.

The image for the tour was suitably grand, the costumes appropriately garish – and the group had no one but themselves to blame for their on-stage fashion disasters, or rather no one but Frida, who had shared responsibility for matters sartorial since 1974 – and the musical ambition also elevated to a new level. The latter was represented by the appearance in the live set of the four-song cycle, of which three songs would appear on the upcoming album as '3 Scenes from a Mini Musical', of which more later.

The 17-date European leg of the tour kicked off on 28 January at the Ekebergshallen in Oslo, where they performed in front of members of the Norwegian royal family. From there the Abba convoy – 52 crew members and around 30 tons of equipment (no wonder Björn complained subsequently that, despite each sizeable venue on the tour being sold out, the tour had barely broken even) – moved on across the continent. The itinerary took in dates in Gothenburg, Copenhagen, Berlin, Cologne, Antwerp, Essen, Hanover, Hamburg, Birmingham, Manchester, Glasgow (this last would come in handy later, providing that elusive rhyme for 'last show' or indeed vice versa), and a two-night stay at the Albert Hall, this at a time before Eric Clapton's annual inflated residency had made such a thing commonplace.

On their previous tour the band's distaste for life on the road had been compounded by some serious self-doubt after public indifference had led to half the tour's being cancelled before they set off, and the Swiss leg's being abandoned in mid-tour – and even when they did get on stage they were forced to perform to patently non-capacity crowds, at least until the return to Scandinavia. This time round, every single venue was sold out well in advance, the Albert Hall shows attracting applications for an astonishing three and a half million tickets.

Part of the group's reluctance to perform live was rooted in the understanding that they wouldn't be able to recreate the distinctive sound that they had gradually developed and perfected in the studio over the previous four years, but, backed up by their regular musicians and aided by a state-of-the-art sound system, they found that replicating, or at least approximating, the lushness of their recordings was not such a problem. Agnetha was, as ever, susceptible to a degree of stage fright (fairly easy to disguise) and a faltering voice (less easy to hide). The reviews of their live performances, when not wholly favourable, matched the criticism of their recordings. The gist of these was that the performances were too perfect, that the emphasis was too much on the clear surface sheen, and that the band's sound, like their music, lacked edge, depth and darkness.

While it is impossible to defend Abba against the accusation that they were at times purveyors of shallow, plastic pop, to criticise their output and their live performances for being too perfect, lacking in emotion, is simultaneously to be unfair and to miss the point. They aspired – and Björn and Benny have always been keen to emphasise the importance of their shared work ethic in their collaborations – to crafting songs based on strong melodies and subtle and dramatic shifts in tone, gilded with complex vocal harmonies. The work continued in the studio during long, temper-fraying recording sessions in which the songs would be constructed layer by layer, instrumental and vocal tracks repeated and distorted, creating their sound, some of which was indeed effectively irreplicable in a live context. Here it should be said, and this is part of the show's appeal, that the full orchestral accompaniment in *Mamma Mia!* is a pretty good substitute. To condemn Abba for having come close to replicating live their glorious recordings, and to criticise these for being too clean and clinical, is to criticise the band for too fully having accomplished what they set out to do.

It is similarly unfair to condemn the band for shallowness or soullessness. They were, after all, a pop band whose central aim was to entertain. Looking at their set list today confirms that the 1977 tour was taking place at a time when the band were, if not quite in the midst of a metamorphosis, then at least in a period of marked maturation. They may have still been peddling such vacuous but irresistible fluff as 'Dum Dum Diddle', but it is misleading to say that they lacked soul. What their songs were increasingly revealing was just a very pop, rather Scandinavian soul, where irresistible pop melodies and harmonies complemented or carried lyrics that explored romantic misery and despair, inner emptiness, artistic exploitation, sexual predation, as well as palm trees, tigers and the queasy desire to be someone's fiddle.

Reviewing the first Albert Hall show in *The Times* on Tuesday 15 February 1977, Richard Williams, one of the most reliable and insightful writers on sport and popular culture, while himself hinting at the occasional lack of humanity in Abba's pristine image and performance, noted that their set included several songs – he selected 'Mamma Mia', 'Dancing Queen', 'S.O.S.' and 'Waterloo' – that were 'already pop classics'. While not impressed with the mini-musical, he did, significantly, assert: 'The arrangements, though, are the real secret: no one in the field can match their outstandingly imaginative deployment of pianos, synthesisers, and tuned percussion derived from the innovations of Brian Wilson and Phil Spector.'

Williams unerringly hit upon the key twin influences on the sound of the group, but he can't have been aware at this time of his own role in helping the band to recreate, or at least create their own version of, these distinctive sounds in the studio. In *Bright Lights Dark Shadows*, Carl Magnus Palm reveals how one day in 1972 Michael B. Tretow had managed to pick up a copy of *Out of His Head: The Sound of Phil Spector*, Williams's seminal account of the life and work of the seriously disturbed, gun-loving pop genius, and had used this as a kind of guidebook and constant source of inspiration for his own innovative work with Abba. Incidentally, and such connections between major pop figures are no surprise, the Beatles had been important figures in the careers of the Beach Boys, Spector and Abba.

Brian Wilson constantly judged his own work against the standards of his transatlantic rivals Lennon and McCartney and was driven to greater efforts, as well as to greater levels of drug consumption, by the Beatles' two masterpieces *Rubber Soul* and *Sgt. Pepper's*. Spector had famously, notoriously, been brought in to make some coherent sense of the recording sessions for *Let It Be*. Björn and Benny were inspired by the Beatles in many ways, not least in their desire to compose their own songs, first separately in their own bands and then together, and Benny would often say in interviews in the middle and late 1970s that, now that he'd already achieved so much with Abba, his greatest remaining ambition was to produce a John Lennon record.

The first half of the tour had, for all the criticism, been little short of triumphant. The Australian leg was, if anything, even more successful (see Chapter 13).

With their Australian success now behind them, Agnetha happily pregnant with her and Björn's second child, and the editing of the film of the tour, which would in time be released as *Abba – The Movie*, going on, the group turned their attention to the new album. At this stage the Abba organisation were in preliminary preparations for their new studio complex, and in order to investigate some up-to-date recording equipment, Björn and Benny travelled to Los Angeles in May 1977. The West Coast vibe they picked up during this short visit proved inspirational to the atmosphere of the new album. There they found a school of soft rock to which they could aspire.

The West Coast rock scene, growing out of the innovative folk-rock fusion of the Byrds and the bluesy rock that had been transmuted into something new in the acid-drenched late 1960s, was headed by the likes of Linda Ronstadt, Jackson Browne, the Eagles and Fleetwood Mac. The last two groups were already particular favourites of Björn's, and the whole music scene was characterised by the very Abbaesque lush productions, a mellow mood belying some darker undercurrents in the lyrics.

At the time of the Abba men's jaunt to LA, Fleetwood Mac

were kicking off the US leg of their Rumours Tour, backing up an album which yielded four hit singles and would go on to sell, depending on who's talking, between 15 and 25 million copies worldwide. The group, formed in the 1960s as a very British blues act but by then transformed into a very American, very West Coast AOR outfit, comprised, like Abba, two couples (vocalist Stevie Nicks and guitarist Lindsey Buckingham; bassist and founder member John McVie and Christine McVie on keyboards and vocals). And, as with Abba, the strain had recently started to show, although in Fleetwood Mac's case the strains had been evident in both relationships. These emotionally fraught circumstances resulted in some of the most notorious recording sessions in rock history, a field not short of tales of excess, and yet these troubled sessions yielded an album of finely wrought, very radio-friendly songs, albeit ones whose lyrics betrayed a degree of romantic animosity.

At the same time the Eagles were enjoying their last hurrah, as a creative force at least, with *Hotel California*. They released one more album, *The Long Run*, in 1979 and then saw their *Greatest Hits* sell an estimated 28 million copies worldwide, making it what is generally accepted to be the best-selling album of all time. (Hard figures for actual record sales are notoriously tricky to come by and unreliable when you do. Universal Records in Stockholm, who refuse to disclose, even if they know, total sales figures for individual records, confidently state that *Abba Gold* has sold around 26 million copies around the world since its release in 1992, a figure that would make it probably the third-biggest-selling album of all time, and yet for mysterious reasons the album features nowhere in such lists.) As with *Rumours*, *Hotel California* was the product of a protracted period in the studio, made by a band on the verge of implosion. And, as with Fleetwood Mac's musical behemoth, so the Eagles managed to shift around 16 million copies of an album whose sensitive, easy-listening vibe belied some rather grim subject matter in the lyrics, not least warnings, as in the title track, of the dangers of recreational drug use.

Benny and Björn already had some ideas for the new record, their mini-musical having been showcased on the recent tour, where it received an uneven reception. But never afraid to mix and match and leap from musical genre to musical genre, they now returned to Sweden, headed off to the isolation of Viggsö, and set to work with their characteristic determination to realise something of the warm, mellow West Coast sound. Although, unlike their American inspirations, they may have been fuelled through their writing and recording sessions by nothing stronger than a few beers and perhaps the occasional shot of spirits, nevertheless the results of their efforts were a couple of Abba's finest moments.

While their new studio was being constructed, the group recorded the album in Stockholm's Metronome and Glen studios, with which they were well familiar, the first a studio in which they had worked individually and together for nearly a decade, and the Bohus Recording Studio in Kungälv, on Sweden's south-west coast.

The album kicks off in wonderful style with the dreamy 'Eagle', an appropriately soaring record that pointed very clearly to the group's desire to be taken seriously as an adult band if only in its un-radio-friendly five-minutes-plus duration, the shift away from the confines of the three-minute pop song being a sure sign of a band in the midst of quest for personal growth. Personal exploration, of however woolly a variety, is the theme of the track, with Björn having been inspired to write the lyrics after picking up a copy of Richard Bach's *Jonathan Livingston Seagull*. The book fitted perfectly with the Summer of Love generation who had turned on, tuned in and dropped out but needed somewhere to go next, now that the world that they had left behind no longer made any sense. The time was ripe for Peter Tomkins's *The Secret Life of Plants* and *Jonathan Livingston Seagull,* the latter exploring the idea that we all have our own spirit animals, a notion that inspired Barbara Hershey temporarily to assume the name Barbara Seagull and Peter Cohon to transform himself for ever into Peter Coyote. It brings to mind a passage from *Money into Light,* John Boorman's book on the troubled production of his Brazilian-set eco-fable *The Emerald Forest.* The director speaks of his mystical encounter and gnomic conversation with Takuma, the shaman of the Kamaiura tribe of the Amazonian rainforest with whom he was working:

'"Everyone is connected with the spirit of a particular creature."

'"What is my animal?" I asked.

'"Your animal," he replied as though it was perfectly obvious and he did not deign to name it. The only intimation I have is that when they painted me it was with the markings of an eagle. This was a strange moment."'

So that's the sentiment of the song, poignant in an Athena-postcard/Leonard Nimoy-poem kind of way. There is also surely an underlying, or rather overlying, meaning to the song, its message being a not-so-cryptic expression of the songwriter's hidden desire. As an avowed fan of the West Coast AOR music scene, and the Eagles in particular, Björn Ulvaeus was dreaming of casting aside his role as a pop performer, spreading his wings and becoming an Eagle alongside Don Henley, Glenn Frey et al.

The intro, which contains a catchy sequence that is repeated throughout the song, inspired the synth-pop band the Human League for their 'dah-dah-da-da-da' – if this isn't becoming too technical – opening passage of 'Don't You Want Me?', their own *A Star Is Born*-riffing monster hit single of the winter of 1981. Responding, in the course of a timesonline webchat on 17 August 2001, to the assertion that the Human League were in effect 'Abba meets Kraftwerk', the Human League's lead singer, Phil Oakey, insisted: 'Abba were a pop band who did some weird stuff which they released as singles, whereas we're a weird band – but our normal stuff was what we released as singles.' 'Eagle' is a very beautiful, rather sad song of escape.

Looking back at the album now, one knows that it must have been created in trying circumstances. It was made on the back of a tour undertaken by a band who hated touring, at a time when the problems in the relationship between Björn and Agnetha had been papered over by the once-trusted method of having a child in the hope that this would bring the increasingly estranged couple closer together. Does this ever work? The schism within their marriage is surely at the heart of the desperately romantic 'One Man, One Woman', a track that begins with the seriously bleak line 'No smiles, not a single word at the breakfast table'. From this deeply unhappy opening, things only get worse, before an unlikely redemptive resurgence of love in the chorus, something that evokes the image in the Beatles 'Things We Said Today' of a couple, together for a long time, being 'deep in love, not a lot to say'. This is clearly a very personal statement, perhaps a chilling commentary on Björn's own marriage, the sudden empty optimism of

> *One man, one woman*
> *Two friends and two true lovers*
> *Somehow we'll help each other through the hard times*

reflecting the last efforts to save the marriage. Significantly, as with 'Knowing Me, Knowing You', it is Frida who sings this heartbreaking song.

But it's certainly not all grim news, and even with the worst will in the world it's hard to read any complex or bleak message into the track that precedes 'One Man, One Woman' on the album, 'Take a Chance on Me', aside from the fact that it contains another of Björn's lewd lyrics featuring, in 'pretty birds have flown', avian imagery of a rather different sort to that of 'Eagle'. We should be glad, though, that Björn for once resisted talking about chicks in one of his 'sexy' songs. It's an exuberant song of hopeful pleading, the slightly electronicised vocal backing 'take a chance' reminiscent of the 'ouga chaka' chant on Blue Swede's 'Hooked on a Feeling' by the group's friend and fellow countryman Björn Skifs. The insistent irresistible rhythm of the track had come to Björn in the course of a run, inspired by the percussive beat of feet hitting tarmac, Björn being a devotee of the jogging craze that was sweeping the Western world in the middle and late seventies.

'Take a Chance on Me' was eventually one of the songs covered by Erasure on their EP *Abbaesque*, one of the key events in the Abba revival of the early 1990s – not that they ever really went away.

On 18 February 1978 'Take a Chance on Me', a piece of expertly realised electro-bubblegum pop, reached the number-one spot in the UK charts, replacing the Abba-imitating Brotherhood of Man's wretched 'Figaro', a rehash of the band's earlier hit 'Angelo', which was itself a pale imitation of 'Fernando'. It was Abba's seventh UK number one, but as magical as it was, it pales, if only a little, beside their sixth, the track that directly follows it, 'The Name of the Game'. This was the other composition on the album, along with 'Eagle', in which Björn and Benny consciously attempted to replicate the laid-back LA vibe that they had tasted earlier in 1977. The result was one of their most spectacular successes artistically and in terms of sales.

After its languid opening, 'The Name of the Game' makes use of both Agnetha and Frida, singing separately and gloriously together, their voices melding in a chorus in which the vocals are complemented by the simple but beautiful acoustic guitar and then the flourish of a 'Penny Lane'-like trumpet. The song's considerable appeal is boosted by one of the more playful of the group's videos, in which they are pictured sitting around a table playing a board game (the name of this game, by the way, is Fia); this section was filmed in Björn and Agnetha's home. The track is one of the towering masterpieces not just of Abba but of the entire pop canon.

As wonderful as *Abba – The Album* undoubtedly is, it is certainly not without its flaws, and after the exceptionally fine opening foursome, there is a dramatic shift of tone – always a feature of Abba records good and bad – although it's genuinely tricky to work out what the mood of 'Move On' is or was meant to be. You wonder if, the mood of LA still strong in their memories, Björn and Benny were going for some meaningful spot of New Age preaching. Perhaps it was allowing Stig to contribute to a track once again – although he is also credited, for what it isn't clear, on 'The Name of the Game'. It is hard to account for the song which, with its panpipe-like flute, has a Hispanic, Andean sound – which made it a natural choice as one of the tracks to be re-recorded with Spanish vocals for the huge-selling *Gracias por la Música* collection. There may be a touch of the Beach Boys' ''Til I Die' to the 'roller in the ocean', 'life is flowing' imagery, and so long as you can ignore the cod philosophy this is rather pretty.

'Hole in Your Soul' is another oddity, for all its catchiness an unholy blend of all the things that Abba did worst – a kind of 10cc-inflected novelty record, one that seems to have had a direct influence on the collaborations a couple of years later of Jon and Vangelis, and, far worse, been the progenitor of Starship's 'We Built This City on Rock and Roll', which in April 2004 was voted by the readers of the American rock magazine *Blender* the worst song of all time.

Then there is another dramatic change of gear as the album

closes with '3 Scenes from a Mini Musical', which represented three-quarters of the musical that had featured strongly in the recent tour. One can perhaps read too much into a song, but there remains something perverse about the most famous of these, the first of the three, 'Thank You for the Music'. This may be a work of theatrical fiction, just a simple celebratory number, sung by an imaginary singer in praise of the music that has elevated her from the mundane to some implicit level of glory. But it is impossible not to be a little disquieted by the idea of Agnetha confessing, thanks to her husband's lyrics, in the song's famous opening couplet: 'I'm nothing special, In fact I'm a bit of a bore.' Not for the first time Björn had written a song for his wife in which she was cast as a thoroughly unexceptional person who comes to life only in performance. One doesn't want to stretch this idea too far, but there does seem something rather peculiar about having your wife thank you and your writing partner for transforming you, however briefly, into something worthwhile.

The second part of the trilogy sees Frida, on stage wearing a blonde fright wig, as is Agnetha, the two being two halves of the same woman, as she belts out 'I Wonder (Departure)', a very stage-musical number in which the woman ponders whether or not to take the plunge and escape from the future that seems to be mapped out for her in favour of a life in show business. The theme of the song, with the contrast between the claustrophobia of domestic life and the perceived freedom of a performer's life, is again pointedly autobiographical and pertinent to Björn's current situation as well as Frida and Benny's own early adulthood. The ambition to break away from their pop moulds, implicit in their desire to create a piece of musical theatre, is emphasised by the song, with the parenthetic subtitle doubly suggestive, of both the singer's desire to escape her own circumstances and the group's desire to escape from the

143

narrow confines of a pop outfit, contrasting with the title of their previous album.

The trilogy and the album end in unusual style with the oddly bitter 'I'm a Marionette', in which the two halves of this hypothetical performer are united to protest against the puppeteers of the music business. The dissonance of the chorus is rather striking, suggesting that Björn and Benny were fed up with the business, and the drudgery of writing pretty, often beautiful pop music. But for those after a spot of nostalgia, Björn proves that, as accomplished as he was becoming in his lyrics, he was still quite capable of producing a stone-bad line with the stunning 'Out of place, like King Kong'.

Abba – The Album is a strange beast, a record that starts out looking as if it may be Abba's most coherent work to date, possibly a great album, one that contains three or four of their finest and best-loved songs, but is ultimately as eclectic, disparate and inchoate as their early records. It may have been incoherent, oddly perhaps less than the sum of its parts, but many of the individual parts were inspired. Aside from bringing to an end the band's extraordinary pop supremacy in Australia, 'The Name of the Game' was, by Abba standards, a relatively minor hit there, the UK being the only territory where it reached number one.

By contrast, its follow-up was one of their greatest successes, its success no doubt enhanced by the engaging video in which scenes of Agnetha and Frida dancing for the benefit of an initially resistant Benny and a stubbornly gloomy Björn are intercut with *Brady Bunch/Celebrity Squares*-style shots of the screen split into four close-ups of the four members of the band. 'Take a Chance on Me' reached number one in Austria, Belgium, Ireland and the UK, and the top ten almost everywhere else it was released, although its top-three place in the *Billboard* chart belied the fact that in terms of sheer sales (more than one million) it was the band's most successful US single release, more successful than their breakthrough number-one hit of the previous year, 'Dancing Queen'.

On 4 December 1977 Agnetha gave birth to her and Björn's second child, a son they named Christian Peter. A little over a year later the couple would publicly announce their decision to separate.

CHAPTER TEN

'VOULEZ-VOUS'

The first couple of months of 1978 saw the UK release of *Abba – The Album* and then *Abba – The Movie*, neither of which met with widespread critical approbation, the *NME*'s review of the first suggesting that: 'Future hits apart, this album could turn out to be Abba's least satisfactory.' But the band was on a roll, the album notching up more than a million sales in advance orders in Sweden, Norway (the album and film were released across Scandinavia in December 1977) and the UK combined. The band were engaged in various promotional duties, the staggered release of the album, their film and their singles creating a ripple effect which culminated in the massive success of 'Take a Chance on Me' in the US.

Perhaps as significant in the continuing global success of the band was the official opening on 8 May of Polar Studios, Abba's very own designer recording space. What should have led to the smoothest period of creativity perversely resulted in Björn and Benny's first-ever experience of writer's block. This being the writer's block as experienced by one of pop music's most prolific and gifted partnerships, it wasn't long before the songs did eventually come, and when they did there were more than enough to fill an album, among them some of their most shimmering efforts, and other near misses.

Where *Abba – The Album*, partly inspired as it was by the Eagles circa *Hotel California* and Fleetwood Mac circa *Rumours*, was their cocaine record without any cocaine having been ingested by any of those involved in the making of it, then *Voulez-Vous* was their Eurotrash disco album, the result of an extended period of recording in which the band were collectively plagued by doubts and uncharacteristic insecurity. The fact that the long production period saw Björn and Benny struggling to find their sound, and consciously, at times self-consciously, aligning themselves with the already widely despised disco movement, means that where much of Abba's music is evocative of its time, their music of this period seems rather rooted in its time. Many of the tracks recorded failed to make it on to the album for one reason or another, but recent releases and re-releases allow us to assess or reassess this troubled period in the group's history.

The first track to emerge from the new, pristine studio was itself one of their most contentious, with what was, unaccountably to this author, dismissed even by Björn and Benny themselves as one of the group's poorest releases. 'Summer Night City' is a very conscious attempt by the Andersson-Ulvaeus partnership to surf the disco zeitgeist – something that they had achieved effortlessly a couple of years earlier with 'Dancing Queen'.

The mood of the album as a whole is set in the rousing opening track, 'As Good as New', which begins with delicate strings, then segues into an authentically funky riff before leading into a very characteristic Abba pop melody. There's often a whiff of dilettantism to Abba's frequent shifts in mood and style, sometimes, as here, within the same song, but in 'As Good as New' they pull off a neat piece of funk-pop fusion which sets the scene for the album, leading almost seamlessly into the album's title track, a lascivious piece of very late-seventies dirty disco. One notably effective treatment for Björn and Benny's writer's block was to dispatch them for an inspirational break in the Bahamas in January 1979. There they soaked up some local music and it all worked a treat. While there, the pair soon came up with two songs, the first of which proved to be the title track for their much-delayed next album.

However reviled disco was at the time – and there were notorious and, however jovial the intention, deeply sinister organised disco-record-burning sessions across America in the late seventies – there were some major talents working within the genre, chiefly Giorgio Moroder, the Bee Gees and Nile Rodgers and Bernard Edwards, these last two the creative team behind Chic. At the time of Björn and Benny's musically therapeutic trip to the Bahamas the top two singles in the US were the Bee Gees' 'Too Much Heaven' and Chic's disco masterpiece 'Le Freak'. Both records helped shape the sound of the next Abba recordings.

Inspired by Chic to write a Franglais disco anthem, Björn and Benny did just that, creating one of their mini-masterpieces, the trashy sexiness of the 'aha's which had by now become a staple of the Abba sound enhancing the idea of the song as lifted from the soundtrack of some imaginary *Disco Emmanuelle* soft-porn movie. The pair were so thrilled with what they had come up with that they hopped across from the Bahamas to the famed Criteria studio in Miami to lay down the backing track for what would become 'Voulez-Vous', with the aid of members of Foxy, who had themselves enjoyed a big US hit a couple of months earlier with the disco classic 'Get Off'.

While the disco/dance movement in general exerted a strong influence on Björn and Benny at this time, and therefore on the record, a particular model for their new sound was the Bee Gees. Throughout 1978 it was all but impossible to escape from their utterly distinctive falsetto vocals, their sound and their intricate harmonies as instantly recognisable as Abba's own. Like Abba, but even more so, the Bee Gees, Mancunians via Australia, were unlikely heroes of the dance scene, all but stumbling into their career-reviving break, to supply much of the soundtrack music for the film of the year, *Saturday Night Fever*, one that, as we saw earlier, dealt at length with the central theme of 'Dancing Queen': the disco as the sole escape for at least one section of bored young urban adults.

The Bee Gees' music, simultaneously cheap and glorious, as redolent of some grotty dive bar as of Studio 54, was the sound to which Andersson and Ulvaeus aspired in 1978. 'Summer Night City', its title consciously evocative of *Saturday Night Fever*, was their attempt, largely successful, to capture the dirty thrills, the vibrancy of the city, the accompanying video, one of Lasse Hallström's finest for the band, capturing some of the atmosphere of Stockholm and perfectly complementing the mood.

If 'Summer Night City' was a relatively oblique homage to the sound and mood of the Bee Gees, then 'The King Has Lost His Crown' is all but a Bee Gees pastiche, with Frida and Agnetha's vocals coming across as a near-imitation of the group's distinctive falsetto sound.

So the trip had precisely the restorative effect on Björn and Benny's writing that it was intended to. By the end of January it had already been a busy year for the band personally and professionally, and indeed the previous four months had witnessed a radical change in both romantic relationships within the band. On 6 October 1978 Benny and Frida had finally got married after a preternaturally extended engagement dating back to 1969, the year they met. In a very conscious attempt to avoid the circus that Agnetha and Björn's wedding day had turned into – with thousands of people in attendance – the pair had gone for an ultra-low-key affair, getting hitched in secret in a church in Lidingö, on the outskirts of Stockholm, close to their home, with no friends or family present, for no one had been told.

The two Abba marriages scarcely overlapped. Björn and Agnetha's relationship had been in terminal decline for years, and their separation was finally announced in mid-January 1979, although the decision had been made even before Frida and Benny's wedding. Both were determined to keep the band going at what was clearly their peak of creativity – however painful the process of creation might be just at that time – and both were emphatic in their insistence that they had achieved that elusive thing, the amicable separation. Many journalists had been frustrated in their dealings with Abba by the band's insistence on presenting themselves as an uncomplicated, friendly group focused almost to the exclusion of all else on their music. While the last part was a fair reflection of the state of their lives, for all but Agnetha perhaps, this shiny, happy veneer was a cause of frustration for those attempting to uncover the real people in Abba. This outer sheen, masking supposed dark undercurrents in their personal lives, mirrored the gloss of their polished recordings, which itself belied the increasingly dark emotional territory that they were exploring in their lyrics.

So, all that was said at the time by Björn and Agnetha, aside from the fact that they were not going to say any more, was that they had gradually drifted apart and the divorce was friendly. This was, as both later admitted, simply untrue. Even in the poptastic world of Abba there really is no such thing as a happy divorce.

For some time there had been strong hints that the relationship was not healthy. Agnetha was a devoted mother, now to two children – Christian was barely a year old at the time of the split – and from the moment of Linda's birth had struggled to reconcile the demands of pop stardom with those of mother-hood. Björn, while no negligent father, was furiously ambitious, utterly determined not to miss out on any avenue for furthering his and the group's career. This produced a serious schism between the pair, and Björn, as ever, would transform his personal experiences into material for his ever more directly personal lyrics, writing the deeply touching 'Slipping Through My Fingers', which was later included on *The Visitors*.

Rather little was said by the couple themselves, and this vacuum created a succession of rumours about the causes and circumstances of their break-up. There was widespread talk of an affair between Agnetha and her therapist Håkan Lönnqvist, but this she vehemently denied, pointing out that this malicious gossip was particularly hurtful and damaging to her, Björn and Håkan, because Lönnqvist had been therapist to both her and Björn in a last-ditch attempt to save their marriage. In lieu of much personal material, we must look to Abba's music for clues as to the state of Björn's mind at the time.

While they were at Criteria, Benny, Björn and the Foxy musicians had an unsuccessful stab at a version of 'If It Wasn't for the Nights', in which Björn writes of the pain of being separated from a new lover, that the pain of separation would be just about bearable if it wasn't for the nights. That he was already writing of the joyous pain of new love at the time of his separation from Agnetha is perhaps not so odd because by the time the news of his and Agnetha's separation was announced to the media in mid-January 1979, he was already engaged in a new relationship, having bumped into Lena Källersjö, whom he had known, but not well, for some time, at a New Year's Eve party at Benny and Frida's.

The positivity, the passion, of this song is in contrast to the mood of 'Angeleyes', which appeared with 'Voulez-Vous' on a double-A-side single, another shimmering pop-disco confection.

151

The lyrics explore the post-separation jealousy to which Björn would return in perhaps his finest-ever lyric, 'The Winner Takes It All', with the couplet from 'Angeleyes'

And the look that he gave her made me shiver
'cause he always used to look at me that way

coming across as a dress rehearsal for the later song's knockout

But tell me does she kiss
Like I used to kiss you?
Does it feel the same
When she calls your name?

The Bahamian trip had galvanised Benny and Björn, restoring them to their full potency as a partnership, but Abba were nothing if not perverse – here in a wholly non-sexual way – and one of the songs that the pair quickly turned out in the aftermath of the trip was 'I Have a Dream', surely the band's lowest moment, a sickly sentimental ditty containing a fatuous, almost meaningless sub-*Imagine* message of hopefulness. If anyone anywhere ever wondered why Björn and Benny never addressed political questions in either their work or their lives, then the answer – that they were, apparently, all but apolitical (although when pushed, the band seemed to share moderate right-wing sensibilities) – is to be found in such bland anthems as this and their earlier 'He Is Your Brother'.

Oddly enough, the earlier song, with its notion of universal brotherhood, not dissimilar to the Hollies' 'He Ain't Heavy, He's My Brother', resurfaced on 4 January 1979 when it was the anthem on which all the artists on the bill of the fund-raising event Music for Unicef (the United Nations Children's Fund) in New York joined together to sing.

That event saw the first performance of the band's next single, which would also appear on *Voulez-Vous*. 'Chiquitita', which had had the working titles of first 'In the Arms of Rosalita' and then 'Chiquitita Angelina' – the name having been dredged up from Björn's memory banks after featuring in the lyrics of one of the Hootenanny Singers' very earliest recordings, 'Ave Maria No Moro' – was in fact a late substitute for 'If It Wasn't for the Nights', to become the follow-up single to the relatively modest, by Abba's standards, hit 'Summer Night City'. The latter, in reaching merely number five, was the group's least successful UK single release since 'S.O.S.' three years earlier, but did achieve some valuable breakthroughs, providing them with their first Swedish chart-topper for a couple of years, and their first-ever Japanese number one, in November 1978, after a concerted promotional push in the country.

Again there is the temptation to read autobiographical intent into everything that Abba do. With 'Chiquitita' it is tempting to see this poor woman who has 'broken a feather' – what is it with Björn and bird imagery? – as perhaps both him and Agnetha, forlorn in the aftermath of their separation, but with the assurance that she will dance again, dancing being another favoured image for Björn. Perhaps the words don't need precise analysis beyond their simple message of defiant hope from a position of apparent hopelessness, all this carried by one of Andersson-Ulvaeus's most affecting melodies, beautiful harmonies and Benny's rousing glissando on the repeated instrumental passage that ends the record.

If 'Summer Night City' had represented a tiny blip in the extraordinary run of success that Abba had been enjoying for several years now, 'Chiquitita' put them right back on top, giving them their last top-five hit in Australia, achieving number one in Belgium, Finland, Ireland, Mexico, the Netherlands, New Zealand, South Africa, Spain (the group's first chart-topper there since 'Waterloo' five years earlier), Switzerland and Zimbabwe, and reaching the top ten virtually everywhere else.

It also marked the beginning of another chapter in the group's commercial life, seeing them exploit a territory that they had thus far neglected, for all the recurrent Spanish and Italian inflections of their music and lyrics. In early March 1979 Frida and Agnetha recorded a Spanish-language version of 'Chiquitita', with lyrics written by Buddy McCluskey, an employee of RCA in Argentina. The resulting record, with the new vocal track replacing the English-language one on the identical backing track, was released in Argentina, Spain and Mexico, at a stroke establishing the band as favourites in each of these underexploited territories. In Argentina the English and Spanish versions of 'Chiquitita' were available simultaneously and both became massive sellers, the latter reaching number one.

On the back of this, Abba achieved their first hit album in Argentina, *Voulez-Vous* eventually topping the charts there. In Mexico, where the band had already had a succession of chart-topping singles, they achieved the notable success of hitting the number-one spot with both versions, while in Spain the Spanish-language version went to number one in the singles charts while the original version reached number three.

The group followed up this success with 'Estoy Soñando', a Spanish-language version of 'I Have a Dream', and when this came close to matching the sales of 'Chiquitita', which ran into the millions, the logical decision was to extend what had ceased to be a tentative experiment and had become a guaranteed money-spinner, into the album format. So was born *Gracias por la Música*, featuring fairly literal translations of established hits – 'Knowing Me, Knowing You' was reborn as 'Conociéndome Conociéndote' and 'Gimme! Gimme! Gimme!' as 'Dame! Dame! Dame!' – and with Latin-inflected numbers ('Hasta Mañana', 'Mamma Mia', 'Fernando') sitting comfortably beside more Anglo-Saxon fare.

154

The album, released in Spain, Argentina, Mexico and elsewhere in Latin America in the spring of 1980, became another prodigious seller, charting not just in the expected territories but also in Japan, this not the result of some hitherto untapped Japanese Hispanophilia but rather a symptom of the Abbamania that was belatedly sweeping across Japan in the aftermath of the band's first and only tour of the country (see Chapter 11).

This temporary extension to Abba's studio work had a secondary impact on their activities, leading them to alter the shooting of their promotional videos, as seen in the bonus material on the *Definitive Collection* DVD. There we see that, just as certain Hollywood studios and producers would make Spanish-language versions of their films using the same sets, crew and often many of the same cast members (for example, Todd Browning's 1931 *Dracula* or many of Laurel and Hardy's shorts of the same era), so Lasse Hallström would make parallel versions of several Abba videos for the Spanish-speaking market.

Abba may not have been a politically engaged band – although a political record of sorts was in the offing – but they were not without a conscience. Aside from anything else, the group were characterised by a decency and a very un-rock-'n'-roll niceness. As grown-ups by the time they hit the big time, as family people, and let's face it, as Swedes, the group had a reputation for being co-operative with colleagues on the road and in the studio. Those who came across them in their many television appearances would invariably remark on how they were as they seemed, charming, well-mannered and utterly professional. Even among members of the press, whom the group treated with a certain suspicion – the Swedish press in general and the British tabloids in particular – there was rarely, if ever, mention of Abba's members being anything other than polite and co-operative. They might sometimes not agree to talk at all, and were always reluctant to open up about the details of their private lives, but they were congenial.

Similarly, there were never any tales of excess on tour, apparently never a suspicion that anyone ever took anything stronger than alcohol. Benny and Frida enjoyed the lively but hardly wild Stockholm nightlife, and were, at the height of the disco era in which they were key players, regular patrons of the city's more exclusive nightspots. Benny and Björn had bonded over a few drinks and their compositions were occasionally facilitated by the odd beer, and Björn was known to overindulge from time to time, but there was never any hint of any dangerous dependency on alcohol or anything else. They didn't trash hotel rooms, they were known for treating members of the tour party with consideration – is this getting monotonous? – and they would go to great pains to ensure that everyone was fairly paid.

A similar attitude was evident in some of the involved financial operations at home during their money-making peak, when they were genuinely concerned that the employees of the various companies that were bought and sold in their name should not be treated like mere pawns in their grand game of fiscal chess. As will be discussed at greater length in Chapter 14, the group collectively had a very sober attitude to their finances, and this after Benny's near-financial meltdown with the Hep Stars.

They could very easily, as many of their high-earning peers had done – Björn Borg decamped to Monte Carlo, for instance, not that it did his finances much good in the long run – have chosen the lives of tax exiles. But instead they stuck it out in Sweden, to a degree took on the chin the implications of the 85 per cent tax bracket into which they comfortably fell (although, as we shall see later, great efforts were made to avoid all their vast revenues' being taxed as straightforwardly taxable income) and insisted, displaying an admirable loyalty to their domestic taxation system, that it was the price you paid for living in a relatively equitable country. In any case, even at this level of taxation they were left with plenty in the bank. It was also around this time that they rewarded Michael B. Tretow with a share of the band's royalties from then on in generous recognition of his invaluable contribution to the sound of the group. However vital Tretow had been to their success, this gesture was still all but unprecedented in the cut-throat music business.

It was in this spirit that the band opened and closed the year 1979. All proceeds from the sales of 'Chiquitita' would go to Unicef. Then, in December of that year, 'I Have a Dream', the fourth single taken from *Voulez-Vous* (embracing the 'Voulez-Vous'/'Angeleyes' double A-side and 'Summer Night City', which didn't appear on the album, this troubled, protracted period of writing and recording ultimately yielded seven single releases), was, with its sickly child chorus, dedicated to Unicef's International Year of the Child. It may make you want to vomit but at least you'd be vomiting in a good cause.

To confirm how surprisingly productive this period in which Björn and Benny had experienced writer's block had been for the group, consider that 'Lovelight' was deemed strong enough only to appear as a B-side to 'Chiquitita'. 'Lovelight' is right up there in the unofficial chart of, if not quite lost, then at least more obscure, Abba gems, a flawed record but, in its chorus, emerging as a small slice of something close to perfect pop. In the aftermath of experimenting with 'The Girl with the Golden Hair', three songs from which featured as extracts from a mini-musical on the second side of *Abba – The Album*, Björn and Benny had seriously toyed with the idea of creating a bona fide stage musical. The almost recitative – to be crueller, faintly monotonous – quality of 'Lovelight's verse betrays some of their then current interests, but from this nearly grey build-up the song bursts into glorious colour in its chorus – one of the prettiest passages of pure pop that Abba ever recorded, graced as ever with a wonderful, intricate melody and beautiful harmonies.

The other two singles from this year, their release separated by 'Voulez-Vous'/'Angeleyes', confirm this as the band's sexiest, danciest, trashiest period. Each album was all but contractually obliged to contain one track in which Björn took the lead vocal duties and this time round he gave himself the more than faintly creepy 'Does Your Mother Know', in which he returned to the subject of dangerous, quite possibly illegal and immoral, transgressive, transgenerational love, which he had touched upon in 'When I Kissed the Teacher'. There were many elements and relationships, factors of timing and sometimes undervalued contributions that all combined to make Abba what they were, but clearly the two most important of these were the songwriting of Björn and Benny and the vocal talents, individually, but even better together, of Agnetha and Frida. In a sense 'Does Your Mother Know' and 'Gimme! Gimme! Gimme!' highlight precisely how important both of these partnerships were.

'Does Your Mother Know' is as winning a tune as Andersson-Ulvaeus came up with when working in their more rock-oriented mode, but the narrative is a little uncomfortable. Ulvaeus was repeatedly drawn to the very rock-and-roll subject of sexual pursuit and heavy flirtation, but whereas 'That's Me', sung by Agnetha and Frida, has a certain playfulness and sexual *frisson*, there is something just a little sleazy in having a man sing about seducing and being seduced by a girl who is barely, if at all, of legal age. One of the simplest but most inspired ideas within Catherine Johnson's simple but repeatedly inspired *Mamma Mia!* is to have 'Does Your Mother Know' sung by a mature woman to a much younger man who has been trying to seduce her, thus at a stroke making the song playful, funny and sexy. 'Does Your Mother Know' also once again featured Björn using the term 'chick' which he so favoured, but it's not all bad news, and to confirm the pervasive influence of Abba on almost everything that followed, the track inspired the stirring guitar riff in the 2002 hit single 'Hindu Times' by fellow Beatles fans Oasis.

The band's fourth out of five UK single releases of 1979 was 'Gimme! Gimme! Gimme! (A Man After Midnight)', which for obvious reasons became something of a kitsch gay classic, and is as sleazy as 'Does Your Mother Know', only this time in a good way. To confirm that writer's block had effectively been banished, in the aftermath of *Voulez-Vous*'s release, while preparing for the imminent tour, Björn and Benny quickly knocked off this minor classic, remaining in the dirty-disco mood. It is impossible to listen to the resulting single without reflecting on the situation within the band at the time, and there is a certain undisguised relish in the way Agnetha belts out this lusty lyric. She had spoken in interviews around this time of feeling lonely and trapped within her home when the children were staying with Björn, but by the time she came to record this track she had at last enjoyed a brief romantic fling, with a Swedish ice-hockey star.

More than a decade before Kathy Burke and James Dreyfus got their hands on 'Gimme! Gimme! Gimme!' (see page 199), in 1986 the Swedish proto-grunge band the Leather Nun covered the song, slowing down the tempo and uncovering its full, lascivious potential – not that this had been hidden to begin with. (The Leather Nun were an outfit who never escaped the level of cultdom despite having an impressively dark live act which in the early days was enlivened by the gimmick of anti-striptease. A woman, naked on stage as the band first appeared, would gradually dress as a nun as their performance progressed.)

In terms of sales, both 'Does Your Mother Know' and 'Gimme! Gimme! Gimme!' were solid, unspectacular successes – and this is unspectacular by Abba's standards of the time in which top-ten international hits were all but guaranteed – the one exception being the latter's emergence as the group's most successful single in France. In terms of cohesiveness, consistency of tone and production values – and you could argue here more than elsewhere that the album is over-produced, and if not chilly, perhaps a tad clinical – *Voulez-Vous* is arguably Abba's greatest album, particularly when graced with the extra tracks that appeared on the 2001 reissue of the CD. So a turbulent, trying but ultimately triumphant 12 months would lead into a tour that would itself turn out to be turbulent, trying and ultimately triumphant.

Although they did from time to time embark on tours, all four members of Abba were avowedly reluctant travellers, none more than Agnetha, whose antipathy to the process was down partly to the unreliability of her voice and her consequentially occasional discomfort in front of an audience, and partly to her profound dislike of flying. This fear would be greatly increased during the tour itself. It must be stressed that the idea that is often conveyed that Abba were a poor or disappointing live band is clearly belied by the evidence of *Abba – The Movie*, and the recently released DVD, *Abba In Concert*, of their rather grand 1979 tour of North America, Canada and the UK, which took in six consecutive nights at the Wembley Arena. (The DVD is actually an expanded version of the Swedish national television company SVT's documentary of the tour.) Reluctant they may have been to go on the road once more, but this was not unnatural in a group who were already veterans of touring, had family commitments and were wary of the imperfections inherent in the live reproduction of songs that had been conceived as studio works and as such had been realised with a meticulousness that was at the same time creative and obsessive.

Each of their three tours had its own unique problems, but they had learned many lessons from the disasters of the post-'Waterloo' tour, which they applied in 1977 and again in 1979. First of all there was the importance of replicating their sound as closely as possible, and so they sourced, as they had in 1977, the finest mobile sound equipment available. Interviewed on the *Abba – In Concert* DVD, Thomas Johansson, who organised and promoted all three of Abba's major international tours, spoke of one of the many joys of working for the group: 'They were never concerned with the fact that they were going to make money, as long as they didn't lose money.' Again this runs counter to an unfair image, particularly current in sections of the Swedish press at the height of the group's international success, that they were a cynical, money-grubbing outfit. Johansson goes on to emphasise how concerned they were that the enjoyment of their fans should always go before the need to make a profit. This extended to ensuring that the tickets for their shows were always affordably priced, and in this they were unique among pop performers, at least in Johansson's considerable experience.

The group set off for the North American leg of the tour in early September 1979, heading first for Canada.

When they were busy on tour, family wasn't all that they missed. While Björn and Benny were still focused on Abba-related activities, they continued to look for other acts to work with, Benny recently having hooked up with Norwegian folk-pop singer Finn Kalvik, on whose album he worked. But Agnetha and Frida had extracurricular activities of their own.

Judging by their respective performances in the videos and indeed their contrasting appearances on stage, Frida was the more naturally gifted actor of the two women in Abba. So, while Benny and Björn were away in the Bahamas and Miami, Frida preceded her singing partner by taking an – equally short-lived – sideways step into a big-screen career. She had accepted a small part in *Gå på vattnet om du kan* (*Walk on Water If You Can*), a romantic melodrama boasting the tagline 'It began as a love story...', of modest ambition, which wasn't granted a release outside Scandinavia. Frida valued the experience a great deal more than she did Stig Björkman's finished film, released on 17 September while she was in Canada with the group.

Nor was Agnetha hard up for distractions from her recent separation, but aside from her young family and preparations for the tour, she had been co-operating with the plans for a retro-spective album of her solo career to date, entitled *Tio år med Agnetha* (*Ten Years with Agnetha*), released in Sweden on 21 September. In fact the collection spanned a little more than a decade, beginning with her first, self-composed hit, 'Jag var så kär' ('I Was So in Love'), and brought her story bang up to date with the recently recorded 'När du tar mig i din famn' ('When You Take Me in Your Arms'), a sweet, wistful, melodic MOR ballad that provides a reminder that Agnetha was an at least modestly talented songwriter as well as a sensitive vocalist with a great gift for portraying heartbreak.

Back in Edmonton, the group and their back-up team – here again Abba insisted on the best, whatever the cost: in Johansson's image, the behind-the-scenes crew on the tour was like the support team for a Formula 1 racing driver – were preparing for the opening date of the tour. To counter the ring-rustiness created by the two-year lay-off since their last live dates, Abba had been rehearsing for more than four months, the group backed up by the core of the musicians who had played on *Voulez-Vous*, including drummer Ola Brunkert and bassist Rutger Gunnarsson, both of whom had worked with the band as far back as *Ring Ring*. Among the more recent additions to the extended Abba family was backing vocalist Tomas Ledin, who was being groomed by Stig as a potential solo star. Ledin will be most familiar to Abba-watchers for 'Never Again', his duet with Agnetha on his 1982 album *The Human Touch*, and which featured on *That's Me*, Agnetha's 1998 greatest-hits collection. He would be given the opportunity of a one-song showcase in the midst of each performance.

To ensure visual as well as musical continuity between the current release and the live show, Rune Söderqvist, the designer of the stylised blue-mountain-cum-iceberg-cum-pyramid on the *Voulez-Vous* cover, was drafted in to create a look for the stage and costumes. This he did by creating a stylised, very cold-blue set to represent the Scandinavian landscape and, in conjunction with Owe Sandström, who had been responsible for/guilty of Abba's on-stage look since 1974, some very seventies figure-hugging bodysuits for Frida and Agnetha (with subtly different coloration and the designs mirror-images of each other, emphasising their complementary/contrasting roles in the band) and for Björn – his tailor would never need to ask him on which side he liked to dress.

Meanwhile, mercifully for Benny, he was given a baggier outfit of slacks and a loose-fitting jacket. Perhaps there's something about Abba that appeals to cultists, but where there was something faintly sinister about the white overalls that the group sported circa *Arrival*, the 1979 tour outfits were lent a retrospectively creepy edge by the uncanny similarity between the triangular shapes of Frida and Agnetha's smocks, when they have their arms outstretched, and the capes worn by the Heaven's Gate members, whose mass suicide was somehow or other triggered by the relative proximity of the Hale-Bopp comet in 1997.

Final preparations having been made over the previous few days, the tour kicked off at the Edmonton Sports Arena on 13 September. The venue was full to capacity – a little under 15,000 people. Stig and the band talked, with some sincerity, about how the tour was a way of giving something to their fans, but there was at least a dual purpose, the central aim of the first leg being a further, perhaps final, attempt to break the US, where, despite some notable single successes, they had failed to establish a nationwide following. In Canada, however, while never quite on the same scale as their popularity in Australia (although that market had almost collapsed since the peak of Abbamania) or their European heartlands, they were a major act, their sales figures generally several times as strong, proportionate to the size of the population, as those south of the border. Consequently the band played significantly larger venues in Canada than in the US, moving from their opening night in Edmonton, where they themselves admitted to a degree of nervousness, which brought them some mixed but far from hostile notices, on to the Pacific National Exhibition in Vancouver, with its capacity of 17,000, by which stage the whole tour party was now into its stride.

As the entourage – the band and their key personnel in a hired Learjet, the stage gear in three lorries – moved down into America – Seattle, Portland and San Francisco – the venues were suddenly, markedly more intimate, with capacities generally between 3,000 and 8,000. However, the gigs were increasingly well received critically, the band generating a warm atmosphere, the nightly accompaniment of 'I Have a Dream' by a choir of local school children being the kind of saccharine entertainment for which American audiences have a greater tolerance. Halfway through the US leg of the tour, the band was joined by film-maker Urban Lasson, who would record several of the shows for what would become *Abba In Concert*. The evidence of this document – and we are assured that it is an accurate record of the Abba sound as it really was, the minor sweetening of the odd bum note notwithstanding – is of a technically impressive show, the band tight, Frida and Agnetha's voices strong and their harmonies impressive.

But what is striking is how physically inert the pair are. Frida is certainly the more mobile, the more confident mover of the two – she had dedicated herself to improving her movement through dance classes, and while hardly dynamic she does move with a degree of confidence. Agnetha, meanwhile, can never fully rid herself of the stage fright from which she always suffered. Her discomfort was possibly the result of, and certainly not helped by, an episode which increased her already marked dislike of life on the road.

In the middle of the tour the band had for a while set up a base in Los Angeles, from which they travelled to a handful of their shows and to which they could return at the end of each day. While there they were joined temporarily by various family members, Agnetha being delighted and relieved to be reunited, if only for a while, with her daughter Linda. But this brief respite over, the tour continued to the East Coast and upwards and back into Canada for the final couple of dates. It was on the flight between New York, where the band had enjoyed a small triumph at the packed Radio City Music Hall, and Boston on 3 October that the Learjet hit some serious turbulence, the plane being rerouted first back to New York, then back to Boston, and finally forced to make an emergency landing in a small airport in the town of Manchester, in the neighbouring state of New Hampshire. Agnetha managed to perform that evening's concert, but perhaps in delayed shock at the trauma of this brush with death – she was not the only one on the flight to be close to hysterics – she fell ill with a flu-like viral infection, thus forcing the cancellation of the planned Washington gig.

This wasn't the only near-death experience of the group's first and only American tour. Thomas Johansson has spoken of events surrounding the group's concert of 24 September at the Aladdin Hotel in Las Vegas, a concert at which Linda Ulvaeus joined the chorus of children on 'I Have a Dream'. In the build-up to the concert, by Johansson's account, he and the band noticed that an extra row of chairs had been set up in front of the stage. This action went against the ethos of the band – it's the group's good-guy image once again, this time clashing with a 'goodfellas' tradition and depriving those who had stumped up cash for their front-row seats of the view for which they had paid. So, acting on

165

Abba's collective instructions, Johansson absolutely insisted, for all the management's urgent pleading, that these extra seats be removed at once. This they were, and when he heard that the seats had been intended for some local mobsters and it was put to him that he leave town at once and never come back, this time he chose to comply.

The tour had been a success, although even with the dates having been carefully selected to coincide with areas of the vast, diverse country in which they had established some form of power base, and more modest-sized venues equally carefully chosen so as not to repeat the disasters of 1974, not all the shows were sell-outs. Most were, but still the tour did little in the short or indeed long term to establish Abba as a major act in the US. It would be more than ten years until this happened, with the massive sales of *Abba Gold*, and then a further decade before Abba's status in North America was cemented by the various permanent and touring productions of *Mamma Mia!* playing to sell-out audiences night after night.

From the tensions, predictable and otherwise, of the North American leg of the tour, the group had a glorious homecoming. In fact they had several, being greeted warmly, indeed rapturously, as returning sons and daughters, right across Europe, from Sweden, where they played before a total of over 18,000 people in their two concerts on consecutive nights in Gothenburg and Stockholm, to France, Germany, Austria and Belgium, this reception building to an unprecedented six-night residency at London's Wembley Arena. There in particular the press notices were far from ecstatic, but while this would not have passed unnoticed by the ever-prickly Björn and Benny, what mattered was the audiences, and wherever they played in Europe their audiences openly adored them. The tour wound up in Dublin, where again the audiences went wild.

To coincide with the tour Polar Music released the band's

Greatest Hits Volume 2 across Europe in late October. The album, boasting an unarguably stronger line-up than the first volume, by virtue of including only genuine hits this time ('Gimme! Gimme! Gimme', 'Knowing Me, Knowing You', 'Take a Chance on Me', 'Money, Money, Money', 'Dancing Queen', 'The Name of the Game' and more besides), failed to repeat the phenomenal success of the first one, but still sold more than respectably, comfortably topping a million copies in pre-sales and topping the album charts in Belgium (of course), Canada and the UK, where it stayed on top for four weeks and remained in the charts for more than a year.

What is most notable in the comparison between the set lists from Abba's three major tours is how their repertoire changed, something that happens inevitably to enduring bands. At first the set list was a showcase for the latest release, in which the lack of consistent, killer material is evident (check out the fact that 'King Kong Song' was a regular in 1974). Then it became one in which filler was gradually dropped, for by 1977 the band had produced a handful of pop masterpieces. And by 1979 they were virtually playing what would become *Abba Gold* ('Lay All Your Love on Me', 'The Winner Takes It All', 'Super Trouper' and 'One of Us' missing for obvious reasons, although 'Mamma Mia' was unaccountably absent from the regular track list). Then again, it ought not to be forgotten that even in 1979 Abba for some reason found space in their set list for 'Hole in Your Soul' from *Abba – The Album*, one of the few seemingly carefree pop records to dip its toe into the troubled waters of depression and existential angst with its message of the restorative powers of rock 'n' roll filling the void at the heart of us all.

It had been an action-packed 18 months: Björn and Agnetha finally split up and Benny and Frida finally got married; they suffered their most troublesome writing and recording session; and they underwent a tour which was not only arduous and inconvenient but included a couple of brushes with death. Yet they emerged from all this stronger than ever, having turned out a succession of hit singles and what was arguably their most satisfying album, and confirmed themselves as the ultimate populist, critic-proof band.

While some critics picked out 'Gimme! Gimme! Gimme!' as the highlight of the band's live show, with Agnetha's violently defiant vocal performance, in retrospect, judging by the material on *Abba In Concert*, the most affecting and most telling moment came in the performance of the unashamedly sentimental 'The Way Old Friends Do', the live version of which would appear as the final track on the group's next album. The rendition sees Abba stripped bare, going unplugged, returning to their individual roots as a *schlager* outfit. Accompanied until the second verse only by Benny on his beloved accordion, the four singers congregate at the front of the stage to sing a song of reconciliation. Not for the first time Björn refers to the silence between a couple who have been together for a long, long time and, more worryingly, to 'words of violence' passing between them, but there is the poignant reassurance that whatever happens they can face it the way old friends do.

So, after it all, after everything that the band have been through during their remarkable personal and professional jour-neys through the 1970s, the decade with which Abba are all but synonymous, the group are seen entertaining, indeed holding rapt, a Wembley crowd, England being the home of one of their most loyal fan bases. After all their personal tribulations, this is a scene of togetherness as the group bid a farewell to their decade via a very Abba, very Swedish song of joy emerging from sadness. And as Urban Lasson's camera sweeps round to film the group from behind, we see Frida, always desperate for affirmation, putting her arm around Benny's midriff and squeezing him towards her, while, aside from a theatrical, almost pleading, look from Björn to Agnetha and his hand alighting briefly, awkwardly, on her shoulder, the pair stand resolutely apart.

CHAPTER ELEVEN

'Super Trouper'

As the 1980s began Abba were once again looking both inward and outward, wondering what they represented and whether now was the time for a change of direction. As they had in the early stages of preparing what would become *Voulez-Vous*, Benny and Björn contemplated writing a musical, gradually feeling their way towards the form that was to constitute at least part of their destiny, and at the same time not realising that they had been writing a musical all along. After the break in the Bahamas that had reinvigorated them and got their creative juices flowing freely once again, the pair once more headed off for the West Indies, this time to Barbados.

The idea for a musical quickly vanished once fellow tourist John Cleese proved uninterested in writing the book for a proposed show built around a number of characters sitting around at a New Year's Eve party, looking backwards and forwards and generally contemplating the state of their lives. But this did result in one album track, 'Happy New Year', which would in time establish itself as a rather gloomily celebratory seasonal staple.

This was just one of five songs that the pair composed in Barbados, four of which ('Happy New Year' being joined by 'Andante, Andante', 'The Piper' and 'On and On and On') made it on to the album that already bore the title *Super Trouper* – the name given to a large stage spotlight – long before the song of the same name had been composed. Björn, Benny, the backing musicians and Michael B. Tretow, now fully *au fait* with the workings of the group's own studio, set to work on the five tracks, 'Elaine' being the fifth. Once the basic musical foundations had been laid down for these tracks, the band set to work on preparing for a short tour of Japan, and what would be their final live appearances outside Sweden. Their very last live appearance as a band would come the following year, with a disappointing TV special hosted by American chat-show host Dick Cavett.

The tour was everything that the band had come to expect and dread from life on the road. The set was essentially the same as on the previous year's American and European jaunt, the hysteria the same only with a slightly restrained, ordered Japanese edge to it, the venues the same size, with an audience of around 10,000 a night over the course of 11 nights. Six of the shows were at Tokyo's celebrated Budokan Hall – most famous for having hosted Bob Dylan in 1969 – scheduled in blocks of two interspersed with appearances at other venues around the country.

The tour was yet another triumph, Abba had found yet another territory to conquer, but much of their life as an outfit had either already lost or was at least very quickly starting to lose its charm. Björn and Agnetha were separated and involved in new relationships, and Frida and Benny's marriage was already starting to look fragile. Always vulnerable, and with the buried traumas of her troubled and lonely childhood to deal with somehow or other, Frida had turned to matters mystical and metaphysical, becoming a devotee of the teachings of

Krishnamurti, one of the celebrity Indian gurus who found a plentiful supply of potential devotees among rich, spiritually unfulfilled Westerners. This interest increased the tensions between her and Benny, who always professed to being perfectly satisfied with a life that allowed him to immerse himself in his abiding passion, music. While both were at or very close to their vocal peak in 1980, it must be said that, judging by the photographic and video evidence, neither Frida nor Agnetha appeared to be at her physical best at the time. Considering the emotional turmoil that, as it only later emerged, both were involved in, this is no surprise.

Meanwhile there was an album to be made. If *Voulez-Vous* was a slick and, by Abba's generally eclectic standards, cohesive work, *Super Trouper* was a massive stride further in this direction, a record created by consummate pop composers, performers and vocalists, working within a high-tech studio over which the three co-producers had achieved mastery. Incidentally, the reputation of the ultra-modern facilities available at Polar Studios spread so fast after their official opening in the spring of 1978 that Led Zeppelin travelled there to produce what was, sadly, their last and, perhaps significantly, over-produced album, *In Through the Out Door*. In terms of technique in songwriting, musicianship, production and vocal clarity, *Super Trouper* is unquestionably the most accomplished of all Abba albums. It is also a record that is produced to within an inch of its life.

As the band gathered in the studio new songs quickly emerged, among them two of their most heart-rending songs of all, 'Our Last Summer' and a number that went by the working title 'The Story of My Life'. Each of these two new songs was – and by this stage of his career, Björn was happy to admit to this element of his compositions – a piece of intense, personal, at times autobiographical work. 'Our Last Summer' is Abba at their sweetest and prettiest, a melancholy, nostalgic piece in which the singer, Frida standing in for Björn, recalls the last, glorious moments of her first great love affair. Much of the mood, if not the details, was drawn directly from a romantic interlude that a teenage Björn and his young paramour had experienced in Paris. The delicate verse yields to an achingly beautiful chorus full of the melancholy sense of longing at which Benny and Björn were adept. The heartbreaking potential of this track was exploited by Catherine Johnson for *Mamma Mia!*, her determination to weave it into the show's narrative leading her to call one of the central characters in the play – one of the three possible fathers – Harry, and establish that he was, as specified in the song, a banker and a family man. While hardly lost, 'Our Last Summer' is one of Abba's less well-known mini-masterpieces of pop.

The album's stand-out song was, and remains to this day, 'The Winner Takes It All', a number that started out as 'The Story of My Life', a song boasting a wonderfully simple melody, the chorus very reminiscent of Michel Le Grand, particularly his beautiful 'If It Takes Forever' from *Les Parapluies de Cherbourg*. It was at this stage that Björn no longer protested at those who saw his lyrics as personal statements reflecting his, and to an extent Agnetha's, emotional state in the aftermath of their much-scrutinised but little-understood separation. He spoke of having struggled for some time with the lyrics and then one evening sat down on his own with a bottle of whisky and got good and drunk. Then the words came flowing and he pretty much had the song nailed in one sitting, or presumably one slumping. It isn't that hard to see the words, as rightly celebrated as they are in part, as the product of a man deep in his cups. There are plenty of gauche moments, from the fumbling couplet

I've played all my cards
And that's what you've done too

to

A big thing or a small

and the grammar police will be wanting to have a word with Björn about the idea of the gods throwing 'a dice', but the very clumsiness of the words makes the whole emotional expression of the song seem more raw and immediate. Completing the peculiar voyeuristic sense that we are all being given, via a pop song, some insight into the pain in the aftermath of a real relationship is the fact that Agnetha takes the lead vocal, to deliver one of her most inspired, heartfelt performances, the sibilance, the precise diction, as ever crucial elements of Abba's appeal, Agnetha's distinctive, winsome delivery rendering the contrivance in the couplet that sees 'tense' made to rhyme with the final syllable of 'confidence' scarcely noticeable.

With this performance, simultaneously vulnerable and defiant, the album's general air of over-production, of Tretow allowed free rein to exploit and have fun with all his new studio toys, is never more apparent than on this number. It is unquestionably, even as it is, one of the band's finest moments, but it would at least have been instructive to hear an alternative take on the track in which the musical flourishes were minimised and the vocal performance was allowed to dominate. In short, one wishes that the group had had the courage to render the song in a similar way to how they dealt with the track's darker musical twin, 'The Day Before You Came', the following year. Still, this is to quibble about one of the most affecting of all Abba's songs, one that boasts lines as deceptively simple and in their way as powerful as anything Björn ever created:

But tell me does she kiss
Like I used to kiss you

Does it feel the same
When she calls your name?

The almost oppressive slickness is common to the three tracks that follow 'The Winner Takes It All' on the album, among them two of the songs that Björn and Benny came up with in Barbados. The first of these is the pumping, bump-and-grind electro-anthem 'On and On and On', in which the lyrics see Björn once again in lecherous mode, the chorus referring to an exhortation on the part of a man whom the female narrator has met at some nightspot to 'keep on rocking, baby', and we think we know what he means by this. The vocals are heavily synthesised and as often, if not always, when artists aspire to a futuristic mood in their work, what they come up with becomes only more rooted in its own time, so there is something very early-eighties about this electro-pop. But it is kind of dirty and fun, the very catchy, richly harmonised chorus lifted directly from 'Do It Again' by perennial Andersson-Ulvaeus faves the Beach Boys.

'The Winner Takes It All' had been a massive worldwide hit for the group, reaching the top ten in Australia, Austria, Canada, Finland, France, West Germany and Italy, number one in Belgium, Ireland, the Netherlands, South Africa and the UK, and entering the top ten virtually everywhere else, in the case of the US this being the last time Abba would enjoy a top-ten single. In several territories the follow-up was 'On and On and On', which proved to be the group's final major Australian hit single.

'Andante, Andante', a piece of soft, sexy MOR fused with an almost *schlager*-ish folk tune, is cheekily juxtaposed with 'On and On and On', this time the request from a woman to her lover being to go gently with her, via an abundance of not altogether comfortable images. Naturally enough with the chorus, she presents herself as his music, his song, which makes it all the more bewildering that he 'tread lightly on my ground'. Like 'Andante, Andante', 'Me and I' is fairly easy on the ear, but a piece of strictly minor Abba in which Benny's keyboards are just too prominent and the voices synthesised just for the sake of it. But for those seeking recurrent themes in Björn's lyrics, here once more he tackles the subject of duality – Frida singing expressly of being a Jekyll and Hyde character – that he had previously explored in 'Nina, Pretty Ballerina' and 'Dancing Queen', among other numbers.

On side two, between the opening two numbers – 'Happy New Year' and 'Our Last Summer' – and the glorious finale – the live version of 'The Way Old Friends Do', recorded during the previous year's tour – come a track that could easily have appeared on *Voulez-Vous* and another in which, finally but elliptically, Björn comes up with a political lyric.

'The Piper' opens like a reprise of Cher's 'Gypsies, Tramps and Thieves', creating the sense of some fifth horseman of the apocalypse, the piper of the title. The song was, according to Carl Magnus Palm's *Bright Lights Dark Shadows*, inspired by Björn's reading Stephen King's apocalyptic horror novel *The Stand*. Here Björn creates an allegory about the dangers for the future of mankind posed by some charismatic Hitlerian figure who will exploit a general weakness to hold sway and do his wicked deeds. Or so Björn claimed. It is tempting to see the song, rather, as an allegory, whether unconscious or not on Björn's part, about the consensus politics in Sweden, the docile electorate blindly fitting in with the politically correct, high-taxing Social Democratic Party, the piper perhaps being, dare one say, Prime Minister Olof Palme. Either way, the song reminds us why Abba so rarely delved into matters political, and also that they couldn't resist experimenting with different musical forms, this song moving from its Western movie-style opening into a very upbeat, poppy chorus and then into some kind of medieval Latin chanting –

'*sub luna saltamus*' – that suggests the influence of Steeleye Span circa 'Gaudete'.

'Lay All Your Love on Me', however, is simply gorgeous, a tale of obsessive, jealous, consuming love told via an electro-pop dance fusion in which the meticulous production suits the track, creating a very sexy, slightly sinister sound. The album as a whole sounds perhaps less glorious and shimmering than it did at the time because of its very success – it became Abba's biggest-selling non-compilation LP – and because of the fact that it influenced virtually every electro-pop album of the 1980s. The influence that 'Lay All Your Love on Me' had on the many synth-pop dance bands of the 1980s is attested to by the loving, sincerely flattering cover on Erasure's chart-topping *Abbaesque* EP.

All that was left to complete the album was to come up with a follow-up single to the globe-conquering pop masterpiece that was 'The Winner Takes It All'. Confirming that the Andersson-Ulvaeus team was still capable of knocking out a piece of infectious, melodic pop drenched in sophisticated harmonies virtually at will, they produced a winsome tune the chorus of which, by good fortune, happened to fit in with the album's title. 'Lay All Your Love on Me' was the group's valediction to the world of trashy, sexy disco music, into which they had all but stumbled only to become one of its leading lights. But it is wholly appropriate that 'Super Trouper' should be the last major hit for the band, because as the final song written on what turned out to be the group's penultimate album, it was their farewell to the field of miserablist power pop, a form that they had all but made their own. The melody was wonderfully, instantly catchy, but in the lyrics Björn finally allowed himself to commit to song what had been one of the few things that always united the band: their shared distaste for life on the road.

In early October the band, some of their closest friends and colleagues, and the members of local circus troupe – this being the unspoken verbal pun underlying the cover shot and the video accompanying the title single – gathered at a Stockholm sound stage to pose for photographers and shoot footage for the videos of both 'Super Trouper' and 'Happy New Year'. (In the case of the second the footage was also used for the video of the Spanish-language version of the song, 'Felicidad'.) The original, and frankly rather optimistic, plan had been to have the shoot take place in Piccadilly Circus. As it turned out, Abba's people were shocked to learn that the London authorities were not happy about the idea of one of the busiest junctions in the capital being taken over, however briefly, by the world's biggest pop band, their entourage, an unspecified number of circus animals and an untold number of fans.

This would be a minor hitch in the promotional plans for *Super Trouper*, compared with what happened later in the year. As it happened, the album scarcely needed much of a promotional push, its advanced sales in the UK alone topping a million copies. In a moment of real-life horror which was echoed nearly a quarter of a century later when Agnetha abruptly cancelled all her promotional activity for her long-awaited 2004 solo album *My Colouring Book*, a press release from Polar Music was issued on 25 November 1981 announcing that all further trips to plug the record had been cancelled. The reason for this was an anonymous letter sent to the company warning that one of the group would be kidnapped. All four members were placed under armed guard.

But nothing could harm the sales of either the album – these topped seven million around the world – or the single, which would hit number one across Europe. By the time the group next set foot in their own, bespoke recording studio the entire dynamic of the foursome would have radically changed once more, thus heralding the beginning of the end for one of the very few pure pop bands to touch greatness.

CHAPTER TWELVE

THE VISITORS

Abba were a band built around various dynamic dualities, creative partnerships. Their diverse but always distinctive sound was built on the compositions of the fertile interaction of Björn the organised, sensible pragmatist and Benny the wilder, prodigiously gifted musical creative force. Their ideas were brought to glorious life by the wondrous chance that their two romantic partners, each strong and vulnerable in her own way, should have looks and, more importantly, voices that both contrasted with and complemented each other's in a way like those in no other band. The immaculate, multi-layered, multi-tracked sound of their recordings was the result of Björn and Benny working in tandem with Michael B. Tretow, Abba's very own George Martin. The relationships of the individual members with their manager, mentor and driving business force Stig were also vitally important, particularly in the early days. But, central to the band, their interaction and, no less importantly, their image for the public, indeed their mythology, were the romantic relationships out of which Abba had been forged.

The strains of being in the same band, their conflicting interests – Björn's ambitions and Agnetha's apparent yearning for a degree of domestic simplicity – and some fundamental incompatibility, which emerged only after years together, had driven the group's golden couple apart. There was something uncanny in how this happened, or at least how the public announcement of their split was made, at around the same time that Benny and Frida finally got married. This synchronicity was to repeat itself in reverse early in 1981. On 6 January of that year Björn Ulvaeus married Lena Källersjö, the restraint of their ceremony standing in stark contrast to Björn and Agnetha's chaotic nuptials of a decade earlier. Then, on 12 February, it was announced in the Swedish press that Benny and Frida were to divorce. It very soon emerged that the immediate cause of the separation was that Benny had fallen in love with another woman, a 37-year-old TV journalist called Mona Nörklit. As it had been for Björn, so with Benny his new girlfriend was someone whom he had known socially for some time, and as with Björn, she was someone who looked strikingly like his wife.

Benny and Frida insisted that they wouldn't be drawn further on the underlying causes of the split, beyond the understandable fact that – and this despite Frida's repeated insistence that she had always relished the intensity of their lives – working and living together had finally placed an unbearable strain on their relationship. As ever, with Björn writing with increasing confidence and from an ever more nakedly, openly autobiographical and biographical perspective, there would be strong clues about the status of the group and their relationships in the lyrics of the album on which he and Benny were already hard at work.

For those after more subtle signs of what was really going on within Abba, there was the rare opportunity for some psychotrichological analysis, with the parlous state of Frida's psyche, a fragile thing at the best of times and for obvious reasons, being revealed through a succession of ill-advised hairdos. Over the previous year, after she had once again opted for the perm that she had favoured in the early years of the band's existence, this style shifted from video to video, from TV show to concert. At times it was bushy, wild, bedecked with ringlets, before settling into the mumsy, prematurely middle-aged version that left her looking uncomfortably like a cross between Tyne Daly of *Cagney and Lacey* fame and Barbara Dickson, this being an oddly prescient look. Then, in her quest for the perfect hairstyle mirroring her pursuit of inner spiritual oneness, she saw the error of her waves and opted for a cleaned-up punk look, in emulation of the pop-rock goddess Pat Benatar, who would be Frida's musical model on her upcoming solo project.

This latter style led to the peculiar situation that when Frida came to do reshoots for the close-ups of her singing 'No Hay a Quien Culpar', the Spanish-language version of the heartbreaking 'When All Is Said and Done', she was sporting her new style, shots that were then intercut with the existing video, this incongruity making the video look like a 'before and after' promotional film for some dodgy hairdressing salon. At least as striking as Frida's rug-rethink is her drawn appearance, the bags visible beneath her eyes, distressing and uncomfortably appropriate for the theme of the song.

This was so because Björn, having already written his own divorce songs, rather prematurely in the case of 'Knowing Me, Knowing You', and then in 'The Winner Takes It All', unapologetically mined the emotional misery of his friends and bandmates. They can't have thanked him for the line 'Slightly worn but dignified and not too old for sex'. Frida boldly took on the song, which was a reflection of her and Benny's split, however oblique. Then again, you can be too oblique, and it is just a touch tricky to work out what Björn is getting at when he talks of the pair as

Birds of passage, you and me
We fly instinctively.

It's Björn with those birds again. In fact there is a strong tendency in Abba's records for themes to be repeated from one album to another. So we have successive albums with their dissection of a painful divorce, 'When All Is Said and Done' being followed by 'Soldiers', a vaguely political song roughly in the style of *Super Trouper*'s 'The Piper'. Indeed, as with the earlier song, this could simply be, with its couplet

Soldiers write the songs that soldiers sing
The songs that you and I don't sing

a call for individual expression in the atmosphere of repressive political, cultural uniformity that was prevalent in Sweden at the time.

The political angle was shared by the album's opening, title track in which Björn said, according to Carl Magnus Palm in *Bright Lights Dark Shadows*, that he was imagining the nightmare of living in the tyranny of a closed society, specifically the Soviet Union, in which there would always be the fear that some dark forces would come for you in the night. Then again, he admitted that the song may just as well have been about what he perceived as the rigid society in his homeland. But, even when delving tentatively into unaccustomed subject matter, Abba were not averse to doing what they always did: playing around with and revisiting various themes and ideas. Whereas *Super Trouper*'s 'On and On and On' lifted the harmonies from the Beach Boys' 'Do It Again', 'The Visitors' begins with a homage to another of their old favourite bands, the dreamy, swirling introductory section containing an emphatic nod to 'Within You Without You' from *Sgt. Pepper*'s. The parenthetic subtitle of 'The Visitors',

'Cracking Up', not only suggests the descent into madness and paranoia which the song's lyrics explore, but also hints at a more general notion of dissolution: of the couples within the group and of the group itself.

The record is in part about divorce and unmistakably indicates, as the band's members freely admitted in interviews at the time and subsequently, that there was little holding them together. At the time of the announcement of Benny and Frida's imminent divorce, they had been keen to emphasise their continuing dedication to the Abba cause, in an almost verbatim reprise of Björn and Agnetha's pledge of loyalty to the band at the time of their split. But, this time round, the recording sessions were, by the band's own accounts, awkward, the sense of a shared mission, a mutual vision, now gone. What is striking – and this is not to say that they were at all a spent force, for both the songwriting and vocal performances are as strong as ever and even display signs of ever-increasing maturity – is that the band were almost consciously falling apart, the songs being allocated to one or the other with fewer of the glorious harmonies that were always intrinsic to the trademark Abba sound.

This idea of falling apart is conveyed, somewhat heavy-handedly, even pretentiously, in the album's cover shot. The members of the group are pictured in an elegant drawing room – the studio in Stockholm of the painter Julius Kronberg – in stiff, awkward poses, all as far apart from one another as possible without actually being out of shot, all expressionless and apparently captivated by something at the edge of the room, although, significantly, they seem to be looking in subtly different directions.

Although they would be distracted with other projects in the years following the end of Abba, 'I Let the Music Speak' made it fairly clear in which direction Björn and Benny were looking. There is something just a touch portentous about the lyrics, with the idea of the songwriter as the medium through which the music speaks, but still this song sounds as though it could easily have been taken from a decent 1980s Broadway musical.

As if to prove that their talents were as diverse as ever, that they were still capable of doing a classic Abba divorce song, they came up with 'One of Us', this time with the twist that the singer is a woman who has left her man and is now desperate for him to have her back. 'One of Us' was the conservative and, as it turned out, wise choice for the first single from these sessions, providing the group with their last international smash hit single, reaching number one in Belgium (their 16th and final chart-topper there, although their next three singles would all enter the top three), Germany (again their final number one, indeed last top-ten placing), Ireland, the Netherlands (their last number one, although their popularity there saw them reach the top five with each of their next three releases) and Spain (only their third number one), the top ten in Austria, France, Norway, South Africa, Sweden, Switzerland and the UK. Aside from their anomalous continuing chart dominance in Belgium and the Netherlands, 'One of Us' marked a glorious final chapter in the extraordinary story of Abba as one of the great singles bands in pop history.

Their final album may have been atypical for the band, their songs becoming ever darker, but advance sales were healthy, approaching two million copies across the key European territories. The follow-up to 'One of Us' would be 'Head Over Heels', a rather sophisticated synth-pop song whose intro can take the credit or blame for inspiring the Thompson Twins' 1983 hit 'We Are Detective'. Incidentally, the number's phrase 'unknown jungles' has a very distinctively Swedish sexiness to it, the hard 'j' not existing in the Swedish language.

The three remaining tracks on Abba's valedictory album confirm just how far they had come, and not always in a good

way. One of the least welcome symptoms of the Abba phenomenon was the success of their most obvious imitators,
Brotherhood of Man. This band had been knocking around for
years before breaking through with their nauseating and rather
dodgy Eurovision winner 'Save Your Kisses for Me'. The supposedly cute conceit of this single, which went on to top the UK
charts, was that the object of this love song, the one whom they
were imploring to save her kisses, was just three years old, and,
one sincerely hopes, their daughter.

Perhaps in some unconscious attempt to repeat this narrative
structure, only this time round with a less uncomfortable twist,
Björn conceived 'Two for the Price of One'. The fact that he and
Benny were clearly now concentrating their efforts on story-
telling in their compositions pointed to their determination to
progress into musical theatre. The choice of their subject matter,
at least in 'Two for the Price of One', pointed to their need for
someone to help them find some appropriate subject matter.
Although the track boasts a catchy tune, the lyrics tell the mirth-
less tale of a cleaner who responds to a lonely-hearts advert which
contains the enticing promise contained within the title, but –
and here's the punchline – the two turn out to be a young
woman and her mother, the revelation of which fact is accompanied by an oompah, folk-brass band.

As if to confound their doubters, this, among the poorest of all
Björn's lyrics, leads directly into another narrative-heavy track,
this one rooted in Björn's own life experiences, and one of his
and the group's finest, albeit neglected, moments. 'Slipping
Through My Fingers' was inspired, as if there were any doubt, by
Björn's watching his daughter go off to school one day – as
Swedish children begin school at seven years of age, she had only
recently started to attend – and pondering on the passing of time.
The song, tinged with the understated guilt of a father who has
struggled to reconcile the obligations of parenthood and career,

is a wonderful, deeply sentimental tear-jerker that provides one of the unexpected highlights of *Mamma Mia!* If you are a parent and can listen to this right through without shedding a tear you might want to check your pulse.

This uneven album, in part excellent and affecting but also oddly chilly, is rounded off in fine style with 'Like an Angel Passing Through My Room', a very adult lullaby, a haunting farewell to love, an entirely fitting finale to Abba's career as an album band. The spare production, and Frida's voice accompanied only by Benny's plinky synth and what sounds like a metronome, leave us to contemplate, for once without the glorious distraction of Abba's trademark glistening harmonies and sumptuous melodic invention, the essential message that 'Love was one prolonged goodbye'. If this seemed to be a perversely apposite send-off from the greatest pop band of the 1970s, one of the greatest of all time, then they had something even darker, even starker and even better in store.

First there were some personal matters to attend to. On 3 December, a week before the UK release of *The Visitors*, Benny and Mona Nörklit were married. Then, at the start of 1982, within a week of each other, Lena Ulvaeus gave birth to a girl and Mona to a boy. The lull afforded by Björn's and Benny's new familial duties allowed Frida to concentrate on her solo career for the first time since 1975 and Agnetha to follow Frida, albeit briefly, into a film career, taking a leading role in *Raskenstam*, a romantic drama based on a true story. The film ended up a modest success, with Agnetha's performance generally well received, although, again like Frida, she had never seen this as the launchpad for a shift of careers. Instead she was planning her own solo album.

But for Abba-watchers the most significant period of the year was the week starting 20 August, when for the last time all four members of the band would be in the recording studio at the same time. The first fruits of this time proved to be their last single. 'Under Attack' is a very slick piece of 1980s pop, again with lashings of synthesised vocals, the main interest coming, aside from its being the group's last-ever single, from the peculiarly prescient, paranoid lyrics, in which Agnetha sings about her terror of being attacked: 'He's on my track, my chasing lover.' If only she'd known.

Abba actually made their last appearance in a satellite link from Stockholm to promote 'Under Attack' on the British TV programme *The Late Late Breakfast Show*. But if the idea of these masters of pop bowing out in the presence of Noel Edmonds is just too much to bear, then it should be remembered that their final recording together was the track that would become their penultimate single release. The B-side was the 'Chiquitita'-like 'Cassandra', but the main show was the simply astonishing 'The Day Before You Came', the starkest recording they ever made. Agnetha, sounding a little like Lotte Lenya – Björn and Benny were coming over a little like Brecht and Weill – tells the haunting, haunted story of the miserable, tiny details of her life, empty until she met her lover.

(While Noel Edmonds is still fresh in the memory, it's worth adding that students of the strange intersection between pop history and conspiracy theory will have noted the malign influence that he and his show seem to have exerted on the careers of the members of Abba. During her appearance on *The Late Late Breakfast Show* to promote 'Wrap Your Arms Around Me' in 1983, Agnetha fell over, injuring her arm, an incident that, in the absence of anything scandalous to write about, justified a chapter to itself in Agnetha's autobiography, *As I Am*.)

The American time-keeping – 'a quarter after ten' – may be disconcerting and calculating, but this aside, 'The Day Before You Came' is a small, grim masterpiece, the chilly and chilling mood of the song suggesting that her life was miserable before the man came and perhaps a whole lot worse after he came. It wasn't just Blancmange, the electro-pop band who had a modest hit with a very straight cover of the song in the summer of 1984, who noticed that Abba bowed out at the very top of their game, with a swansong oddly rich in promise.

CHAPTER THIRTEEN

'BANG-A-BOOMERANG' AND 'DANCING QUEEN'

Abba were a truly international pop phenomenon. They spread like a horde of notably polite, clean-living Vikings and gradually conquered the planet. No country was immune – although the US proved a more stubborn conquest than most and the Latin countries of Europe and Central and South America only belatedly yielded to their charms. Some territories were more loyal in their devotion than others, West Germany, the Netherlands and especially Belgium sticking with the band even more doggedly than their fans in the UK. The Scandinavian countries, the launchpad of their international success, proved inconsistent, oddly fickle, while always fascinated by their private lives as much as by their music.

But while Japan belatedly and briefly erupted into an orgy of Abba love, there was one country where Abbamania truly took root, where the national devotion to the group's music in their early peak years approached a collective madness, reaching a level of intensity that could not possibly be sustained. Abba were often described as the new Beatles, as is every new pop band who provoke an intense, even violent level of attention and love in their fans. Nowhere was the analogy more apposite than in Australia in the mid-1970s.

As everywhere else, the secret of the band's success was simply the band – the songs and the singers – but their most spectacular breakthrough was the direct result of the Australians' being exposed to their music not through live appearances (although these would follow and further fuel their popularity) nor through radio airplay – although, of course, this played a role. At the end of 1973 'Ring Ring' had been released in Australia, but the single had made barely a ripple, just sneaking into the lower reaches of the top 100. Then, despite the meaninglessness of the Eurovision Song Contest outside Europe – not that it is imbued with any profound meaning *in* Europe – 'Waterloo' was propelled into the top ten in the summer of 1974, as it had been in the US.

Then the follow-ups repeated roughly the same pattern as had been established in Europe and America, with 'Honey Honey', the re-released 'Ring Ring' and 'I've Been Waiting for You' exciting little interest among record buyers. But at this stage something remarkable happened, and it was all thanks to the relative novelty of the music video. Here is the time to pay tribute to one of the half-dozen or so figures outside the core of the band without whom the Abba story would have been so different.

Lasse Hallström, born in Stockholm in 1946, was a precocious film-maker who created his first movie, an 8mm short entitled *The Ghost Thief,* when he was just ten. By 1974, the year that also saw his feature-film debut, he was already a veteran of television, having spent ten years churning out comedy and pop-music clips when he came to the attention of Björn and Benny, who were looking for someone to make a promotional video for 'Waterloo'. Hallström was well used to working very quickly and with minimal budgets, so he was the perfect candidate for the job. Aside from the jump-cuts between close-ups of the band members and a bust of Napoleon – reminiscent of the Beethoven's bust jump-cuts in *A Clockwork Orange* – his first job for the band was rather straightforward, but he accomplished what the group wanted of him, simply to concentrate on the four members of Abba themselves, and he was from then until the group's final two videos their official video director.

Hallström's contribution to the band's international break-through came in April 1975, when, in a pragmatic move to showcase Abba's new self-titled album, and to allow cheap, international promotion, he was commissioned to come up with videos of four tracks from the record: 'I Do, I Do, I Do, I Do, I Do', 'Mamma Mia', 'S.O.S.' and 'Bang-a-Boomerang'. The four videos were made in just two days with a budget set at a modest 50,000 kronor, the equivalent of a little over £5,000. It proved to be one of the wisest investments Abba ever made, although, considering their various financial misadventures of later years, this isn't saying much.

The videos were shipped off as a package to the group's Australian record company, and from there to the popular music show *Countdown*, not to be confused with the UK's long-running Channel 4 game show of the same name. This programme's producers, finding ready-made, crowd-pleasing filler, quickly became champions of the group. First of all they played the video for 'I Do, I Do, I Do, I Do, I Do', a straighter version of the Chevy Chase-Paul Simon video for the latter's 'You Can Call Me Al', with its whimsical blend of Björn and Benny miming the sax parts while Agnetha and Frida looked impassioned as they sang their *schlager* love song. It was all fairly simple but it was effective, with its shots of good-looking women and a couple of funny-looking guys in the background singing an easy-on-the-ear ballad. The reaction was instantaneous, the single beginning its rapid rise up the charts.

Then *Countdown* tried out 'Mamma Mia'. Among many other

turning points in the Abba story, you could point to the inspired moment when Hallström decided that the first chorus of 'Mamma Mia' should be illustrated by a dramatic close-up – one directly inspired by Ingmar Bergman's intense drama *Persona* – of Agnetha and Frida's faces perpendicular to each other. It was a neat visual gimmick that Hallström would repeatedly return to in subsequent videos for the band, in which he would continually invent new ways of placing the members in various combinations aligned in complementary or contrasting directions.

The impact of 'Mamma Mia' was perhaps even more dramatic than that of 'I Do, I Do, I Do, I Do, I Do', the broadcast leading to an extraordinary public clamour, with a substantial proportion of the show's estimated two million viewers asking at their local record shops for this single as well. 'Mamma Mia' hadn't been selected as a potential single in Australia or anywhere else, but the pressure from the Australian record company on Stig and others at Polar Music was such that the bigwigs relented and 'Mamma Mia' was released while 'I Do, I Do, I Do, I Do, I Do' was still making its way inexorably to the top of the Australian singles charts. So it was that when 'I Do, I Do, I Do, I Do, I Do' finally hit number one, 'Mamma Mia' was just behind it, and when the former slipped from the top slot it was replaced by 'Mamma Mia', which stayed there for the following ten weeks. When it finally yielded the number-one position it was replaced by 'S.O.S.'.

From a position of relative obscurity, propelled by nothing more than four cheaply produced pop videos and without ever having set foot in the country, Abba had become the biggest pop band in Australia, *Abba* riding high in the album charts and their last three singles having hogged the top spot for 14 consecutive weeks. Abbamania had begun in earnest. It all happened very much more quickly and more intensely than it had done anywhere else, and everyone knew from the start that it couldn't possibly maintain this level, that sooner or later it had to run its course. Stig was always acutely aware of this, warning about the dangers of saturation from the start, this fear having been behind his reluctance to rush-release 'Mamma Mia'.

A national obsession had been created, with Abba, their music, their image. So flexible was this image that the band could embody fidelity and wholesomeness to the family audience and also, specifically through the presence of Agnetha, who was generally Abba's visual focus, the fantasy of the sexually available, sexually voracious Swedish blonde. To stoke up the fires of this fixation what was needed was for the group to visit the country in the flesh. This they did in March 1976. The promotional tour, with the band inciting something close to hysteria wherever they went, took in the usual rounds of press conferences, signing sessions and photo-ops and built to the broadcast of a TV special called *The Best of Abba*, which attracted an audience of more than half of the viewing public, the highest-ever rating for a show on Australian TV.

The visit, in which the band were thoughtful, breezy and at all times polite in interviews, had the desired effect, continuing the Australians' frenzied love affair with them. Lasse Hallström expressed some doubt about his ideas for the 'Fernando' video, feeling with some justification that it was all rather too plodding and literal, with the firelight of the lyrics evoked by the image of a campfire and stars by a shot of stars. Yet nothing could hinder Abba's progress, and before long the single went to number one where it stayed for 14 weeks. They would be back the following year, this time on a fully-fledged concert tour, and along with them would be Hallström and his film crew to commemorate the music and the phenomenon, but, as ecstatic as their reception would be, by that stage Abbamania would have passed its peak, at least in terms of sales, the band having already enjoyed, with

'Dancing Queen' and *Arrival*, their last ever chart-toppers on both the single and the album fronts.

There were various factors militating against the project that would in time become *Abba – The Movie*, not least the foursome's perceived limitations as actors. As it turned out, Frida and later Agnetha would prove to be at least competent screen actors, but the cautious decision was made early on that to whatever limited extent the four members would be called upon to perform at all, they would be playing themselves. The film marked a significant boost to Hallström, who, used to the modest, actively stingy budgets for the videos, was given a healthy sum – estimated at around six million kronor (more than £600,000) – to allow him to realise the plan to expand his remit from creating a straightforward tour documentary to directing a feature film, this decision taken only shortly before the band set off for Australia. This indecent haste is apparent in what passes for the drama sections that serve to link the main attraction: separate scenes of the band in and around their live appearances.

The plot, such as it is, centres on the increasingly desperate measures undertaken by a young DJ played by Robert Hughes to secure an interview with Abba which is scheduled to be broadcast the day the band leave Australia at the end of their jaunt. He pursues them from concert hall to outdoor arena, always narrowly missing them, repeatedly failing to secure press accreditation. Eventually, after a fantasy sequence in which he hangs out with the band and frolics with Agnetha and Frida to the strains of 'The Name of the Game', while convinced that he has missed his chance, he literally stumbles upon the foursome in a hotel lift. So, just in the nick of time, he gets his interview and, as Abba's plane heads back to Europe, all ends happily. These linking sequences are pretty lame, dismissed by David Robinson in his review in *The Times* on 17 February 1978 as 'a very childish anecdote'. Indeed it is astonishing that the script was the work of Hallström (who would go on to create the wonderful *My Life as a Dog*, which in turn would serve as his calling card to Hollywood, where he would turn out the likes of *What's Eating Gilbert Grape?* and *The Cider House Rules*) and Robert Caswell, who would later write the scripts for *A Cry in the Dark* and *The Doctor*.

Nevertheless, as a document of Abba live and the fervid interest they still attracted in Australia, the film is invaluable. The vox-pop comments, while not necessarily a wholly reliable source of information, emphatically confirm the idea that it was Abba's white-bread heterosexual wholesomeness that made them such unthreatening favourites, while others were simply fixated on Agnetha's celebrated derrière. One bizarre question at a press conference, asking how she herself reacted to her elevated position as the owner of the world's most shapely arse, was batted off with good humour, belying the true feelings of Agnetha and the rest of the band about the unnatural concentration on this anatomical detail. Quite reasonably, she pointed out that she could hardly comment because she had never seen it herself.

There is an amusing moment in *Abba – The Movie* when, with their minder (played by Tom Oliver, aka 'Larrikin' Lou Carpenter from *Neighbours*), the band examine the newspaper reports of their opening concert, chiefly the headline 'AGNETHA'S BOTTOM TOPS SHOW'. As is pointed out on the Abba: Memories of the 1977 tour website, Benny's thumb is tactically placed over the word 'Dull', which appears between 'Tops' and 'Show' in the actual headline.

Abba arrived in Sydney on 27 February 1977. Crowds greeted them at the airport, as they would at every location where the band appeared. The arrival on this date gave them nearly a week to acclimatise, perform various promotional duties and prepare for the first gig at the city's Showground Arena. The first concert, before 20,000 ecstatic fans, ought to have been a disaster, performed as it was in the midst of a torrential downpour, but the rain, which affected the sound equipment and Hallström's cameras so that little of the event was recorded, failed to dampen the fans' ardour.

As for Abba themselves, they were by this time far from enamoured of touring, as they make clear in both *Abba – The Movie* and later in *Abba In Concert*, the film of their 1979 tour, and now the spookier extremes of the hysteria they encountered, the limitations placed on their freedom of movement, only exacerbated this distaste. Agnetha felt moved to swear, not for the first or last time, that she would never go on the road again. Here there is another parallel with the Beatles, for the hysteria that greeted all the Fab Four's concerts from 1963 onwards was such that neither fans nor the group themselves could hear any of the music, one of the factors that led them to give up live performances in 1966.

Another occupational hazard that Abba encountered, for neither the first nor the last time, in Australia in 1977 was a credible terrorist threat. On this occasion it came during their appearance on 10 March at the Perth Entertainment Centre, the first of a three-night residency that would wind up the tour; they had played sell-out shows in Melbourne and Adelaide in the interim. A bomb scare caused the show to be interrupted in midflow, but once the venue had been evacuated and searched and the 8,000 fans had been allowed to return to their seats, Abba, ever professional, returned to the stage and finished their act, relatively unflustered.

By the end of the tour it was estimated that one in three Australian households owned an Abba record, and more than one per cent of the country's population, around 145,000 people, had seen the band in their 11 sold-out live shows. Even so, the end of the tour seemed to mark the end of the Abba phenomenon in Australia, and in the scene where the band members bid a fond, relieved farewell to their fans at the airport they were also bidding a farewell, similarly relieved, to Abbamania.

Abba – The Movie received its world première in Australia on 15 December, and over the following months was given a staggered release around the world, in Sweden, the Netherlands, Finland, the UK, West Germany, France and Japan, even receiving a limited release in the Soviet Union. Precise and reliable details of box-office grosses are impossible to come by but some authorities have claimed that the film was one of the ten highest-grossing films worldwide in 1978. This confirmed that Abba were a critic-proof act in the face of generally unfavourable reviews of *Abba – The Movie*. David Robinson's sniffy piece in *The Times* was fairly typical of the film's reception, concluding condescendingly: 'For their part the Abba are sweet and clean and Scandinavian; and their music, with its clockwork beat, shows all the scars of having won the Eurovision Song Contest.'

Back in Australia, after the astonishing run of *Abba, The Best of Abba* and *Arrival*, which had together spent a total of 35 weeks at the top of the national album charts, and 'I Do, I Do, I Do, I Do, I Do', 'Mamma Mia', 'S.O.S.', 'Fernando', 'Dancing Queen' and 'Money, Money, Money', which had together topped the singles charts for 42 weeks, the bubble had burst. A backlash began, and while Abba's records would continue to sell, the band would thenceforth have, by their standards, only modest hits. But, as happened in other territories in the aftermath of the peaceful demise of the band as a working outfit, Abba became a sleeping giant. Perhaps more than anywhere else, certainly more intensely than anywhere else, Abba had got under the national skin, had become part of the fabric of Australia for a while at least, having all but dominated the country's pop-cultural life for a couple of years. In the process they had, as they would elsewhere, become synonymous with, and instantly evocative of, a certain kind of very mid-seventies, very clean, very

Swedish, very garish, very badly dressed, very camp, very kitsch and, for a certain constituency of their loyal fan base at least, very gay entertainment.

There are now many different Abba tribute bands plying their trade and making a good living around the world, at the very least 30 outfits spread across Australia, Canada, Germany, Ireland, Sweden, the UK and elsewhere. But it is fitting that the most famous of them all, the group who could reasonably lay claim to being partly responsible for, as well as symptomatic of, the remarkable renaissance of Abba in the 1990s, should be a bunch of Australians. 'Bjorn Again's a tribute to Abba, but it's a tribute with a twist.' This is the assessment of the Aussie group's co-manager Rod Leissle, interviewed for the documentary *Abba: Bjorn Again*. One day in the early 1990s, while working in a Melbourne research lab, Leissle and John Tyrrell were struck with the inspired idea that what Australia needed was an Abba tribute band.

We live in a strange, post-modern, ironic world, something that Christopher Guest, aka Nigel Tufnel of Spinal Tap, explored when I spoke to him about the tours undertaken by him and the other members of what is, with the possible exception of Bjorn Again, the world's most famous 'fictional' group: 'The Spinal Tap tours were incredibly surrealistic. Here we were playing live shows to an audience who behaved as if they were in the film.' This notion was echoed by Leissle, who said of the bizarre experience of Bjorn Again: 'We're pretending to be Abba, and these people in some bizarre way are pretending to be the fans of Abba.'

Bjorn Again, who narrowly missed out on being called Abbattoir, somehow encapsulate the status of Abba, their appeal managing to be simultaneously sincere and ironic. Like the actors behind Spinal Tap, so the members of Bjorn Again are reluctant to be interviewed or otherwise appear out of character, and so

Bjorn Volveus, Benny Anderwear, Agnetha Falstart and Frida Longstokin maintain their peculiar caricatures of the band members, playing on the notion of marital and sexual tension between them, including a not-understated suggestion of a certain lesbian tension between Frida and Agnetha. But what they do they is fulfil a need, one that is catered to by *Mamma Mia!* and by all the other tribute acts with their wildly varying degrees of accuracy and authenticity, that people have to hear Abba's music live, to be transported back in time. Here there is no apparent irony – Bjorn Again have made an awful lot of money through their immaculate sound-alike act. They are confronted with the same problems that Abba were when performing live, in struggling to recreate the Abba studio sound, but, unlike the originals, they usually rely on a backing tape for the full sound.

But, also unlike their models, the band face no danger that they will be split apart by divorce or a change in musical direction, nor is there at present any suggestion that they will go out of fashion any more than Abba will. Just as the Bootleg Beatles have lasted more than twice as long as the Beatles did, so Bjorn Again have been around for longer than Abba were, and have by now played live to far more people than the real Abba ever did.

Bjorn Again almost performed in front of more people than Abba ever did in the course of a single gig, when they played at London's Gay Pride concert in 1996, where considered estimates put their audience at around 300,000 people, every one of whom knew all the words to 'Dancing Queen'. Aside from having created this gay anthem – right up there with Gloria Gaynor's 'I Will Survive' and 'Gimme! Gimme! Gimme! (A Man After Midnight)' – Abba had seemingly been made into icons of gay adoration with their ludicrous, fancy-dress stage outfits and the soap-opera story of their real lives, in which the women were cast in the role of Judy Garland-lite divas of suffering done ill by their men. Indeed 'Gimme! Gimme! Gimme!' eventually inspired the critically reviled but cultish and very gay sitcom of the same name in which James Dreyfus and Kathy Burke starred as a gay, perennially unemployed actor and his OTT fag-hag flatmate.

In 1992, around the time that Bjorn Again were emerging as an internationally recognised pop phenomenon, the Abba revival received a serious boost with Erasure's *Abbaesque* EP. Vince Clarke was a leading light in the generation of British synth-pop bands of the early 1980s, all of whom took inspiration from Abba. Having left Depeche Mode after their first couple of hits, he joined forces with Alf, aka Alison Moyet, for a brief fertile period as Yazoo, then got together with Feargal Sharkey in the short-lived, best-selling the Assembly, before striking gold for a fourth time with Erasure alongside the camp, gay Alf sound-alike Andy Bell. Since the mid-1980s the band had notched up a dozen hit dance singles before inspiration struck and the pair paid tribute to their shared idols via their EP featuring four Abba cover versions, led by 'Lay All Your Love on Me', backed up by 'Take a Chance on Me', 'S.O.S.' and 'Voulez-Vous'.

This loving, sincere, fun-filled tribute gave these tracks a respectful but emphatically dance-floor treatment, supported by pastiche videos in which the pair impersonated all four Abba members. The success was instantaneous and dramatic, *Abbaesque* reaching number one in the UK singles charts in June 1992 and staying there for five weeks. The EP's massive sales in the UK and across Europe paved the way for the *Abba Gold* collection, as well as inspiring an act of revenge from Bjorn Again, who made their own minor ripple on the world of record sales with their own EP, *Erasur-ish*, with its selection of Erasure songs done in the style of a bunch of Australians impersonating Abba.

The re-emergence of Abba in Australia was apparent in the film *Muriel's Wedding*, in which the eponymous heroine (played

199

by Toni Colette) dreams of escaping the mundane misery of her native small town of Porpoise Spit, heading for the city and eventually marrying her dream man. Her fantasies are fuelled by Abba songs, which litter the soundtrack ('Waterloo' featuring in a lip-sync sequence, 'Mamma Mia', 'Fernando', 'Dancing Queen' and, of course, 'I Do, I Do, I Do, I Do, I Do').

In perhaps the ultimate fusion of Abba's iconic status in both Australian and gay culture, 'Mamma Mia' appears prominently in the climactic sequence of *The Adventures of Priscilla, Queen of the Desert*, the cult kitsch road movie in which three drag queens, Bernadette (Terence Stamp), Mitzi (Hugo Weaving) and Felicia (Guy Pearce), travel across Australia in the eponymous coach. Felicia is, much to the annoyance of her travelling companions, an Abba nut with an unhealthy interest in Agnetha's movements. After one fateful near-encounter with his idol when he followed her into a public toilet he found floating in the bowl what was apparently one of her turds, which he retrieved and has lovingly kept as a token of his devotion ever since.

When you become the instantly recognisable shorthand for the escape from the miseries of everyday life into a glorious, garish fantasy world, when you inspire dozens of bands around the world to make their living impersonating you, when one of these groups can hold hundreds of thousands of people entranced as if having summoned up some divine spirit, when, albeit fictionally, your excrement is treated like some holy relic, then you know that you have attained iconic status, even immortality.

CHAPTER FOURTEEN

'Money, Money, Money'

*It's a lot of money coming in, but there's a lot of tax to pay if you're
a Swedish citizen, which is fair. But still, it's a matter of hard
work, and the money isn't that important, really. It's more a
matter of pleasing yourself in what you're doing.*
Benny Andersson, in response to an Australian
journalist's question in *Abba – The Movie*

In the summer of 1966 Benny Andersson and his bandmates
took what was apparently the shrewd, calculated business decision to found an organisation called Hep House both to handle
all the group's business affairs and to act as a publishing company
for their, i.e. Benny's, compositions. In this one instance at least
the Hep Stars were way ahead of the Beatles, whose own Apple
Corps, handling recording and other sundry business affairs,
wouldn't be launched until May 1968. If the decision to set up
Hep House gave the suggestion of some keen financial acumen,
then that suggestion was misleading. Unfortunately, like Apple,
Hep House proved to be of little use for anything but leaking
cash. Nineteen sixty-six, the band's most successful year, saw
them reportedly pay precisely nothing in tax. Needless to say,
this was a big mistake.

Their financial difficulties were exacerbated when they were
persuaded to follow in the footsteps of the Beatles and find a
movie vehicle for their rock-star charms. The project turned out
to be disastrous both fiscally and artistically. The film, given the

unenticing working title 'Habari-Safari', attracted a reasonable budget – all set against the band's royalties, as they would discover in time – but no script, a situation that would be repeated a decade later during the preparations for *Abba – The Movie*, a project about which Benny was wary, owing to his deeply unhappy celluloid experience with the Hep Stars. The patent lack of preparedness didn't stop the band and their small entourage of film-makers from heading off to Kenya in early 1967, where much footage was shot but precisely nothing came of it, despite the attempts of the young Lasse Hallström, then just starting out in the film-making business, to lick it into some sort of shape. The general financial recklessness, not to say cluelessness, of the Hep Stars was bound to come back to haunt them eventually, and this it did. Over the following couple of years the band collectively and individually faced a succession of financial shocks, including a sea of tax debts that led to the demise of Hep House.

Benny's tax debt would remain a burden for years to come. In the spring of 1969 he and Frida would be compelled to move out of their plush, five-bedroom flat in central Stockholm and into a nearby studio apartment. At this time he had come under the umbrella of Stig Anderson and Bengt Bernhag through his association with their protégé Björn. Now convinced of the potential of this dynamic new songwriting duo, Stig, no fool when it came to spotting a money-making idea, suggested that the four of them forge a publishing business based on the Andersson-Ulvaeus product. This they did under the Union Songs banner. Equally significantly, it was at this time, in 1969, that Benny sought the assistance of Stig's formidable wife, Gudrun, who sorted out a repayment scheme which saw to it that his onerous tax debt would gradually be repaid over a period of time – and it proved to be four years, with the result that the final instalment was paid shortly before Benny was established as a hit-maker on the international stage.

Clearly this fiscal crisis was down to a combination of poor advice and, on Benny's part, an absence of financial responsibility. But even without this recklessness, for Swedes in the 1960s making money, or at least keeping your hands on the money that you were making, was tricky enough, and it would become harder still by the middle of the following decade, when Abba had become successful on such a scale that for several years the income they were generating rivalled, in proportion to turnover, if not in actual terms, that of Sweden's leading brands, Saab and Volvo among them. More of which later.

To place the ever-confused state of Abba's finances in context and to understand something of the society and culture that spawned them, now is perhaps the time for...

A Very Brief History of Sweden

Sweden finds itself at the centre of the Scandinavian peninsula, sandwiched, often uncomfortably, between Norway to the west and Finland to the east. More uncomfortable still is the umbilical connection at the north of the peninsula to Siberia. Sweden was settled by hunter-gatherers moving northwards with the thawing of the last Ice Age from around 10,000 BC. By the middle of the second millennium BC Swedish traders had opened up routes to the south. By the middle of the following millennium the Svea tribe had become the dominant force in the land, having occupied the central region of the country, then pushed southwards, ousting the Goths. The Svea would give their name to the new nation, Sverige, the Swedish for Sweden, which derives from *Svea rike*, or 'land of the Svea'.

Although there was trade between the Svea and Rome, Sweden remained untroubled by the spread of the Roman Empire. In the age of the Vikings, from the ninth to the eleventh centuries AD, while the Danish and Norwegian Vikings headed west, the Swedes turned their attentions eastwards, launching a pattern of skirmishes for control over Finland and the Baltic that would continue in one form or other for the next thousand years – incidentally the influence of Sweden on its near neighbour to the east was such that they were responsible for its name, Russia, which derives from Rus, the name given to these early Swedish invaders.

Sweden was visited by Christian missions intermittently throughout the Dark Ages, and a German Christian mission was established in the mid-ninth century. Very early in the 11th century King Olof became the first Swedish monarch to be baptised and he decreed that Christianity was from that time the country's official religion, but Sweden was not officially Christianised until the appointment of the first Archbishop of Lund in 1104.

Over the following centuries the hold of Christianity became ever firmer, trading routes were consolidated – particularly with Germany – and Sweden, along with Norway, fell under the dominion of Denmark, under what was known as the Kalmar Union. Also in this time, slavery was abolished (1355) and the University of Uppsala was founded (1477). The Kalmar Union was always fragile and was finally dismantled by the accession to the throne of Gustav Vasa in 1523, which launched a royal dynasty that would rule the country for the next 200 years. Aside from driving out the Danes, Gustav Vasa played a vital role in the formation of modern Sweden by adopting Lutheranism, a strict, dour and joyless strand of Protestantism, as the national religion, strengthening the bond between Church and nation, indeed making one indivisible from the other, and setting in place the complex bureaucracy that survives in modified form to this day. Sweden became ferociously anti-Catholic, and although the influence and importance of the Church has receded dramatically over the centuries, the history of Catholic persecution is perpetuated to the present day, if only in anti-papist children's games.

The organisation of national bureaucracy and the power of the Church were enhanced through successive Vasa monarchs until the turbulent rein of Charles (Karl) XII. This charismatic, in many ways heroic, although eccentric figure – among his odder endeavours was the unsuccessful attempt to establish an elk cavalry – brought a period of glorious expansion to an end when, as Napoleon and Hitler would in their turn, he pursued a disastrous campaign against the Russians that led to a humiliating defeat. The era following Charles XII's death in 1718 was an inward-looking one, in which Swedish bureaucratic law was further consolidated and the power of the monarch diminished.

Arguably having even more profound an impact on the history and culture of Sweden than the little corporal himself serving as inspiration for a mid-1970s planet-conquering pop waxing, was the offering of the Swedish throne – in the aftermath of King Gustav III's final, misguided attempt to tame Russia, and the travails of the Napoleonic Wars, presided over by his son Gustav IV – to Napoleon's marshal Jean-Baptiste Bernadotte. He accepted, and was crowned King Karl-Johan, thus launching the Bernadotte royal dynasty, which survives up to the current king, Carl Gustav, the monarch blessed with his very own dancing queen, both of them friends of Frida. The most significant event of the 19th century was the mass emigration of the middle years, which saw around one million Swedes head for America, creating enclaves in the Midwest that remain largely if not exclusively Swedish-American communities to this day, notably exemplified in the Coen Brothers' film *Fargo*. The exodus would inspire Vilhelm Moberg to create his tetralogy of novels named after the first volume: *The Emigrants* (*Utvandrarna*), *Unto a Good Land* (*Invandrarna*, literally *The Immigrants*), *The Settlers* (*Nybyggarna*)and *The Last Letter Home* (*Sista brevet till Sverige*). This work would in turn would inspire Björn Ulvaeus and Benny

205

Andersson to create their own hit musical *Kristina från Duvemåla* (*Kristina from Duvemåla*).

The early years of the Bernadotte era were significant in that they saw the end, thus far at least, after the 1814 aggression against Denmark, of Sweden as an actively warlike nation – although it boasts a long and highly lucrative if not noble tradition of arms manufacture and export. Since then the country has played no active role in any war for nearly two centuries other than its participation in UN peace-keeping operations. This determined neutrality – Sweden's record of disengagement is matched only by Switzerland's – has come at a price. The union between Sweden and Norway, in which the former was the dominant partner, ended in 1905. During the Second World War, while Norway and Denmark faced the ignominy of German occupation, the sting of which is still keenly felt in both countries, and Finland endured occupation by Russian forces and aggression from German ones, Sweden remained steadfastly disengaged. Even so, it was a breed of neutrality that allowed thousands of Nazi troops to use the country's rail networks at the height of the war.

After all the expansions and contractions of the various Scandinavian countries, with first Denmark and then Sweden emerging as the dominant nation, establishing lengthy dominion over first Finland and then Norway, the four countries – so long as you accept that there are only four countries in Scandinavia, excluding Iceland and others with more spurious connections – were decisively defined, and borders that survive today were ultimately established. Following all this conflict, close links remained – trade, a degree of shared culture, and the Danish, Norwegian and Swedish languages' being closely related to one another. (Finnish belongs to an entirely distinct linguistic family, but Swedish is still spoken alongside it throughout Finland.) But there were enduring tensions too, for instance the Norwegians' remaining the butt of Swedish jokes in the same way that the Irish have been for the British and the Poles for the Americans.

If you take the view of Roland Huntford, as expressed in his highly controversial book *The New Totalitarians*, a study of the background to and history of the rise to power of social democracy in Sweden in the 20th century, you will imagine the average Swede as a meek conformist, and Sweden in the 1970s as – despite its many achievements in industry, culture, sport and elsewhere and apparent enlightened attitude to many social issues – an almost closed society in which a strongly left-wing orthodoxy held dominion and was barely open to question. One can only hope that those familiar with the book, and the subsequent revelation of Huntford's political allegiances – rather right-wing – will have taken what he says with a large pinch of salt.

Yet Huntford's hostile attitude to Sweden and the Swedes is in itself revealing. In the midst of his book-length diatribe he says of Swedish people in general: '... among them the concept of individuality and the development of personality have been grossly retarded down the centuries'. He had certainly not missed the fact that the notion of society – to spell it out, the vital importance for the health of a society of its members' understanding what they owed to and could expect of the commonwealth – was and is absolutely central to the Swedish character. Note the moment in *Abba In Concert* where Björn, with a slight air of resignation, says that, whatever his unspoken position as *de facto* leader, should he be outvoted by his bandmates at any given moment, then the majority prevails. As he adds with a shrug: 'It's the Swedish way.'

But Huntford also points to something rather significant in the way that Sweden and Swedes are often perceived and treated. His words are patently racist, but as Swedes are not under any yoke of disadvantage or impoverishment – or have not been for some time at least – such attitudes are less grave than other expressions of race hatred. In this hinterland, this grey area between legitimate social commentary and outright bigotry, there are a number of perceptions of what Swedes are like. For example, Swedes abroad routinely encounter the notion, when they are not confused with the Swiss, that they come from a land with a population that manages to be simultaneously emotionally chilly and sex-mad, a bunch of alcoholic, suicidal depressives, people either simply dull or entirely lacking in personality, whose essential frivolity of mind is reflected in their faintly absurd, singsong accents, a land where all of the women are statuesque, blonde Viking goddesses, the men denim-bedecked geeks. This isn't an entirely accurate picture.

Nevertheless, however rebarbative Huntford's views may be, there is no doubt that Sweden has long been a profoundly bureaucratic country and that the general reliance upon and trust in central, state control has had some deeply unfortunate results. Among the worst of these was – and this grim, shameful episode shines some light on the less healthy political and cultural links between Sweden and Germany in the first half of the 20th century – the government-sponsored eugenic programme of forced sterilisation of those citizens deemed unfit for reproduction for reasons of racial or mental inferiority, a policy that saw up to 60,000 women sterilised between the mid-1930s and the mid-1970s. This policy was grimly linked to the state-sponsored persecution of the *tyskebarna* in Norway, a living nightmare from which Frida narrowly escaped.

Certainly the ever-diminishing power of the monarchy and the acceptance of, if not outright fondness for, consensus politics, advanced bureaucracy and state control in a sense culminated in the birth of the Social Democratic Party. The party that would dominate the Swedish political scene through much of the 20th century and beyond, although latterly in a much-diluted form, was born in the late-19th century. Committed from the outset to the equitable distribution of assets, a widespread social welfare system and universal or near-universal employment via a rigidly planned economy, involving the careful nurturing of industry which was heavily state-controlled if not state-owned, the Social Democrats first came to power in the 1932 general election in the aftermath of the disastrous events in Ådalen in 1931. As depicted in the 1969 film *Ådalen 31*, Bo Widerberg's lyrical, sentimental take on this pivotal episode, the tension surrounding a strike organised by workers at a paper mill in this northern Swedish town escalated, finally exploding into violence with the fatal shooting of five workers at the hands of the soldiers who had been struggling in vain to contain the unrest. This notorious event created shock throughout this pacific country, a shock that would be matched, on the domestic front at least, only by the murders of Prime Minister Olof Palme in 1986 and Foreign Minister Anna Lindh in 2003.

From the early 1930s Sweden was all but a one-party state, the Social Democrats' hold on government interrupted only by the odd term in opposition. They were occasionally obliged to form coalition governments, but their principles prevailed. After the depression of the late 1920s and early 1930s the Swedish economy was quickly turned around and soon began to flourish through the application of a carefully honed economic policy which saw the encouragement of industrial expansion and a thriving export trade aided by the efficient exploitation of the country's natural resources. Sweden, a country rich in minerals, notably iron and soft wood, had long been a producer of iron and steel goods, timber and wood pulp.

In the post-war years – and Sweden had done rather well economically out of the war itself – the economy was thriving, unemployment was at a barely significant level, union membership was almost universal and yet industrial disputes were all but unknown. Sweden was one of the world's economic success stories, the general standard of living high, poverty effectively obliterated, the welfare state extraordinarily beneficent. It was a society that functioned well and harmoniously. Incidents of social unrest were infrequent and the crime rate in general was relatively low, although there were the problems of suicide – the notoriously high suicide rate in Sweden has been at least partly due to the greater levels of honesty with which these statistics have historically been collated in Sweden relative to many other countries – and alcoholism.

Heavy drinking was the one foible to which both Björn and Benny have both admitted being prone, especially during the early, touring years, and has been a historic problem for Swedes. The problem of widespread alcoholic dependence, one common to all countries of Northern Europe, led to the creation of the so-called Bratt System, which was introduced in 1914, leading to the strict rationing of alcohol in bars and restaurants and the restriction of the sale of alcohol for home consumption to government-run shops, known as *Systembolaget*.

In the early 1970s high taxation was introduced across the board, with a top rate of tax on earnings of 85 per cent. By the middle of the decade taxation seemed to be reaching genuinely punitive levels, and top earners – among them children's authors Astrid Lindgren and Inger and Lasse Sandberg – were shocked that they were apparently being taxed at a rate of more than 100 per cent. But, this still being a society that was in many ways liberal and open, Lasse Sandberg was able to pick up the phone and call Olof Palme to ask for some clarification, which he duly received.

The notorious experience of Ingmar Bergman, Sweden's greatest film-maker and a major theatre director, illustrates just how zealous the country's tax officials were at the time. On 30 January 1976 Bergman's rehearsal of Strindberg's *The Dance of*

bove Abba at the height of their sartorial offensiveness, their look reflected with only a hint of
xaggeration in, *below,* the 2004 London production of *Mamma Mia!* (pictured: Kim Ismay,
ivien Parry and Lara Mulcahy).

Scenes from two marriages: *inset* Björn and Agnetha on their blissful wedding day and, *above,* pictured in chillier times; *below left* two couples at their happiest and, *below right,* in more sombre mood in 1982 when all had been said and done.

ba today: *Above left* an all too rare glimpse of Agnetha; *above right* Björn and, *below left,* Benny
oking increasingly like brothers; and *below right* Frida finally going blonde.

Abba at their peak. As Quentin Crisp once said: 'Dressing in fashion is like signing a petition, dressing with style is like publishing your manifesto.'

Death (if you're not familiar with this gloomy masterpiece, just imagine 'Knowing Me, Knowing You', only with the couple having unwisely decided to stay together) at the Royal Dramatic Theatre in Stockholm was interrupted by the unexpected arrival of two plainclothes police officers. He was whisked off and questioned by members of the police department dealing with tax matters about a possible tax-avoidance scheme dating back several years, which, if proven against him, could leave him liable to a tax bill for an amount equivalent to hundreds of thousands of pounds or a couple of years in prison. His plea was, according to Peter Cowie's *Ingmar Bergman – A Critical Biography*: 'I am an artist. I know nothing about money,' an argument that, unsurprisingly, didn't cut much ice with the taxman. The matter was eventually settled, but not before Bergman briefly went into exile in Bavaria and threatened to retire from all creative endeavours. He lashed out against those who had condemned him, for in some quarters he had indeed been accused of tax-dodging.

This peak of taxation coincided with the period when Abba began to generate a prodigious income. While all four members refused even to contemplate the most straightforward solution to the taxation problem, i.e. leaving Sweden as tax exiles, with the help of Stig Anderson and various financial advisers over the years they put in place a number of rather bizarre financial arrangements, setting up a succession of unusual businesses and colourful tax-avoidance schemes, some more successful and less risky than others. They spoke at various times of their willingness – and this was the Swedish way – to pay the taxes that supported Sweden's remarkable social welfare system, and these were not empty statements, and over the years they contributed massively to the national economy. But they were at the same time eager that not all of their vast income from international sales should come to the band members directly as such, thus leaving it all open to direct income tax. So they invested in property, and set up Abba Invest to handle their ever more complex investment portfolio.

As time passed, the Abba organisation, under various names which were in the overall control of Abba Invest, sank money into an art gallery, their own lavishly equipped recording studio and an import company specialising in sports goods; they branched out in the hope of establishing a wing of the Abba organisation as a general investments company; acquired a bicycle company for what was a quite legal but patently opportunistic buyout (a tactic that, when extended still further in an involved deal several years later, would come back to haunt Stig and Abba); they bought a wealthy real-estate company; a huge leasing company; and bought into a large investment company, among many other deals large and small.

From these many and complex transactions which saw them, Stig in particular, rather out of their depth in the murky world of international business, several deals stand out as especially colourful. Chief among these was the establishment of the Abba organisation's oil-trading company, Pol Oil, set up as a means of instantly translating some of the revenues generated in Eastern Europe, where the band had a strong core following, into a tradable asset which could then be liquidated. Apparently a foolproof plan; but, as it turned out, far from it. The company had been limping along for a couple of years when one spectacularly unfortunate turn of events, with the international price of oil plummeting in the immediate aftermath of a massive acquisition of crude oil which anyway proved all but unsaleable, led to a loss running into several million dollars and the collapse of Pol Oil.

Abba's financial deals had for some time been the object of fascination among the Swedish press. Sometimes the results of detailed journalistic investigations, often carried out with the co-operation of the band – however frustrating they found the focus on their money rather than their music – would be picked up by other countries' media. This led to at least one common misapprehension, as is succinctly explained by Carl Magnus Palm in *Bright Lights Dark Shadows*, a book that tackles in some detail the ever-complex finances of the group. In the financial year ending April 1978, Polar Music's profit was an impressive 50 million kronor on a turnover of 86 million, a profit of 70 per cent on working capital. The latter figure was vastly superior to the performance of Sweden's major industries, Saab and Volvo included, thus creating the false impression that Abba were generating more profit than these industrial giants, rather than merely surpassing them in their profit-to-capital ratio.

While not financially ruinous, the Pol Oil débâcle was certainly not something Abba welcomed, and in the aftermath of their demise – although no official announcement of the band's dissolution was ever made – their business ventures got only messier, their relationship with Stig ever more strained, eventually reaching breaking point. The tension between the former band members and the man who was still technically their manager – it would be years after the release of Abba's last album, *The Visitors*, before Stig finally came to understand that they were truly defunct as a working band – concerned both the specific deals relating to the royalties that they received from sales of Abba records, and more general business dealings which, while often undertaken without their full knowledge, were still their ultimate responsibility.

Many details of the contentious financial dealings of the band were already familiar to Swedish newspaper readers, but a newspaper article which appeared in the UK on Saturday 21 July 1984 proved that the fascination with the contentious fiscal transactions undertaken in Abba's name was now international, and confirmed just how grave the situation had got for the group. Under the headline 'Abba faces £4.6m tax allegations' *The Times* published a story about the controversial aftermath of

Pol Oil's collapse and resultant tax liability. A further allegation concerned the dealings of the property company Stockholms Badhus, in which Abba were involved, wherein companies were repeatedly bought and sold by other institutions, all of which fell under the umbrella of the Abba organisation.

As the experience of so many bands – not least the Beatles, once more the inescapable model for Abba – has proved, pop groups are uncannily, often uncomfortably, like marriages (the analogy particularly appropriate in Abba's case), unions that, although embarked upon out of a sense of boundless optimism, intense emotional connections, shared visions and goals, all too often end in bitter mutual recriminations, and frequently in court.

For some time the various members of the group had sought to simplify their involvements in business and ultimately to sell their share of the Polar organisation – something that Frida had already done by this stage. Agnetha followed suit, but she, Björn and Benny were still caught up in the fallout from the Stockholms Badhus affair, as well as being involved in a protracted legal dispute with Stig that would drag on into the 1990s.

Parallel with this bitter dispute was an equally unseemly contest, one that also came to court, in which the former band members individually sought from their former manager a more favourable share of the royalties, as had, they alleged, been promised to them in negotiations conducted shortly after the release of *The Visitors*. Stig always insisted that the reason the band continued to receive payments in line with an earlier agreement was that the improved deal was contingent on the recording of new material by the group, which, of course, never happened. Whatever the ultimate truth of the case, the courts found at least partly in favour of Agnetha, Björn, Benny and Frida.

While Stig managed to remain on relatively congenial terms with Frida, who was less involved in the legal actions than her former bandmates, the falling-out between him and the others proved to be irremediable, this end to a long partnership seeming particularly sad in the case of his one-time protégé Björn. There was to be no reconciliation – feelings of betrayal were too strong on both sides – although Björn continued attempting to renew contact into the 1990s, but Stig simply refused to take his calls. Stig, having long since come clean about his problems with alcohol – an open secret in the Swedish music scene, and in particular in the Polar offices, where his drink-fuelled rages were regular if unwelcome occurrences – continued to work in the music industry but with little success, his enthusiasm long gone, as was his seemingly instinctive connection to the record-buying public.

His one remaining contribution to the music scene was the establishment of the Polar Music Prize, an annual award financed by a fund extracted from the money that he got from the sale to Polygram of Sweden Music, including the royalties from the entire Abba catalogue. Long since divorced from, but then belatedly reconciled with, Gudrun, Stig died of a heart attack on Friday 12 September 1997, at the age of 66. As Pierre Perrone wrote in the obituary in the *Independent* on 15 September: 'In the music business, the pop entrepreneur is a much maligned creature, often seen as either a Svengali pulling the strings or a financial wizard investing money on his charges' behalf. Then there are the true visionaries who actually see something in artists and help them realise their vision, even beyond their wildest dreams. The impresario Stig Anderson was the perfect embodiment of all these tendencies.'

Stig and his former charges were at last reconciled after his death when all of them but Agnetha, who, because of an unspecified malady, was too ill to attend, turned up at his funeral. His recklessness, his relentless pursuit of financial gain, the very quality that had been his driving force, along with the shame of his illegitimacy, throughout his life, propelled him from his humble origins in the small town of Hova to modest success as a composer, lyricist and – his speciality – as a translator/transposer of proven foreign-language pop hits. But while he may have dreamt of making it as a musical star, his particular genius lay elsewhere, his entrepreneurial flair having been evident from early on.

He was a product of his country and of his time as much as, perhaps more than, his most celebrated clients, colleagues and collaborators. It is tempting to see Björn, Benny, Agnetha and Frida as part of a sudden, intense flowering of Swedish talent – witness Björn Borg and Ingemar Stenmark, the dominant force in slalom and one of the few superstars of that sport – perhaps in reaction to the long national tradition of favouring the team over the individual. Certainly Abba, as Borg did for Swedish tennis, opened up the field of pop music for the following generations, showing that Swedes could make it on the international stage, breaking ground for dozens of Swedish pop stars, including Europe, Ace of Base, Neneh Cherry, Eagle-Eye Cherry, the Cardigans, the Abbaesque Roxette, the even more Abbaesque A* Teens.

But Stig was also a reaction against the Sweden of the mid-20th century. He was infuriated at the levels of taxation he and Abba were forced to pay, or somehow avoid paying, was equally irked by the attitude of the Swedish press to his band once they had made it big internationally, bemoaned the smallness of his native country and insisted that he would one day leave to find pastures new. But he was very Swedish, not just in his drinking habits, but in his love for his native land. He may have been out of tune with the pervasive leftist politics of his time (he was some distance to the right of the members of Abba with their tacit soft-right stance) but he always felt he belonged in Sweden. Indeed, for all his loudly and frequently expressed problems with his country, unlike Frida, and later Björn, both of whose departures were at least partly precipitated by their disputes with their former manager, Stig never took the easy option of leaving Sweden as a tax exile.

Stig may have fallen out with the band, and his contribution to their celebrated and much-loved compositions may be hard to determine and perhaps of questionable significance, but without him, without his support, without his enthusiasm (and the expertise of his doomed partner Bengt Bernhag) for the then West Bay Singers, would Björn have pursued a career in music? Without his contagious enthusiasm and faith in the then largely unproven songwriting talent of Björn and Benny, would the pair have had the self-belief to write international hits, as he always assured them that they would? This is just to scratch the surface, and these are rhetorical questions. The story of Abba is all but unthinkable without Stig Anderson, the band's 'fifth member'.

CHAPTER FIFTEEN

'S.O.S.'

But you seem to be so sad
Like a fairy tale gone bad
From 'Strangers', on Frida's album *Something's Going On*

In the aftermath of *The Visitors*, Frida looked set for a successful solo career, and her plans began to take shape promisingly enough. As Agnetha would for each of her solo projects, so Frida carefully hand-picked a sympathetic celebrity producer for her first venture outside the band since *Frida ensam* in 1975. She turned to Phil Collins, Genesis's drummer and lead vocalist, who had himself only recently begun to emerge as a solo star with 1981's monster hit *Face Value*. Collins was happy to travel over to Polar Studios, so the sessions for the album began in February 1982, the week after the UK release of 'Head Over Heels'.

Something's Going On has a generic, slightly tiresome 1980s rock-chick feel, but there are several good moments. Chief among them is 'Threnody', an unlikely musical version of a Dorothy Parker poem. Its composer, Per Gessle, came up with a pretty melody that owes something to Led Zeppelin's 'Stairway to Heaven' and even more to the 1979 Euro-smash 'Driver's Seat' by Sniff 'n' the Tears, while also bearing a passing, and what must be a purely coincidental, similarity to Tears for Fears'

'Mad World', which was released around the same time as Frida's album. Collins's signature emphatic drumming, which earned him the nickname 'Thumper', is evident throughout *Something's Going On*, as are his distinctive vocals, which provide backing on most of the tracks.

The album is far from a disaster, but again – something that would be a persistent problem with Agnetha's solo work – there is too little of Frida's personality, her characterful singing, the 1980s rock-ballad style choking out this expressiveness. It would perhaps have benefited from more of Collins's compositions – his one contribution, the penultimate track, 'You Know What I Mean', at last allowing Frida to display her gift for dramatic interpretation – and could certainly have done without the final track, 'Here We'll Stay', a wretched duet between Frida and Collins.

Frida, generally more willing to become involved in promotional activities than Agnetha, was keen to promote the album fully and, on its release in September 1982, went on a mini-tour of Europe and North America, giving TV and press interviews everywhere she went. The tactic paid off, and *Something's Going On* survived the shocking cover illustration – a rather peculiar, undoubtedly eye-catching sketch of Frida apparently modelling herself on David Bowie circa *Aladdin Sane*, only with slightly less make-up – and became a hit across Europe. In fact its success was surpassed by the near-title single, a Joan Jett/Pat Benatar-style soft rock-out with an almost self-parodic Collins drum beat. 'I Know There's Something Going On' reached an impressive number 13 in the US, entered the top ten right across Europe, although UK buyers proved notably resistant to the track's subtlety-free charms, and occupied the top spot in Belgium, France and Switzerland.

By the time of her next solo project Frida had turned her back on Sweden, having settled temporarily in London, and it was apparent to all – except Stig Anderson – that Abba were unlikely ever to record together again. Her choice of producer suggested that she retained her superstar status but also that she was, perhaps ill-advisedly, determined to make it as a chick pomp-rocker. Steve Lillywhite was one of the superstar producers of the decade, creating a signature stadium-rock sound, helping to turn U2, Big Country, Simple Minds and, briefly, the Alarm into monster international rock bands.

Whatever Frida had expected from it, the collaboration was something of a disappointment, and, when released in September 1984, *Shine* fared rather poorly, selling well only in Belgium, Norway and Sweden. The title track, a frankly monot-onous, drum-machine-heavy rocker that could easily have been a Simple Minds album-filler, reached the top ten only in ever-loyal Belgium and Sweden. This failure and the dramatic change in direction that Frida's life was taking led her to take a near-total break from the music world for the next decade.

But when she returned she did so in some style, collaborating on a Swedish-language project with Anders Glenmark, the former protégé, along with his sister Karin, of Benny and Björn in the Gemini project (see Chapter 17). Glenmark, taking his inspiration from the key events of Frida's life, composed much of what was effectively Frida's somewhat portentous biographical concept album (check out the poetic floral imagery of the stand-out track, 'Även en blomma' ('Even a Flower'), with its talk of kisses from the rain and clouds reflecting Frida's passion for the environment), which would be released in the autumn of 1996 under the title *Djupa andetag* (Deep Breaths). Released only in Scandinavia, the album constituted a remarkable career renais-sance, being critically well received, selling solidly and quickly establishing itself, along with *Frida ensam*, as her fans' favourite of her solo projects.

Frida's private life was every bit as rich in colour and controversy, peaks and troughs, as her music career. A disproportionate number of famous pop musicians lost or were otherwise abandoned by one or both of their parents in childhood. Frida fits into a long line that includes John Lennon, Paul McCartney, Bono, Bob Geldof and countless others, the desire to perform apparently fulfilling a need for approval to fill the void created by the absent parent. The profound sense of insecurity and the depression from which Frida would suffer through much of her life with Abba were clearly at least partly the result of this lack of any parental influence in her life from the age of two.

As if her family background wasn't complex enough already, Frida also belongs to a more exclusive group of unfortunate celebrities stars whose perception of their own family life is turned upside down after they have attained a degree of fame and wealth. Like Cary Grant, who, having become an international movie star, was shocked to learn that his mother was not dead, as he'd been told, but in a psychiatric hospital in his native Bristol, and like Jack Nicholson, who learned in adulthood that the woman he had always thought of as his sister was his mother, and his mother his grandmother, Frida discovered at the height of Abba's success that the father who she thought had been dead for more than 30 years was alive and well and living in Germany.

The revelation came in August 1977, when the German magazine *Bravo* published a profile of the group in which it related the story behind Frida's birth and early life, a story not widely reported until that time. A young fan of the band, a girl called Andrea Buchinger, noted that the man in the story had the same name as her uncle, Alfred Haase, a pastry chef. A message got through to Haase's son, who asked his father if he had ever known a Synni Lyngstad. When it became clear that Alfred had known her, the son there and then let him know that he was the father of one of the world's most famous pop stars.

Shortly thereafter Haase put a call into Polar Music's offices in

Stockholm, and in time the message reached Frida that a man claiming to be Alfred Haase was trying to contact her. Frida naturally assumed the man to be a crank, but eventually took the call. Still sceptical, but her certainty wavering, she probed the man, who was able to furnish details about Synni and the small town of Ballangen, details that he couldn't have known without having at least visited the place and somehow gained some knowledge of her family. She was sufficiently intrigued, if not yet wholly convinced, to invite Alfred to stay with her and Benny in Stockholm.

So it was that Alfred Haase arrived at Stockholm airport one day in early September, where he was met by Benny, Frida feeling too nervous to confront him straight away. When Frida and Alfred did at last meet face to face they immediately embraced, and the physical resemblance, a photograph he had of himself from his army days and further revealing details banished all further doubt. She had found her father, and announced that she was thrilled.

But, as so often with Frida, the happiness was not to last. The relationship between Alfred Haase and Anni-Frid Lyngstad followed the pattern familiar in such reunions between family members reunited in bizarre circumstances after a long time, or indeed meeting for the first time. The early closeness and joy gave way to doubt, the shared genes all but irrelevant and certainly unable to compensate for the painful lack of any shared life experiences. In Frida's case this problem was greatly exacerbated by a lingering suspicion, confirmed by various family members, that her father had abandoned her mother, fully aware that she was pregnant at the time he left Norway to return to Germany in the winter of 1944.

Whatever her precise reasons for doing so, with their meetings and conversations anyway becoming ever more infrequent over time, five years after they first made contact Frida made it known that she no longer wished to be in regular touch with Alfred, a situation that persists to this day, more than 20 years later. Poignantly, the reluctance to maintain contact seems to be a one-sided thing. Interviewed in the Swedish national newspaper *Svenska Dagbladet* in 2001, Alfred Haase, then 82, said: 'I have every record that Abba released. Most of them I got from Anni-Frid. "Fernando" is my favourite song. I am proud of her and hope we will see each other again soon.'

In the aftermath of her divorce from Benny, Frida enjoyed a serious romance with a Swedish billionaire businessman by the name of Bertil 'Bobo' Hjert. Their relationship lasted a couple of years, and shortly after that ended she took up with Prince Heinrich Ruzzo Reuss von Plauen, a German aristocrat. Having by this stage moved from London to Switzerland, she soon moved in with Reuss at his mansion in Fribourg, near Berne. As Agnetha would later, Frida retreated from the music business after the relative disappointment of *Shine*, but while it was occasionally said that she had also become something of a recluse, this was clearly a case of mistaken identity. Whereas Agnetha led a genuinely solitary existence, Frida was always socially active and quickly found a cause that more than compensated for the lack of music in her life. She became a committed, impassioned environmentalist working for Det Naturliga Stega (The Natural Step), the organisation out of which grew the fund-raising body Artister för Miljö (Artists for the Environment). At a concert in 1992 for the latter, Frida once more performed live on stage, as part of an ensemble, and on her own sang a version of Julian Lennon's lachrymose hit 'Saltwater'.

Away from her environmental and other charitable work – she would later become involved in fund-raising activities on behalf of a charity for the handicapped – her private life had been transformed beyond recognition by her relationship with Reuss, who in 1992 became her third husband. The Swedish royal couple,

King Carl Gustav and his German-born wife Queen Silvia, for whom Frida and her bandmates had performed 'Dancing Queen' while garbed in frankly ridiculous period costumes back in 1976 in a special gala concert, were now her friends. Reuss, whose mother was from the southern province of Skåne, where he and his wife now had a second home, had been educated at the ultra-posh Värmland boarding school of Lundsberg, where he befriended the future king.

After her turbulent life and her bouts of depression, Frida at last seemed to have arrived at a level of contentment with a real-life prince; she was entitled to call herself Princess, although she rarely did. She was settled, was by all accounts very much in love and had, after years of problems with her two children, eventually been reconciled with them. She had discovered her calling, her cause, and had by the mid-1990s found a way to return to a style of music-making that satisfied her. Wealthy in her own right and married to an aristocrat, she seemed, in her early fifties, to be looking better, more beautiful than ever. The stress that had been evident in her face and the bags beneath her eyes, the ever-changing hairstyles that marked the final years of Abba and the time of her divorce from Benny, were now long gone. She seemed finally to have found peace and happiness – but it wasn't to last, fate delivering two cruel blows in quick succession. On 13 January 1998 her daughter, Lise-Lott, was killed in a car crash in the United States. Then, in October the following year, after a long battle with cancer, Reuss died.

It was a long and remarkable journey for Anni-Frid Lyngstad, who, although she narrowly escaped the miserable suffering and state-sanctioned persecution that was the lot of so many of her fellow Norwegian *tyskebarna*, experienced her own kind of misery as an orphan brought up by her brusque and frosty grand-mother. She repeated the pattern of emotionally reserved parenting with her own children, whom she felt compelled to leave with their father in pursuit of her career ambitions. Now a millionaire activist, semi-retired pop star, a widow, bereft of her one daughter, after a period of introversion she is active once more. If we bear in mind that she has recently branched out into opera, recording a duet from Offenbach's *Tales of Hoffmann*; that she has renewed her business interests by investing in *Mamma Mia!*; that a reunion, even if only with Agnetha, is still possible, if unlikely; and finally, that she has gone blonde, it seems there is still a lot to come from Princess Anni-Frid Lyngstad-Reuss.

CHAPTER SIXTEEN

'I Know Him So Well'

Sometimes it was awful. I felt as if [our fans] would get hold of me and I'd never get away again. It was as if I was going to be crushed. No one who has experienced facing a screaming, boiling, hysterical crowd could avoid feeling shivers up and down their spine. It's a thin line between ecstatic celebration and menace.
Agnetha Fältskog in *As I Am*

It's almost unfair that I've been given so much.
Agnetha Fältskog

If there were such a thing as a guidebook on how to be a reclusive celebrity then surely the golden rule would be, above all else, do not get emotionally involved with your number one fan. Agnetha Fältskog, rivalled only by J.D. Salinger for the mantle of most celebrated recluse since Garbo, failed to heed this unwritten rule.

It is the last week of March 2004, and in the London *Evening Standard* of the 25th, Abba, this long-defunct band, once dismissed as purveyors of cheap, throwaway music, merit two news stories even though it is more than 20 years since they last recorded together. In one, the newspaper's show-business correspondent reports on an item in the upcoming issue of *Q* magazine in which Abba appear at number 41 – alongside the likes of the Sex Pistols and the Wu-Tang Clan, as well as more natural stable-mates like the Beatles, the Beach Boys and the Bee Gees – in a chart of the 50 bands who have had the most profound effect on the world. An arbitrary judgement, perhaps, but indicative of the status of the band and yet another acknowledgement of their back catalogue of enduring pure pop gems.

A little further on comes a two-page spread headlined 'Can the Abba girl ever return?'. At this time it is just a couple of weeks before the members of the group are due to be reunited for one night only, and even then with absolutely no prospect of even a fleeting performance, at London's Prince Edward Theatre, to mark both the fifth anniversary of the first performance of the global phenomenon that was *Mamma Mia!* and the 30th anniversary of Abba's victory in the Eurovision Song Contest.

Every bit as significant as these two notable milestones was the news that had all the world, or at least the Abba- and Agnetha-fixated part of the world, panting in anticipation: that Agnetha was about to release a solo single, 'If I Thought You'd Ever Change Your Mind', followed by an album of cover versions, *My Colouring Book*, a full 17 years after her last studio album. She had planned, if not an extensive schedule of promotional duties, then at least a handful of public appearances and the odd interview. And yet, as this story revealed, none of this publicity was actually going to happen, and although the record releases would go ahead as planned, she would resolutely not be breaking her silence and would not be joining her former colleagues and her ex-husband in London.

The reason for this sudden change of heart and mind was not some fit of diva-like pique or Garboesque truculence, although it was, perversely, connected to her notorious, obsessive desire for solitude. It was, it began to be clear, all down to the reappearance in her life of a man who had long been Agnetha's own recurring nightmare in a long-running episode that had fuelled tabloid stories around the world for nearly a decade. This story constitutes one of the oddest, darkest chapters in the action-packed story of Abba.

Over the two decades and more since Abba had very quietly and unspectacularly ceased to be, Agnetha had increasingly withdrawn from the spotlight. The yearning for celebrity, to fulfil the dreams of performing in front of an audience that she had had since childhood, when she would sing in front of her bedroom mirror using her hairbrush as a mike, was more than sated by her eight years as the co-focus of the biggest pop band in the world. From the start her desire for recognition was balanced by a degree of shyness, of reticence. By the time Abba came into being, all the members were veterans of the Swedish, and to a limited degree, international music scene and life on the road. Agnetha, more than her bandmates, who for their own reasons were themselves generally not keen to embark on tours, increasingly disliked singing in public and both loathed and feared the flying that touring entailed.

She was also determined to give her children as normal a life as was possible, to be a good mother to them. To begin with she attempted to fuse her personal and professional lives, as for so long she had with Björn, and indulged herself with a couple of vanity projects, recording two albums, one with each of her children. She had also made tentative steps into the world of screen acting with her well-received co-starring role in the feature film *Raskenstam*. In 1982 she had collaborated with Tomas Ledin, one of Stig's protégés, who had sung backing vocals on Abba's 1979 tour, the result being the modest hit single 'Never Again', a pleasant enough but rather bland romantic ballad that sounds uncomfortably like a middling Eurovision contender. But all these projects were one-offs. If she was to continue working it would be as a solo singer, and so, following Frida's example, she set to work to find the appropriate collaborator. But, in another echo of Frida, the results, despite Agnetha's having apparently found the right man for the job, were rather disappointing in terms of quality if not of sales.

Agnetha was shrewd enough to see that the natural candidate was Barry Gibb, the Bee Gees being Abba's musical soulmates. Gibb's producing skills, most recently employed by Barbra Streisand, had attracted Agnetha's attention, but negotiations foundered on Agnetha's unwillingness to travel to Miami, where Gibb was accustomed to working – in the same Criteria studios where Björn and Benny had worked on a couple of tracks for *Voulez-Vous*. Instead she turned to Mike Chapman, one of the great figures of 1970s pop music.

Working at Mickey Most's RAK label, in conjunction with Nicky Chinn in a partnership that became known as Chinnichap, Chapman was responsible for writing and producing a succession of hits for a breed of soft-rock-inflected pop stars of the glam era and beyond, among them Sweet ('Ballroom Blitz'), Suzi Quatro ('Devil Gate Drive'), Mud ('Tiger Feet') and Smokie ('Living Next Door to Alice'). In the late seventies Chapman decamped to America, where he brought his pop sensibilities to the art-punk band Blondie, aiding their transformation into one of the best-selling pop groups in the world. Other notable clients were Frida's idol Pat Benatar, Toni Basil and Patti Smith.

Chapman was eager to work with Agnetha and, no less importantly, willing to travel to Stockholm to record at Polar Studios, Agnetha's home territory. However, they didn't quite gel as a partnership, the resultant album, *Wrap Your Arms Around Me*, being oddly reminiscent of Abba at their least inspired, and lacking consistency and cohesiveness. Agnetha and Michael B. Tretow, working as an engineer to provide some continuity, expressed frustration with Chapman's unfocused approach, which was in stark contrast to the ferocious work ethic prevalent in the Abba days.

The album may pale beside her work with Abba – what wouldn't? – but it was far from a disastrous experience and boasted several stand-out tracks. 'The Heat Is On' (a cover version of the Manfred Mann song 'On the Run', credited to Manfred Mann's Tony Ashton and Florrie Palmer, but featuring amended lyrics) has a lilting warmth in its recreation of the atmosphere and sounds of a Caribbean beach party, with Chapman bringing to it some of the glow and sheen of Blondie's 'The Tide Is High'. The song proved to be a big hit single in Sweden and in others of Abba's old European heartlands, and 'Can't Shake Loose', a Pat Benatar-like soft rocker with a relentless, thumping beat, was designed as a US radio-friendly number and promptly became a moderate hit there, peaking at number 29.

The outstanding number was the title track, Chapman's sole writing contribution to the album, its exquisite chorus at last exploiting Agnetha's particular talent for conveying a sense of sadness, of yearning, of broken-heart romanticism, all this making it one of the few recordings from Agnetha's solo career, at least until *My Colouring Book*, that bears comparison with her best work with Abba.

Wrap Your Arms Around Me sold more than respectably, notching up over a million sales, reaching number one in Sweden, Belgium and Norway, and generally faring solidly if unspectacularly across Europe, peaking at number 18 in the UK chart, but signally failing to break into the US top 100.

In the midst of a promotional tour to support the album, Agnetha's tour coach was involved in a crash, the force of which threw her out of a broken window. She narrowly avoided serious injury, the incident a rather cruel irony in the light of the fact that she favoured coach travel because of her profound fear of flying, a fear that had earlier been exacerbated by the near-crash of Abba's private jet during the 1979 tour of North America.

Although increasingly frustrated by the intrusion of the press into her private life – Agnetha had enjoyed several serious romances since her split from Björn but not as many as the news-papers speculated – and becoming ever more withdrawn from public life, jealously guarding her privacy as best she could, Agnetha was not yet ready to withdraw fully from the world of show business. For her follow-up album, she chose to work with Eric Stewart, of Wayne Fontana and the Mindbenders and 10cc fame, who would go on to successful collaborations with Paul McCartney among others. The fruit of their collaboration was *Eyes of a Woman*, a more cohesive record than its predecessor, well- if over-produced, but crucially lacking in any exceptional songs.

The title track itself is bouncy and catchy, and the opening number, 'One Way Love', a mildly pleasing Jeff Lynne composition. Although not the best, the most interesting song on the album is 'I Won't Be Leaving You', written by Stewart. This tepid romantic ballad (rather beautifully performed) is far from the usual standards of Stewart, at his best an outstanding song-writer, but one that aspires in its lyrics to the sad love stories that were Agnetha's speciality. The lines 'I want you, don't let me go slipping through your fingers again' are a conscious or uncon-scious nod to her glory days.

The lilting 'The Angels Cry' was written by Justin Hayward (the Moody Blues guitarist, who was a long-time admirer of Abba and was one of the celebrity guests, along with Joe Strummer, Ron Wood and assorted Blockheads, who attended the band's Wembley dates on their 1979 tour), while the anthemic 'I Won't Let You Go', co-written by Agnetha and Stewart and uncharacter-istically belted out by her, provided a reminder that she was a proficient if rarely inspired songwriter. 'I Won't Let You Go' was released as a single, and this track, along with the winsome, schmaltzy B-side, also co-written by Stewart, constitutes the last time to date that Agnetha committed any of her own compositions to record, although 'The Queen of Hearts', a much-improved version of 'När du tar mig i din famn', with English lyrics written by Ingela Forsman, was subsequently discovered and included on her 1998 greatest-hits collection, *That's Me*.

A worrying pattern of diminishing sales was beginning to become apparent in Agnetha's solo career, certainly by the time of 1987's *I Stand Alone*, which would prove to be her last recording until *My Colouring Book*.

Again her choice of producer was solidly AOR/MOR, in the shape of Peter Cetera. As lead singer with Chicago and in his solo work, Cetera specialised in the kind of soft-rock ballads that Agnetha seemed to favour, as proved by her 1986 single, the power ballad 'The Way You Are', in which she duetted with Ola Håkansson, a Swedish pop star turned music entrepreneur. (As managing director of Stockholm Records, a subsidiary of Universal Music, Håkansson oversees such current Swedish bands as the A* Teens and the Cardigans.) Cetera gave the album a very 1980s, fatally blanded-out sheen, Agnetha's expressiveness muted by the characterless production, the strongest track being 'I Wasn't the One', a duet with Cetera. *I Stand Alone* constituted a fairly uninspired collection of soft-rock ballads and, further hampered by Agnetha's reluctance to do all but the bare minimum of promotional work, was a relative commercial failure, shifting around 500,000 copies internationally.

The prospect of turning out an album full of anonymous ballads every other year was not enough to maintain Agnetha's interest in her career, and after the disappointment of *I Stand Alone*, she began to retreat, or at least attempted to retreat, from the public eye. Over the years that followed she refused all requests for interviews and, aside from taking long walks through Stockholm, a habit that she shared with Garbo (in New York), shunned appearing in public at all. Like Frida, Agnetha took solace in Eastern mysticism, specifically the teachings of Deepak

Chopra and Ayurvedic medicine, as well as developing an interest in astrology.

She was married for barely two years from 1989 to Tomas Sonnenfeld, a surgeon a few years older than her about whom she revealed nothing, although in 1997 she gave herself the chance to do so. Perversely – and there is a distinct pattern in Agnetha's life of repeatedly opening up and then withdrawing, her actions propelled by the apparent and irreconcilable forces within her both to seek attention and to be left alone – Agnetha is the only member of Abba thus far to have written her autobiography. In an attempt to counter the effects of misleading stories in the media and in particular Andrew Oldham, Tony Calder and Colin Irwin's 1995 book *Abba – The Name of the Game*, she revived a project mooted a decade earlier, and agreed to an 'as told to' memoir, published in 1997. *As I Am*, co-written by her friend, now former friend, Brita Åhman, turned out to be a fairly anodyne, wilfully unrevealing book, as suggested by the declaration/warning in her foreword: 'I don't intend, for example, to disclose anything about the men in my life.' She was as disappointing as her word, and although the book has become something of a favourite among hard-core Abba fans, it was dismissed by critics and sold rather poorly.

There was the brief suggestion of a reunion on record with Frida, but this has never materialised – at least not thus far. And then, after a 17-year gap, Agnetha returned to the recording studio, and following a delay caused when engineer and long-time Abba collaborator Michael B. Tretow suffered a stroke, April 2004 saw the release of *My Colouring Book*, a collection of cover versions. After all the disappointments of her 1980s solo ventures, the idea of selecting 1960s classics, standards and more obscure numbers that were suited to her voice was a simple but inspired one, even if some of the choices themselves were not. But at its best *My Colouring Book* is a glorious return showcasing

Agnetha's voice, a wondrous, pure instrument when on top form. 'If I Thought You'd Ever Change', selected as the first single from the record, and 'Sometimes When I'm Dreaming' prove that she was singing as well as ever and that, when given the right material, she had lost none of her talent to project vulnerability.

Sales of the album were promising and the reviews generally positive, if stopping a little short of ecstatic. Caroline Sullivan, in the *Guardian* on 6 April, was fairly typical, enthusing: 'The soaring sentimentality evokes Cilla Black and Sandie Shaw in their mini-skirted pomp, and I don't say that lightly.'

My Colouring Book represented a widely welcomed return of a much-loved pop star, but any sense of triumph had been negated even before the album made it to the shops. The pre-release announcement that Agnetha would not be supporting the record with any promotional activity was prompted by threats to her made by Gert van der Graaf, a Dutch man in his late thirties.

The stalker is one the darker symptoms of modern celebrity-obsessed culture. The grim, unstated joke is that you know you're not famous until you've got your first stalker, but Steven Spielberg, Michael J. Fox, Madonna, Björk, Jodie Foster, Meg Ryan, Jerry Lewis, Linda Ronstadt, Lenny Kravitz, Britney Spears, Axl Rose and the many other celebrity victims aren't laughing.

The truth about the bizarre relationship between Agnetha and her obsessive fan Gert van der Graaf first began to emerge just days before she celebrated her 50th birthday on 5 April 2000. Newspapers reported that she had sought police assistance and a restraining order against van der Graaf, who was said to have written her hundreds of letters and otherwise harassed her over the previous three years.

Van der Graaf had in fact been arrested on 31 March, and in police interviews admitted to his uncontrollable passion for the reclusive pop diva. He talked of having first and for ever fallen in love with Agnetha when – the tale is horribly reminiscent of the prologue to some 1980s stalker-slasher movie – as an eight-year-old boy in the Netherlands he sat transfixed by Abba's Eurovision contest-winning performance. He instantly became obsessed with her and promised himself that he would one day marry her.

By the time Agnetha made her reports to the police asking for protection from van der Graaf, she had been living for more than a decade in a mansion on the island of Ekerö, where she hoped she would be able to avoid the attentions of her more persistent fans. This tactic had been a signal failure. Van der Graaf had first appeared in Agnetha's life in 1997, after he finally resolved to act on the fantasies that he had harboured for nearly 25 years. He left his job as a fork-lift truck driver and headed to Ekerö, before long buying a shack close to where the object of his fantasies lived. It is here, as it emerged only several days into the police investigation in 2000 and then only after van der Graaf released a letter that he claimed to have received from Agnetha, that the story deviated from the established trajectory of the stalker-celebrity relationship.

Unbelievably, although this was apparently confirmed in the 2000 court case, van der Graaf's persistence paid off for him, and he eventually met Agnetha. The pair embarked on the unlikeliest of love affairs, which she, belatedly realising precisely how unbalanced her lover was, broke off, only and repeatedly to revive it over the next couple of years. The precise details of the relationship are impossible to ascertain, given that of the only two people who know the truth one refuses to speak and the other is scarcely reliable, although van der Graaf was quoted as saying: 'I thought we had the perfect relationship.'

What is certain is that Agnetha didn't agree and the court case ended with van der Graaf's being fined, deported and ordered not to return to Sweden for two years. But return he did, to experience a second arrest and a second deportation in June 2003, at which time he was quoted in the Swedish daily paper *Expressen* as commenting: 'I love her still. I will never forget.' It seems he was as good as his word and acted on it in April 2004, forcing Agnetha to cancel her plans to break her stubborn silence – plans that included a proposed interview on *Parkinson* – and to retreat once more into isolation.

Around the time of the publication of *As I Am*, Agnetha had complained of the appalling loneliness she felt in the aftermath of her parents' deaths. It says something about her state of mind at the time that rather than face solitude, she embarked on a relationship with a man who turned out to be disturbed.

For all her efforts to be taken seriously, to be appreciated for her music alone, Agnetha will be remembered, and by some revered, for many things: for having the most celebrated bottom of the seventies pop scene; for being the object of an intense and enduring fascination on the part of the press and her more passionate fans; for being a shy celebrity whose withdrawal from public life only increased the fascination she held for these inquisitive souls; for having an incomprehensibly intense relationship with a stalker; but also, and more than all this, for possessing a fragile, expressive, sometimes heartbreakingly beautiful voice, which, much aided by her enigmatic, sexy/shy persona and her very Nordic beauty, made her a vital component in one of the most beloved of all pop bands.

CHAPTER SEVENTEEN

'THE WINNER TAKES IT ALL'

There was no explicit suggestion that the group would do other than carry on writing and recording together – the divorces, new relationships and remarriages and the solo projects of both Frida and Agnetha notwithstanding – but, by the end of 1981, the writing was on the wall for Abba. Indeed their fate may well have been effectively sealed even before then, but at a dinner meeting in mid-December of that year, Björn, Benny and Stig sat down for a serious chat with producer Richard Vos and Tim Rice, the lyricist who, in collaboration with Andrew Lloyd Webber, was responsible for the hit musicals *Joseph and His Amazing Technicolor Dreamcoat* (in fact this, their first collaboration, wouldn't become a bona fide smash until its revival in the early 1990s), *Jesus Christ Superstar* and *Evita*. As had been evident for some time, Björn and Benny were eager to branch out into musical theatre, and saw in Rice the ideal collaborator.

Before the Andersson-Ulvaeus-Rice partnership produced its first fruits there was yet another compilation, the, in retrospect, disingenuously named collection *The Singles – The First Ten*

Years (like a eulogist at a memorial service paying tribute to the first three score and ten years of the deceased), released in November 1982. The image of the group on the sleeve of the gatefold double LP was wilfully un-pop, the four of them dressed as if on their way to the opera, looking very much what they were, four very wealthy, well-groomed individuals hurtling towards middle age. Abba fever, or at least its first wave, had come to an end, the ever gloomier run of recent final singles having alienated some of their record-buying fan base. *The Singles – The First Ten Years* sold pretty well, squeezing some solid sales out of a market that was by that stage saturated in Abba vinyl, although the collection did reach the top spot in the UK, for just one week, and, it goes almost without saying, in Belgium.

Many inferior collections would follow over the years, generally budget-priced and invariably boasting a handful of hits and a lot of filler, but the story would be very different a decade later when, in the aftermath of the CD revolution, the next official Abba-hits package was released on an unsuspecting world.

The story of *Chess* was loosely inspired by the celebrated clash for the World Chess Championship held in Reykjavik in 1972 between the wayward and subsequently seriously odd American chess genius Bobby Fischer and the Russian Boris Spassky. This was just one of the ideas that Rice suggested to Andersson and Ulvaeus, and it was the one in which they instantly saw the most promise. Much of 1983 would be spent by Benny and Björn bashing out the structure, the tunes and the words both alone and with Rice. The premise was to present a tale of love and politics set around the world of chess, where the game could be used as a metaphor for both the endless complexities of love and the battle between diametrically opposed political ideologies. One way and another, *Chess* would occupy Björn and Benny for much of the next five years.

The story opens in the small town of Merano, in the Italian Tyrol, in the days leading up to the World Chess Championship between the two unnamed opponents, the American and the Russian. Each has his representative, the brash, self-centred, just slightly mad American being assisted by Florence, a Hungarian-born, English-raised woman who, when not looking after her tiresome charge, is desperate to learn what happened to her father, who 'disappeared' at the time of the 1956 uprising, when she and her mother were forced to leave the country. The Russian's second is Molokov, a KGB agent who is both a manipulator on behalf of the state and himself a victim of state control.

The games begin, but soon descend into chaos. While engaged in efforts to have the match restarted, the Russian and Florence meet and fall in love almost at once. The Russian becomes World Champion and soon afterwards defects to the West, turning his back on Svetlana, his wife in Russia.

The second act begins a year later in Bangkok in the run-up to that year's championship, in which the Russian, now aided by his lover Florence, will take on a younger Russian, a near-autistic chess prodigy. The American is also in town, in order, it quickly emerges, to derail the Russian's attempts to retain his crown. He is desperate to revive his partnership with Florence and revive his own career, and with this in mind he has arranged for Svetlana to be flown over from Russia.

He attempts to blackmail the Russian to throw the match, promising him that if he does then he, the American, will keep from Florence the information that he has uncovered concerning her father: that, far from being the hero that she always believed him to be, he was a traitor responsible for many deaths. The Russian rejects the deal and goes on to win the game with single-minded ruthlessness, in the process ending any chance of reconciliation with Svetlana and quite possibly destroying his relationship with Florence, who has herself rejected the offer of working again for the American, the full extent of whose moral bankruptcy is revealed at the musical's climax.

The appeal of the story to all three composers is plain to see. The particular elements of *Chess*, the shifting moods and locations, the themes of the fragility of romantic relationships, the political background, allowed them to explore further and to exploit favourite themes, ideas and working practices. Björn and Benny were always drawn to pastiche of diverse musical styles, and *Chess* gave them the opportunity to evoke through music the Tyrol and Thailand, Eastern Europeans and Americans, allowing them to flex their compositional muscles and exploit their eclectic musical tastes. Rice had, in *Evita*, previously tackled political themes, the contrast between open and closed societies, although that musical was really more about the nature of what was effectively a show-business style of charisma than it was an examination of the nuances of South American political machinations. There was also just a hint of the strange circumstances of Frida's conception and early life in the character of Florence. But most of all, the story's romantic complications, chiefly the theme of abandonment and the ultimate impossibility, or at least unlikeliness, of enduring love, allowed Björn and Benny to continue to mine the rich seam that had been at the heart of so much of Abba's finest work.

But, as Björn was eventually forced to admit, there was something essentially flawed about *Chess* from the start. It looks like a musical and sounds like a musical – it is at its best highly proficient, full of ideas, some wonderful moments and several fine tunes – but, and this was so often a problem as well as a virtue of Abba's recordings, it lacks cohesion. The game of chess is indeed an endlessly flexible metaphorical device, but there is something fatally unresolved about the plot. The failure of the story to hold our interest is connected to the weakness of some of the lyrics. However underrated Rice may at times be, here he was carried, his lyrical gaucherie disguised, by Andrew Lloyd Webber's gift, one in many ways similar to Benny's, for the felicitous melody and the shrewd musical borrowing or stylistic pastiche. Rice is at best – and some of his collaborative efforts have been undeniably pleasing – a modestly talented lyricist who has a strong tendency to be flippant and a fondness for absurd verbal contrivances, but is rather weaker when it comes to more substantial material. Aside from the fact that the story lacks, however deliberately, any satisfactory romantic conclusion, the show is hamstrung by the rather simplistic politics of the central Cold War theme.

Although they are far from the only stand-out songs in the show – 'Where I Want to Be' and 'Nobody's Side', for instance, are also both rather fine – it is telling that the two strongest songs are unquestionably 'One Night in Bangkok' and 'I Know Him So Well', which became the two hit singles from the 1984 studio recording of the show. They are two of the types of song of which Benny and Björn were most fond during their Abba days, and which had provided them with many of their greatest successes. 'One Night in Bangkok', which gave Murray Head (in the role of the American) an international hit (topping the chart in Australia, Belgium, Canada, West Germany, South Africa and Switzerland, and peaking at number three in the US), was an inspired rehash of the old, dirty, sexy, atmospheric urban numbers that Björn would often sing himself, among them 'Summer Night City', 'Does Your Mother Know' and 'Gimme! Gimme! Gimme!'. 'I Know Him So Well', which became a best-seller for Elaine Paige (Florence) and Barbara Dickson (Svetlana) in the UK, staying at number one for four weeks in early 1985, could so easily have been an Abba record, indeed was elaborated from an idea that Björn and Benny had been working on for the never-recorded follow-up to *The Visitors*.

These two recordings were lifted from the 1984 *Chess* album, which Benny and Björn insisted on recording as an elaborate and, as it transpired, best-selling method of testing the show's structure before exposing it to the rigours of a stage production. Aside from the performances of Head, Dickson and Paige, who was at the time engaged in a long-term, and at that point still secret, affair with Rice, the cast of the recording was filled out by Swedish singer Tommy Körberg as the Russian, Björn Skifs, an old friend and sometime collaborator of Björn and Benny, as the Arbiter of the first match, and Dennis Quilley as Molokov. Largely recorded in Polar Studios under the control of the faithful and ever-creative Michael B. Tretow, *Chess* went on to sell more than two million copies around the world, providing a promising – as it turned out, misleadingly so – launchpad for *Chess* as a stage musical.

The problems that had been there from the start remained through the troubled pre-production of the London stage version. In fact there would be one further showcase for *Chess* before its official opening as a stage musical. This took the form of an international stage tour of the show, performed, shortly before the release of the album, at London's Barbican Centre, then in Paris, Amsterdam, Hamburg and Stockholm. What looked like a further costly extravagance – this mini-tour was expected to make a loss of over £400,000 – was in fact underwritten by Saab, who used the show to promote a new model. The auspices of the opening at the Barbican Centre were not so promising. Anthony Masters, reviewing it in *The Times*, sarcastically gave the Americans the names of Boris and Bobby, and talked of the 'sub-Lloyd Webber' quality of some of the compositions. Condescending if not outright disparaging, Masters did capture one of the show's enduring problems, namely its lack of narrative dynamism: 'One inbuilt flaw of the show is that the action is so negative: affairs that come to nothing, chess matches abandoned, Molokov threatening, Bobby snarling.'

After much tinkering, a belated change of directors – Trevor

Nunn taking over the reins from the ailing, sadly terminally ill Michael Bennett – and a serious health scare for Tommy Körberg, *Chess* finally opened in mid-May 1986 at the Prince Edward Theatre, which would, a little over a decade later, provide a long-term home for *Mamma Mia!* Some of the changes that had been wrought had clearly had a beneficial effect on the production, and although the show was not universally praised, it garnered some appreciative notices. *The Times*, for instance, had softened its position, Irving Wardle generously commenting: '*Chess* turns out to be a fine piece of work that shows the dinosaur mega-musical evolving into an intelligent form of life.' In the *Daily Mail*, Jack Tinker, while he had certain reservations, praised the show for the 'strength of its ambition'.

For all the problems of its genesis, *Chess* was a long-running show, staying at the Prince Edward Theatre for nearly three years, eventually recouping its substantial costs and turning a small profit. Sadly, this wasn't the case for the Broadway production, which was savaged by the notoriously powerful *New York Times* theatre critic Frank Rich. The show opened in New York on 28 April 1988 but closed after just 68 performances, Ulvaeus, Andersson and Rice all suffering a considerable loss on their seven-figure investment in the production. This wasn't the end of the *Chess* story, though, for the concert version became a regular on the international tour circuit, and the Swedish-language production, which opened in Stockholm in February 2002, ran for nearly a year and a half and was seen by a little under half a million people, leading to the renewal of plans to revise the show and try it out once more in the West End of London and on Broadway.

Back in the 1980s *Chess* hadn't exhausted the surplus of Abba material that Björn and Benny were left with after the demise of the band. Some of this they used as the starting point for their collaboration with Gemini, a duet consisting of the brother and sister vocalists Anders and Karin Glenmark, both of whom had known and worked with the Andersson-Ulvaeus partnership before, most recently in different capacities in the various incarnations of *Chess*. The Gemini project saw Benny and Björn resume the roles that they had briefly adopted in the early 1970s as Polar's in-house composers and producers. The result was two albums, *Gemini* and *Geminism*, which were minor successes in Sweden but failed to excite interest elsewhere. The two songwriters' collaboration in the early 1990s with the young pop singer Josefin Nilsson was even less successful.

The soullessness of the work with Gemini and Nilsson stands in stark contrast to Benny's next project, the album *Klinga mina klockor* (*Ring My Bells*), a treat well worth tracking down for anyone interested in European folk-music traditions in general and the roots of Benny's enduring love for his national folk music in particular. For fans of Abba it also reveals the musical provenance of Benny's instrumental interludes on Abba's album, in particular the much-covered title track from *Arrival*. 'Arrival' had the working title 'Ode to Dalecarlia', and Benny's main musical collaborators on *Klinga mina klockor* are the Orsa Spelmän (Orsa Folk Musicians), Orsa being one of the famous four centres dotted around Lake Siljan (along with Mora, Rättvik and Leksand) of folk music and folk culture generally in the province of Dalarna, known to Anglophones as Dalecarlia. Benny has professed that he is never so happy as when he is making music and was never happier making music than with the Orsa Spelmän. The joy of the experience comes through in every track, several co-written with Björn (Björn Skifs, Tommy Körberg and Karin Glenmark also contribute), the album building to the wonderful, extended, lush and romantic finale provided by the title song.

What could have seemed an extravagant indulgence actually marked the beginning of what would become a series of recordings, together constituting perhaps the most accomplished and satisfying of all the former bandmates' post-Abba projects, and at least rivalling *Kristina från Duvemåla*, more of which later. If not a vanity project, *Klinga mina klockor* was a labour of love, a relatively modest undertaking begun with no hint of commercialism. It was embraced by a considerable portion of the Swedish public and went on to sell more than 150,000 copies, an impressive achievement for a collection of folk songs.

Benny's follow-up, *November 1989*, did equally well, cementing his reputation as a guardian of Sweden's musical traditions, but the success of the first two records was surpassed in 2001 by *Benny Anderssons Orkester*, which became a number-one hit. Although, as Benny makes clear in his sleeve note, this album was effectively recorded live, it is perhaps even more accomplished, more lush than the earlier records, Björn's contribution restricted to the lyrics on two songs, 'Vår sista dans' ('Our Last Dance') and 'Lätt som en sommarfjäril' ('Light as a Summer Butterfly'). Again, it's wonderful stuff, revealing the links between Swedish folk music and that of central and even Southern Europe. Nevertheless, this recommendation comes with the warning that these records may cause offence to those with an aversion to oompah music.

But it wasn't just these albums that marked a dramatic change in Andersson's fortunes, financially and in terms of his and Abba's standing around the world. Of the four former Abba members, Andersson, as the group's musical motor and creative heart – although Ulvaeus's role must never be underestimated – has expressed the greatest frustration with the fact that he and his former bandmates are frozen in time, in many people's minds exclusively associated with a group that ceased to exist nearly a quarter of a century ago. He and Björn were both bewildered by their anointment as gay icons and even more by the rash of Abba tribute bands such as Bjorn Again. Indeed Benny regarded this latter phenomenon as symptomatic of a general torpor in the world of pop music. But, despite this apparently curmudgeonly verdict, he welcomed the effect on his already healthy fiscal situation.

Aside from the countless, generally shoddy compilations, the only remotely fresh Abba product in the 1980s was the 1986 release *Abba Live*, a CD compilation of live performances (a condensed version of their greatest hits: 'Dancing Queen', 'Take a Chance on Me', 'Chiquitita', 'Fernando', 'Super Trouper', 'Waterloo', 'Money, Money, Money', etc.) culled from the 1977 Australian tour, the 1979 Wembley shows and the band's disappointing farewell to live performance, the 1981 TV special *Dick Cavett Meets Abba*. Michael B. Tretow had worked his magic on the recordings, getting rid of the odd duff notes and generally cleaning them up, thus making them closer to the Abba recognisable from their meticulous studio work. This work, of course, shows up the problem with the record: that Abba live, however thrilling the idea of seeing a beloved group performing in the flesh, were at one remove from the real Abba magic, and a recording of this, however digitally enhanced and polished, is a further remove from the ideal Abba, making *Abba Live* the only non-essential official Abba record, a fact reflected in disappointing sales.

The Abba revival itself, their critical and commercial rehabilitation, which had been, if not quite an underground movement, then certainly a slow, subtle and gradual process – Erasure's success with *Abbaesque* and Bjorn Again being its most obvious manifestations up to early 1990s – exploded in the autumn of 1992 with the release of *Abba Gold*. Polygram, having acquired Abba's back catalogue in a deal in 1989, set to work preparing a grand collection of their greatest recordings. First they had to wait until the rights in various international territories reverted to them, and then, when the temptation might have been to go for the ironic, kitsch angle with an image of the band in their 1970s pomp, they came up instead with the classy gold-and-black CD, one that has been much imitated in other subsequent 'best of' collections. The collection pointed to, and to some extent helped reinforce, the impression that Abba had been purveyors of some of the most beautifully written, crafted and performed popular music of the 20th century.

The marketing angle, helped by what was on the actual CD itself, paid off gloriously. Around the world people were rediscovering their love for the band, their music and the association with a simpler time, while another generation was discovering them for the first time. It became officially OK to like Abba, almost *de rigueur* for every CD collection to include a copy of *Abba Gold*. The album was a best-seller around the world, topping the album charts in many countries, and even where it didn't, selling consistently, indeed continuing to sell to this day. In America, while it never came close to the number-one spot, it nevertheless stayed in the charts for a couple of years, notching up sales of more than three million copies, to become by some distance the most successful Abba record there. It is in fact the most successful Abba album of them all, the most recent cumulative international figures to be released by Universal Music's Stockholm office putting sales at an extraordinary 26 million copies.

Inevitably the success of the original led to a sequel, 1993's *More Abba Gold*, which included the singles not featured on the first album (among them 'The Day Before You Came', 'Summer Night City' and 'Head Over Heels') and a selection of the band's finest B-sides and album tracks, such as 'Lovelight' and 'Our Last Summer'. In lieu of *Even More Abba Gold*, 1994 saw the release of the four-CD box set *Thank You for the Music*, a must for all Abba completists, and the closest thing thus far to a definitive compilation, featuring all the singles, assorted B-sides and a smattering of obscurities and foreign-language medleys. But, best of all, it contains 'Abba Undeleted', in which Michael B. Tretow knits together into one cohesive 20-odd-minute epic track some unfinished Abba recordings, among them alternative and early versions of well-known hits, including 'Fernando', 'Rock Me', 'Take a Chance on Me' and 'Summer Night City'. This light-hearted assortment also belies the notion that this group of perfectionists were a dour, humourless bunch in the studio.

Every year brings more and more evidence of the extent of the continuing Abba revival. In 2001 alone all eight Abba albums were re-released on CD, each boasting sleeve notes from Abba expert Carl Magnus Palm and bonus tracks. In that same year came *Abba Live*, the DVD version of the documentary *The Winner Takes It All – The Abba Story* and then *The Definitive Collection*, a double CD featuring all the official singles. Then 2002 saw the release of the DVD version of *The Definitive Collection*: a compilation of all the Abba videos that Lasse Hallström directed, plus the clip of 'Chiquitita' from the Swiss TV special and the final two videos for 'The Day Before You Came' and 'Under Attack', these last two the slick work of director Kjell Sundvall and cameraman Kjell-Åke Andersson. Among the bonuses on this release was the opportunity to see Abba decked out in their ridiculous outfits performing 'Dancing Queen' for the Swedish King and Queen. In 2004 *Abba In Concert*, a film of the band's 1979 tour of Europe, here specifically their Wembley Arena shows, and of the US, was released on DVD.

As if to prove that in the midst of this orgy of money-spinning nostalgia Benny Andersson and Björn Ulvaeus were still an active, creative musical force, there came their belated follow-up to the mixed success of *Chess*. *Kristina från Duvemåla* marked a substantial improvement on their previous musical and was an altogether happier experience, not least in that from the outset they were working with proven material, indeed a major work of literature, Vilhelm Moberg's quartet of novels collectively entitled *The Emigrants*.

The musical tells the tragic story of Kristina, her family and her fellow emigrants, who head to Minnesota to escape from the grinding poverty of rural Sweden in the mid-nineteenth century. As they arrive in America they are all trapped between the uncertainty of the future in a new country whose language and culture are alien to them and a nostalgia for the past, however miserable it was, a longing for a romanticised homeland. After many small tragedies and triumphs, the new settlement that the immigrants have made for themselves is abandoned by everyone but Kristina, who has ignored warnings that should she ever get pregnant again she will certainly die, and her husband Karl-Oscar. With Karl-Oscar at her side, Kristina dies.

Björn and Benny worked patiently at *Kristina från Duvemåla* for five years, the finished musical receiving its première at Malmö's Musikteater on 7 October 1995. It was warmly received by critics and public alike, the same production moving between Malmö and Gothenburg before enjoying a final run in Stockholm and eventually coming off in 1999, by which time it had been seen by around one million people. It is, without doubt, as it should be, the most assured and mature creation from the prolific Andersson-Ulvaeus team, although Björn is not above making a 'fart' joke in the jocular bilingual 'Tänk att man som han kan finnas' ('Can You Believe That a Man Like That Could Exist'), the Swedish word '*fart*' meaning a very innocuous speed or rate or way. The pop-musical style of *Chess* having been left behind, *Kristina från Duvemåla*, with its nods to a broad spectrum of classical music, stage musicals and the folk traditions in which Björn and Benny had been involved all their lives and in which Benny was increasingly immersing himself, is a

249

triumphant achievement, one that Björn has long promised to translate into English for a proposed run in the West End and on Broadway.

As *Kristina* was coming towards the end of its long, successful Swedish run, final preparations were being made for a further stage musical, *Mamma Mia!*, the staggering success of which would, in terms of simple commercial gain, surpass everything that Abba had achieved in their first flush of fame and their dramatic afterlife. The huge success of the original London production proved to be just the start of a global phenomenon. A *Sunday Times* magazine profile of producer Judy Craymer pointed out that at the time of the article, the end of February 2004, there were ten productions of the musical around the world, with a further six planned to open over the following 18 months. The ones that were already running were generating for the producer's company, Littlestar, weekly sales of $7.5 million.

Although there is apparently nothing new in the offing, Björn and Benny remain a creative force, with the English-language version of *Kristina från Duvemåla* a prospect to relish, as is whatever they choose to do afterwards. There have been some words of disappointment among commentators and interviewers, including suggestions that the pair's enduring working relationship, in which each has previously characterised the other as a best friend-cum-brother, seems to extend less and less into their private lives. Whether or not this is true, what is remarkable is that they have remained such a loyal, reliable and prolific partnership since writing their first song together, 'Isn't It Easy to Say', nearly 40 years ago, their professional relationship already having lasted longer than those of Rodgers and Hart, Lennon and McCartney and Morrissey and Marr combined.

So 2004 represented something of a high point for the members of Abba. They had all experienced at least their fair share of tragedies and heartbreak. Frida had lived a life straight out of an airport novel, losing her father, until an unsatisfactory reunion in mid-life, before she was even born, and her mother shortly thereafter. She was estranged from her children for many years, and when they were finally reconciled, she lost her daughter tragically young to a car crash, her beloved aristocratic husband to cancer the following year. Agnetha, in the midst of her notorious withdrawal from public life, had ended up having a relationship with a deranged fan. There were the famous marriages and the even more famous divorces.

Yet, from all this chaos, these four plutocratic grandparents have seen not just the restoration of their reputation but indeed its elevation to a level far beyond what it was while they were still a working band. Besides this, all four have enjoyed a second flowering of their professional lives, each having found, after the disappointments of their careers in the 1980s, personally satisfying ways of expressing themselves through their work. It has raised eyebrows, in fact caused widespread disbelief, that they have rejected the offer of a rumoured $1 billion for a year-long reunion tour – and Björn has never contested this figure when confronted with it in interviews, as he so often has been in recent years. The four of them did at least take the proposal seriously before collectively deciding that they could only do their reputation harm by accepting the offer.

It is just the latest instance of how the Abba story has become almost inextricably linked with the money that they make, have made, could make, are alleged to make, and what they do with it. Björn, who lamented in his Abba days that they had responded so candidly to the financial questions with which they were repeatedly confronted, has joked that they may reconsider if the offer were raised to a cool $2 billion, but it was just that, a joke. There really is no incentive for the band to reform, however insane the money they are promised. They are already very wealthy and getting wealthier by the day. The music that they continue to make, but, far more than this, the music that they made together in the past, still finds an audience all around the world. It delights and, yes, moves people. They have nothing left to prove.

FINALE

A rather dismal March evening on Hackney's Mare Street, an east London thoroughfare that hardly glistens at the best of times. An expectant crowd has gathered outside the Hackney Empire, the recently lovingly, painstakingly refurbished theatre. It is an odd mixture of people, many middle-aged and elderly couples, some young hipsters, a scattering of gay men, several large and mildly raucous hen parties, a few families. Everyone has been drawn by the lure of an evening of unashamed, undiluted kitsch and nostalgia, a show that would not be out of place on the stage of a cruise ship. The evening opens with a tribute to the golden age of Motown, before segueing smoothly into a Bee Gees tribute band who manage to sound uncannily like the group with which Abba are destined for ever to be associated.

After that it's a short selection from *Grease* before the main attraction, Abba Magic, one of dozens of acts making a decent living performing an extended sound-alike, if notably not – for all the carefully replicated costumes – look-alike recreation of some of Abba's greatest moments. This is a show built around audience participation and, as happens at the climax of every performance of *Mamma Mia!*, wherever it is playing round the world, the whole audience, at least all those still capable of rising from their seats, are on their feet dancing and singing along throughout the show. Abba Magic are not even a great tribute act, but they are efficient enough in their pastiche to bring back, for those among the audience old enough to remember, the spirit of the supposed golden days of the mid-1970s, and presumably to inspire in the younger ones fond recollections of the halcyon days of the early 2000s when the A* Teens were still the Abba Teens.

So, as this very mixed crowd makes its way back out on to drizzly, dreary Mare Street, there is an unmistakable, shared sense of exuberance that is almost comically at odds with the surroundings. Once again Abba's music has overcome its alleged shallowness and ephemerality, and has worked its magic, bringing an odd, deceptively simple kind of happiness to an audience who have been transported by songs of boomerangs, birds and 19th-century heroes, of love, marriage and divorce, of isolation and despair, but also of fragile, defiant hope.

DISCOGRAPHY

UK singles

Ring Ring/Merry-Go-Round 1973 [charted 1974]

Waterloo/Watch Out 1974

So Long/I've Been Waiting for You 1974

I Do, I Do, I Do, I Do, I Do/Rock Me 1975

S.O.S./Man in the Middle 1975

Mamma Mia/Intermezzo No. 1 1975

Fernando/Hey, Hey Helen 1976

Dancing Queen/That's Me 1976

Money, Money, Money/Crazy World 1976

Knowing Me, Knowing You/Happy Hawaii 1977

The Name of the Game/I Wonder (Departure) 1977

Take a Chance On Me/I'm a Marionette 1977

Summer Night City/Medley (Pick a Bale of Cotton, Old Smokey, Midnight Special) 1978

Chiquitita/Lovelight 1979

Does Your Mother Know/Kisses of Fire 1979

Angeleyes/Voulez-Vous 1979

Gimme! Gimme! Gimme! (A Man After Midnight)/The King Has Lost His Crown 1979

I Have a Dream/Take a Chance On Me [live] 1979

The Winner Takes It All/Elaine 1980

Super Trouper/The Piper 1980

Lay All Your Love On Me/On and On and On [12-inch] 1981

One of Us/Should I Laugh or Cry 1981
Head Over Heels/The Visitors 1982
The Day Before You Came/Cassandra 1982
Under Attack/You Owe Me One 1982
Thank You for the Music [live]/Our Last Summer [live] 1983

Albums

[Digitally remastered versions of the nine studio albums – *Abba*, *Abba Live*, *The Visitors*, *Super Trouper*, *Voulez-Vous*, *Abba – The Album*, *Arrival*, *Waterloo* and *Ring Ring* – were released in 2001.]

Ring Ring 1973

Ring Ring; Another Town, Another Train; Disillusion; People Need Love; I Saw It in the Mirror; Nina, Pretty Ballerina; Love Isn't Easy (But It Sure Is Hard Enough); Me and Bobby and Bobby's Brother; He Is Your Brother; She's My Kind of Girl; I Am Just a Girl; Rock 'n' Roll Band. *Bonus tracks:* Merry-Go-Round; Santa Rosa; Ring Ring [in Swedish].

Waterloo 1974

Waterloo; Sitting in the Palmtree; King Kong Song; Hasta Mañana; My Mama Said; Dance (While the Music Still Goes On); Honey Honey; Watch Out; What About Livingstone; Gonna Sing You My Lovesong; Suzy-Hang-Around. *Bonus Tracks:* Ring Ring [US remix]; Waterloo [in Swedish]; Honey Honey [in Swedish].

Abba 1975

Mamma Mia; Hey, Hey Helen; Tropical Loveland; S.O.S.; Man in the Middle; Bang-a-Boomerang; I Do, I Do, I Do, I Do, I Do; Rock Me; Intermezzo No. 1; I've Been Waiting for You; So Long. *Bonus tracks:* Medley (Pick a Bale of Cotton, On Top of Old Smokey, Midnight Special).

Greatest Hits 1975 [not reissued as a CD; Fernando was added in later pressings]

S.O.S.; He Is Your Brother; Ring Ring; Hasta Mañana; Nina, Pretty Ballerina; Honey Honey; So Long; I Do, I Do, I Do, I Do, I Do; People Need Love; Bang-a-Boomerang; Another Town, Another Train; Mamma Mia; Dance (While the Music Still Goes On); Waterloo.

Arrival 1976

When I Kissed the Teacher; Dancing Queen; My Love, My Life; Dum Dum Diddle; Knowing Me, Knowing You; Money, Money, Money; That's Me; Why Did It Have to Be Me; Tiger; Arrival. *Bonus tracks:* Fernando; Happy Hawaii.

Abba – The Album 1977

Eagle; Take a Chance On Me; One Man, One Woman; The Name of the Game; Move On; Hole in Your Soul; The Girl with the Golden Hair; 3 Scenes from a Mini Musical: Thank You for the Music; I Wonder (Departure); I'm a Marionette. *Bonus track:* Thank You for the Music [Doris Day version].

Voulez-Vous 1979

As Good as New; Voulez-Vous; I Have a Dream; Angeleyes; The King Has Lost His Crown; Does Your Mother Know; If It Wasn't for the Night; Chiquitita; Lovers (Live a Little Longer); Kisses of Fire. *Bonus tracks:* Summer Night City; Lovelight; Gimme! Gimme! Gimme! (A Man After Midnight).

Greatest Hits Volume 2 1979 [reissued as a CD in 1983]

Gimme! Gimme! Gimme! (A Man After Midnight); Knowing Me, Knowing You; Take a Chance On Me; Money, Money, Money; Rock Me; Eagle; Angeleyes; Dancing Queen; Does Your Mother Know; Chiquitita; Summer Night City; I Wonder (Departure); The Name of the Game; Thank You for the Music.

Super Trouper 1980

Super Trouper; The Winner Takes It All; On and On and On; Andante, Andante; Me and I; Happy New Year; Our Last Summer; The Piper; Lay All Your Love On Me; The Way Old Friends Do. *Bonus tracks:* Elaine; Put On Your White Sombrero.

The Visitors 1981

The Visitors; Head Over Heels; When All Is Said and Done; Soldiers; I Let the Music Speak; One of Us; Two for the Price of One; Slipping Through My Fingers; Like an Angel Passing Through My Room. *Bonus tracks:* Should I Laugh or Cry; The Day Before You Came; Cassandra; Under Attack.

The Singles – The First Ten Years 1982 [reissued as a CD in 1983]

Ring Ring; Waterloo; So Long; I Do, I Do, I Do, I Do, I Do; S.O.S.; Mamma Mia; Fernando; Dancing Queen; Money, Money, Money; Knowing Me, Knowing You; The Name of the Game; Take a Chance On Me; Summer Night City; Chiquitita; Does Your Mother Know; Voulez-Vous; Gimme! Gimme! Gimme! (A Man After Midnight); I Have a Dream; The Winner Takes It All; Super Trouper; One of Us; The Day Before You Came; Under Attack.

Abba Live 1986

Dancing Queen; Take a Chance On Me; I Have a Dream; Does Your Mother Know; Chiquitita; Thank You for the Music; Two for the Price of One; Fernando; Gimme! Gimme! Gimme! (A Man After Midnight); Super Trouper; Waterloo; Money, Money, Money; The Name of the Game/Eagle; On and On and On.

Abba Gold 1992

Dancing Queen; Knowing Me, Knowing You; Take a Chance On Me; Mamma Mia; Lay All Your Love On Me; Super Trouper; I Have a Dream; The Winner Takes It All; Money, Money, Money; S.O.S.; Chiquitita; Fernando; Voulez-Vous; Gimme! Gimme! Gimme! (A Man After Midnight); Does Your Mother Know; One of Us; The Name of the Game; Thank You for the Music; Waterloo.

More Abba Gold 1993

Summer Night City; Angeleyes; The Day Before You Came; Eagle; I Do, I Do, I Do, I Do, I Do; So Long; Honey Honey; The Visitors; Our Last Summer; On and On and On; Ring Ring; I Wonder (Departure); Lovelight; Head Over Heels; When I Kissed the Teacher; I Am the City; Cassandra; Under Attack; When All Is Said and Done; The Way Old Friends Do.

Thank You for the Music 1994

Disc 1: People Need Love; Another Town, Another Train; He Is Your Brother; Love Isn't Easy (But It Sure Is Hard Enough); Ring Ring; Waterloo; Hasta Mañana; Honey Honey; Dance (While the Music Still Goes On); So Long; I've Been Waiting for You; I Do, I Do, I Do, I Do, I Do; S.O.S.; Mamma Mia; Fernando; Dancing Queen; That's Me; When I Kissed the Teacher; Money, Money, Money; Crazy World; My Love, My Life.

Disc 2: Knowing Me, Knowing You; Happy Hawaii; The Name of the Game; I Wonder (Departure) [live version]; Eagle; Take a Chance On Me; Thank You for the Music; Summer Night City; Chiquitita; Lovelight; Does Your Mother Know; Voulez-Vous; Angeleyes; Gimme! Gimme! Gimme! (A Man After Midnight); I Have a Dream.

Disc 3: The Winner Takes It All; Elaine; Super Trouper; Lay All Your Love On Me; On and On and On; Our Last Summer; The Way Old Friends Do; The Visitors; One of Us; Should I Laugh or Cry; Head Over Heels; When All Is Said and Done; Like an Angel Passing Through My Room; The Day Before You Came; Cassandra; Under Attack.

Disc 4: Put On Your White Sombrero; Dream World; Thank You for the Music; Hej gamle man; Merry-Go-Round; Santa Rosa; She's My Kind of Girl; Medley (Pick a Bale of Cotton, On Top of Old Smokey, Midnight Special); You Owe Me One; Slipping Through My Fingers/Me and I; Abba Undeleted; Waterloo [French/Swedish]; Ring Ring [Swedish/Spanish/German]; Honey Honey [in Swedish].

259

ABBA The Definitive Collection 2001

People Need Love; He Is Your Brother; Ring Ring; Love Isn't Easy (But It Sure Is Hard Enough); Waterloo; Honey Honey; So Long; I Do, I Do, I Do, I Do, I Do; S.O.S.; Mamma Mia; Fernando; Dancing Queen; Money, Money, Money; Knowing Me, Knowing You; The Name of the Game; Take a Chance On Me; Eagle; Summer Night City; Chiquitita; Does Your Mother Know; Voulez-Vous; Angeleyes; Gimme! Gimme! Gimme! (A Man After Midnight); I Have a Dream; The Winner Takes It All; Super Trouper; On and On and On; Lay All Your Love On Me; One of Us; When All Is Said and Done; Head Over Heels; The Visitors (Crackin' Up); The Day Before You Came; Under Attack; Thank You for the Music. *Bonus tracks:* Ring Ring [1974 remix, single version]; Voulez-Vous [1979 extended remix].

SOURCES

Books

Bergman, I, *Images – My Life in Film*, Bloomsbury, London 1994

Boorman, J, *Money into Light*, Faber & Faber, London 1985

Britten Austin, P, *On Being Swedish*, Secker and Warburg, London 1968

Brown, T, Kutner, J, and Warwick, N, *The Complete Book of the British Charts – Singles and Albums*, Omnibus Press, London 2002

Cowie, P, *Ingmar Bergman – A Critical Biography*, Secker and Warburg, London 1982

Davies, H, *The Beatles*, Jonathan Cape, London 1985

Fältskog, A, and Åhman, B, *As I Am*, Virgin Publishing, London 1997

Fodor, E (ed.), *Fodor's Scandinavia 1970*, Hodder and Stoughton, UK 1970

Hawksley, L, *The Virgin Illustrated Encyclopaedia of Rock*, Virgin Publishing, London 1998

Huntford, R, *The New Totalitarians*, Allen Lane, London 1971

Hutchings, J (project ed.), *Insight Guide – Sweden*, Apa Publications, UK 1999

Linnér, B, *Sex & Society in Sweden*, Jonathan Cape, London 1968

McAleer, D (compiler), *The Warner Guide to UK & US Hit Singles*, Carlton/Little Brown, London 1996

Norman, P, *The Stones*, Corgi Books, UK 1985

Oldham, A, Calder, T, and Irwin, C, *Abba – The Name of the Game*, Pan Books, London 1995

Palm, CM, *Bright Lights Dark Shadows – The Real Story of Abba*, Omnibus Press, London 2002

Potiez, J-M, *Abba – The Book*, Aurum Press, London 2003

Savage, J, *England's Dreaming – The Sex Pistols and Punk Rock*, Faber & Faber 1991

Scott, GW, *The Swedes – a Jigsaw Puzzle*, Sidgwick and Jackson, London 1967

Scott, R, *Abba: Thank You for the Music (The True Stories Behind Every Song)*, Carlton Books, London 2002

Stallings, P, *Rock 'n' Roll Confidential*, Vermilion, London 1985

Strong, MC, *The Great Rock Discography*, Canongate Books, Edinburgh 1996

Warner, O, *A Journey to the Northern Capitals*, George Allen and Unwin, London 1968

Magazine and newspaper articles

'Olivia hits out: The song was wrong for Europe', Brian Wesley, *Sun*, 6 April 1974

'It's Nice Here. . .', report on Eurovision Song Contest; Andrew Tyler, *New Musical Express*, 13 April 1974

'Eurovision: 500 million viewers can be wrong', Jeff Ward, *Melody Maker*, 13 April 1974

'Waterloo Victory for CBS – 400,000 Demand Expected', Graham Punter, *Music Week*, 13 April 1974

Review of 'Ring Ring', Charlie Gillet, *New Musical Express*, 29 June 1974

Review of *Waterloo*, Greg Shaw, *Phonograph Record*, August 1974

'Have We Got the Eurosong at Last?', Brian Wesley, *Sun*, 6 April 1974

'Abba: Oompah?', profile of Abba; Mick Farren, *New Musical Express*, 24 April 1976

'Frayn's Sweden', Michael Frayn, *Observer*, 21 April 1974

'How Abba got into the money, money, money', Robert Parker, *The Times*, 5 February 1977

Review of Abba concert at Albert Hall, London, Richard Williams, *The Times*, 15 February 1977

Review of *Arrival*, Robot A. Hull, *Creem*, April 1977

'Abba and the class system', review of *Arrival*, *Melody Maker*, 4 December 1977

Review of *Abba – The Album*, Bob Edmunds, *New Musical Express*, 14 January 1978

Review of *Abba – The Movie*, David Robinson, *The Times*, 17 February 1978

'Abba-Cadabra', Barbara Graustark, Janet Huck and John Herbert, *Newsweek*, 5 June 1978

'21 views of Abba', review of *Voulez-Vous*, Brian Case, Susan Hill, Christopher Petit, Jon Savage, Richard Williams et al., *Melody Maker*, 12 May 1979

Review of *Voulez-Vous*, Tony Parsons, *New Musical Express*, 12 May 1979

Review of *Super Trouper*, Richard Williams, *The Times* (Christmas round-up), 22 November 1980

'The Abba route to easy escapism', review of *Super Trouper*, Lynden Barber, *Melody Maker*, 22 November 1980

News-in-brief report of marriage of Björn Ulvaeus and Lena Källersjö, *The Times*, 8 January 1981

'Rude Boys', interview with Joe Strummer and Robert Fripp; Vic Garbarini, *Musician*, June 1981

Review of *The Visitors*, Graham Lock, *New Musical Express*, 16 January 1982

Review of *The Visitors*, *The Times*, 18 January 1982

'The Story of Pop from A to B and Back Again', review of *The Singles – The First Ten Years*, Richard Cook, *New Musical Express*, 4 December 1982

'Mates again', *Diary*, *The Times*, 6 April 1983

'Oil's Well That Ends Well', Mike Gardner, *Record Mirror*, 15 January 1983

'Abba face £4.6m tax allegations', *The Times*, 21 July 1984

'Gambling on a £425,000 opening gambit', article on *Chess*; David Hewson, *The Times*, 8 October 1984

'The Kiss of Death, Survived', interview with Murray Head; David Hewson, *The Times*, 16 October 1984

'Borrowed Innocence', review of *Chess* (concert performance) at Barbican Centre, London; Anthony Masters, *The Times*, 29 October 1984

'A Long Game of Chess', review of *Chess* (musical); Jack Tinker, *Daily Mail*, 15 May 1986

'Fable with a Moral Centre', review of *Chess* (musical); Irving Wardle, *The Times*, 16 May 1986

Article on music banned in first Gulf War (including 'Waterloo'), *Daily Telegraph*, 6 July 1994 (the principal source of this article was a piece in *Independent*, 29 January 1991)

'The super troupers' success is Swede all over again as Björn's band bounces back to No. 1 in the charts', Ricky Sky, *Daily Mirror*, 2 October 1992

'Super Troupers: What's Going on?', Simon Garfield, *Independent on Sunday*, 21 February 1993

Review of *More Abba Gold*, Barry McIlheney, *Q*, May 1993

'In Praise of Pop's Perfect Palindrome', review of *A for Abba* on BBC1; Lynne Truss, *The Times*, 21 July 1993

'Funny, Funny, Funny', review of *A for Abba* on BBC1; Giles Smith, *Independent*, 21 July 1993

'How We Met: Björn Ulvaeus and Benny Andersson', Martin Palmer, *Independent on Sunday*, 26 April 1996

Review of CD reissues in 2001 of *Abba*, *Abba Live*, *The Visitors*, *Super Trouper*, *Voulez-Vous*, *Abba – The Album*, *Arrival*, *Waterloo* and *Ring Ring*; Robert Yates, *Q*, March 1997

'ABBA: Welcome to the Palindrome', review of CD reissues of *Abba*, *Abba Live*, *The Visitors*, *Super Trouper*, *Voulez-Vous*, *Abba – The Album*, *Arrival*, *Waterloo* and *Ring Ring*; Nick Hornby, *Mojo*, June 1997

'Super Trouper', article on Agnetha Fältskog and *As I Am*; Penny Wark, *Sunday Times*, 14 September 1997

Stig Anderson obituary, Pierre Perrone, *Independent*, 15 September 1997

Stig Anderson obituary, *The Times*, 16 September 1997

Stig Anderson obituary, *Daily Telegraph*, 18 September 1997

'Keeping Abba on Song', Stig Anderson obituary; Dave Laing, *Guardian*, 25 September 1997

'Thank You for the Music', Anna Blundy, *The Times* magazine, 8 November 1997

Love Stories, review of Abba compilation album released under this title in 1998, Nick Duerden, *Q*, October 1998

Björn Ulvaeus interview; Ally Ross, *Sun*, 1 April 1999

'Abba: Not Together Again', profile of Abba, *Sunday Telegraph*, 6 February 2000

Stephin Merritt (the Magnetic Fields) interview, *Independent*, 14 April 2000

'Does This Picture Prove Abba's Agnetha Really Did Love Her Stalker?: Mystery of Swedish Star's "Affair" with Deranged Fan Who Now Makes Her Fear for Her Life', Paul Henderson, *Mail on Sunday*, 9 April 2000

Review of *25th Anniversary Singles Collection 1972-1982*, Peter Kane, *Q*, October 2000

Abba Gold, review by John Aizlewood, *Q*, October 2000

'Brentwood, Vould You Like to Dance?', article on Bjorn Again; Brian Viner, *Independent*, 18 December 2000

'The Stars Who Kept Me from Knocking on', Johnny Gold, *Daily Express*, 16 October 2001

Review of Benny Anderssons Orkester at Old Fruit Market, Glasgow; Bob Flynn, *Guardian*, 26 October 2001

Definitive Collection, review by Steve Lowe, *Q*, March 2002

'Torment of the Abba star with a Nazi father', profile of Anni-Frid Lyngstad, *Observer*, 30 June 2002

Björn Ulvaeus and Benny Andersson interview; Peter Paphides, *Guardian*, 8 June 2002

'Lebensborn 2620', Kirsty Lang, *The Times* magazine, 1 February 2003

'Sleeping with the Enemy', article on the Norwegian 'Lebensborn' (*tyskebarna*) children; Julia Stuart, *Independent on Sunday*, 2 February 2003

'We Turned Down $1bn to Get Back Together', Barbara Davies, *Daily Mirror*, 4 July 2003

'Sweden's euro choice', Christopher Brown-Humes, *Financial Times*, 7 August 2003

'Why I love Frida Fältskog [sic]', Peter Paphides, *Guardian*, 14 October 2003

Moby interview; Will Hodgkinson, *Guardian*, 14 November 2003

'"Mamma Mia!" here we go again', Björn Ulvaeus interviewed by Joe Gross, *Austin American Statesman*, 16 March 2003

'Abba stalker arrested in Sweden', article, BBC news online, 24 June 2003

'Agnetha: reclusive, afraid and alone', *Australian Women's Weekly*, July 2003

'Abba's Björn Reveals Secret Comeback', interview with Björn Ulvaeus; Barbara Davies, *Daily Mirror*, 4 July 2003

'Love Is the Best Thing to Write Songs about', interview with Björn Ulvaeus; Andrew Billen, *The Times*, 29 July 2003

'Abba to Z', A–Z of Abba, *Sun*, 27 February 2004

'Pop Turns Sour: Blue for You', article on Abba and the Carpenters; Mark Paytress, *50 Years of Rock 'n' Roll*, special edition of *Q*, March 2004

'Chancing Queen', profile of Judy Craymer; Lesley White, *Sunday Times* magazine, 29 February 2004

'Stage Struck', Jay Rayner on fifth anniversary of *Mamma Mia!*, *Observer Music Monthly*, March 2004

'Bjorn Again', profile of Agnetha Fältskog; Barbara Davies, *Daily Mirror*, 13 March 2004

'The 50 bands that changed our lives', Richard Simpson, London *Evening Standard*, 25 March 2004

'Can the Abba girl ever return?', article on Agnetha Fältskog; Richard Hewitt, London *Evening Standard*, 25 March 2004

'Abba dabba do', review of *My Colouring Book*; Liz Hoggard, *Observer Music Monthly*, April 2004

'The 50 Bands That Changed the World', *Q*, April 2004

'Björn Ulvaeus: The Winner Rakes It in', Björn Ulvaeus interview; James Rampton, *Independent*, 2 April 2004

'Abba Recording Studio to Shut Its Doors', Associated Press story posted on CentreDaily.com, 7 April 2004

My Colouring Book, review by Alison Moorer, *Daily Mirror*, 8 April 2004

My Colouring Book, review by Andy Gill, *Independent*, 16 April 2004

'No Super Trouper', article on Agnetha Fältskog; Peter Paphides, *The Times* magazine, 16 April 2004

My Colouring Book, review by Dave Simpson, *Guardian*, 16 April 2004

'Mamma Mia! Here we go again...', *Radio Times*, 15–21 May 2004

Articles on websites

'Swedish Music Exports', Holger Larsen, www.sweden.SE

'A Historical Overview of the Swedish Economy', Richard Holgersson (SAAB Centre for Scandinavian Studies), www.ssn.flinders.edu.au/scanlink/nornotes/vol6/articles/holgersson2.htm

Videos and DVDs

Abba – In Concert (directed and produced by Urban Lasson), Polar Music, SVT and Universal DVD

Abba – The Definitive Collection (remastered videos), Polar Music, Universal DVD

The Winner Takes It All – The Abba Story (directed by Steve Cole and Chris Hunt; produced by Chris Hunt), VVL DVD

Abba – The Movie (directed by Lasse Hallström; produced by Reg Grundy and Stig Anderson) MGM/UA Home Video

TV documentaries

Abba's Biggest Secret: Revealed (directed by Tom Sheahan; produced by Andrew Braddel)

Abba: Bjorn Again (directed by Michael Clifford; produced by Natasha Carlish)

Abba's Greatest Hits (produced by Paul King)

Show programmes

Programme for *Mamma Mia!* musical at Prince Edward Theatre

Souvenir programme for *Mamma Mia!*, the touring show (not the stage musical of same name) incorporating Abba Magic

Liner notes

Abba In Concert DVD, Carl Magnus Palm

ABBA The Definitive Collection DVD, Carl Magnus Palm

Thank You for the Music CD box set, Abba, Stig Anderson, Fred Bronson, John Tobler, Dennis McNamara, Carl Magnus Palm and Michael B. Tretow

2001 CD reissues of *Abba*, *The Visitors*, *Super Trouper*, *Voulez-Vous*, *Abba – The Album*, *Arrival*, *Waterloo* and *Ring Ring*, Carl Magnus Palm. Palm did not write liner notes for *Abba Live*, also reissued at this time.

Frida 1967–1972, translated into English on Carl Magnus Palm's website (see below)

Websites

Abba – the Site
www.abbasite.com

The Abba Internet Database
www.abbafiles.com
Abba Mail
www.abbamail.com
Abba: Memories of the 1977 Tour
http://www.geocities.com/SunsetStrip/Studio/5073/tour/mem1.htm
Abba – The Worldwide Chart Lists
www.zip.com.au/~callisto/abba.html
Agnetha
www.agnetha.net
AMG All Music Guide
www.allmusic.com
Arts4All Newsletter
www.arts4all.com
Axess magazine
www.axess.se
BBC News
http://news.bbc.co.uk
CentreDaily.com
www.centredaily.com
Chess the musical
www.geocities.com/miss_florence_vassy/index.html
The Elvis Costello Home Page
www.elviscostello.info
The Eurovision Song Contest site
www.eurovision.tv
FilmForce
http://filmforce.ign.com
Guardian Unlimited
www.guardian.co.uk
Independent
www.Independent.co.uk

The Internet Movie Database
www.imdb.com
Daily Mirror
www.mirror.co.uk
NewsBank
http://infoweb.newsbank.com
New York Times
http://nytimes.com
Carl Magnus Palm
www.carlmagnuspalm.com
Q magazine
www.q4music.com
soc.culture.nordic (Swedish history)
www.lysator.liu.se
Stacy's Musical Village
http://theatre-musical.com
Sweden.SE
www.sweden.se
Union Songs
http://members.home.n1/union.songs

PICTURE CREDITS

p.1 Rex Features

p.2 London Features International *top left*; Rex Features *top right, bottom left, bottom right*

p.3 Redferns *top and bottom*

p.4 mirrorpix/Syndication International *top and bottom*

p.5 Redferns *top*, Rex Features *bottom*

p.6 Rex Features *top left*, mirrorpix/Syndication International *top right, bottom left, bottom right*

p.7 mirrorpix/Syndication International *top left*, Rex Features *top right, bottom left*, London Features International *bottom right*

p.8 mirrorpix/Syndication International

INDEX

NEIL DIAMOND
The biography
Laura Jackson

Neil Diamond has been responsible for writing some of the most memorable songs in pop music history and he has sold in excess of 120 million albums.

After years of anonymity in Tin Pan Alley churning out hits for other artistes, Neil Diamond burst onto the scene in his own right in 1969 with 'Sweet Caroline' and has continued to reign as one of the top five most successful solo artistes in pop music.

However, superstardom has come at a personal cost – he is a star who has suffered periods of crippling self doubt. He is an intriguing blend of contradictions – a massively charismatic dazzling live performer, yet deeply introspective off stage.

This fascinating portrait of Neil Diamond, his life, his music and his passions are explored from his childhood struggle to get out of Brooklyn, through five decades of global stardom, to the present day. *Neil Diamond: the biography* provides a definitive insight into one of the most enduring, creative, and prolific singer-songwriters of his generation.

ROGER DALTREY
The biography
Tim Ewbank and Stafford Hildred

The wild life of The Who's legendary lead singer

The charismatic lead singer for uncompromising supergroup The Who is one of rock's great survivors; at the age of 60 he's presenting a television series and masterminding a new album with long-term partner Pete Townshend.

Roger Daltrey's life is extraordinary from start to finish; he was expelled from school and written off as a violent thug before music and The Who became his salvation. For many years he was the sex-symbol lead singer, strutting bare-chested on stage at their dynamic concerts – while fighting the other group members backstage.

The authors, Tim Ewbank and Stafford Hildred, are both veteran showbusiness journalists who have collaborated on a number of biographies.

A SELECTION OF BOOKS AVAILABLE FROM PIATKUS BOOKS

THE PRICES BELOW WERE CORRECT AT THE TIME OF GOING TO PRESS. HOWEVER PIATKUS BOOKS RESERVE THE RIGHT TO SHOW NEW RETAIL PRICES ON COVERS WHICH MAY DIFFER FROM THOSE PREVIOUSLY ADVERTISED IN THE TEXT OR ELSEWHERE.

0 7499 5029 3	Roger Daltrey	Tim Ewbank and Stafford Hildred	£17.99
0 7499 5025 0	Neil Diamond	Laura Jackson	£16.99
0 7499 5023 4	Jon Bon Jovi	Laura Jackson	£7.99
0 7499 5033 1	Home Before Daylight	Steve Parish	£8.99
0 7499 5004 8	Rod Stewart	Tim Ewbank and Stafford Hildred	£16.99

ALL PIATKUS TITLES ARE AVAILABLE FROM:
PIATKUS BOOKS C/O BOOKPOST
PO Box 29, Douglas, Isle Of Man, IM99 1BQ
Telephone (+44) 01624 677237
Fax (+44) 01624 670923
Email; bookshop@enterprise.net
Free Postage and Packing in the United Kingdom.
Credit Cards accepted. All Cheques payable to Bookpost.
(Prices and availability subject to change without prior notice. Allow 14 days for delivery. When placing orders please state if you do not wish to receive any additional information.)

OR ORDER ONLINE FROM:
www.piatkus.co.uk
Free postage and packing in the UK (on orders of two books or more)